Restorative Justice and the Law

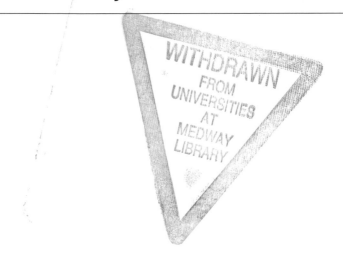

Restorative Justice and the Law

Edited by Lode Walgrave

WILLAN
PUBLISHING

Published by

Willan Publishing
Culmcott House
Mill Street, Uffculme
Cullompton, Devon
EX15 3AT, UK
Tel: +44(0)1884 840337
Fax: +44(0)1884 840251
e-mail: info@willanpublishing.co.uk
website: www.willanpublishing.co.uk

Published simultaneously in the USA and Canada by

Willan Publishing
c/o ISBS, 5824 N.E. Hassalo St,
Portland, Oregon 97213-3644, USA
Tel: +001(0)503 287 3093
Fax: +001(0)503 280 8832
e-mail: info@isbs.com
website: www.isbs.com

First published 2002

ISBN 1-903240-97-2 (cased)
ISBN 1-903240-96-4 (paper) √S√b

British Library Cataloguing-in-Publication Data
A catalogue record for this book is available from the British Library

Printed by T.J. International, Padstow, Cornwall
Project management by Deer Park Productions
Typeset by GCS, Leighton Buzzard, Beds.

Contents

List of figures and tables

I. Figures:

II. Tables:

Notes on contributors

Gordon Bazemore is Professor of Criminology and Criminal Justice and Director of the Community Justice Institute at Florida Atlantic University. He has published many articles in several international journals, and has co-edited *Restorative Juvenile Justice: Repairing the Harm of Youth Crime* (with Lode Walgrave) (Criminal Justice Press, 1999) and *Restorative and Community Justice: Cultivating Common Ground for Victims, Communities and Offenders* (with Mara Schiff) (Anderson Publishing, 2001). He currently is principal investigator of two national studies on restorative justice issues for juveniles, funded by the National Institute of Justice (NIJ) and the Robert Wood Johnson Foundation, and by the Office of Juvenile Justice and Delinquency Prevention, U.S. Department of Justice (OJJDP).

Hans Bouttelier is strategic policy advisor at the Dutch Ministry of Justice; he is also affiliated with the Department of Criminal Law and Criminology at the Vrije Universiteit of Amsterdam. He was managing editor of the *European Journal on Criminal Policy and Research* and published among others *Crime and Morality: the Moral Significance of Criminal Justice in Postmodern Culture* (Kluwer, 2000) and (in Dutch) *Safety Utopia: Contemporary Uneasiness and Desire around Crime and Punishment* (Kluwer, 2002).

John Braithwaite is Professor, a member of the Centre for Restorative Justice at the Australian National University and Chair of its Regulatory

Institutions Network. He is author of a number of publications which belong to the foundations of restorative justice, and has won a number of awards. His most recent book is *Restorative Justice and Responsive Regulation* (Oxford University Press, 2002).

Adam Crawford is Professor of Criminology and Criminal Justice at the University of Leeds. Amongst his publications are *The Local Governance of Crime* (Clarendon, 1997), *Crime Prevention and Community Safety* (Longman, 1998), *Integrating a Victim Perspective within Criminal Justice* (with J. Goodey) (Ashgate, 2000) and *Crime and Insecurity* (Willan, 2002). He is participating in research to evaluate recent restorative reforms into the youth justice system in England and Wales.

Jim Dignan (LLB, MA) is Professor of Criminology and Restorative Justice at the Centre for Criminological and Legal Research, University of Sheffield and has written several reports, articles and book chapters on a variety of theoretical, practical and policy issues relating to the development of restorative justice.

Antony Duff was educated at the University of Oxford, and has taught in the Philosophy Department at the University of Stirling since 1970; he works on issues in the philosophy of criminal law. His most recent book was *Punishment, Communication, and Community* (Oxford University Press, 2001); his current major project is on the structures of criminal liability.

Sandra O'Brien is Director of the Center for Public and Social Policy at Florida Gulf Coast University and Assistant Professor in the Division of Public Affairs, College of Professional Studies. She previously served as Project Administrator with the Balanced and Restorative Justice Project at Florida Atlantic University, and as Associate Director of the Center for the Study of Youth Policy at Nova Southeastern University, Shepard Broad Law Center. Her interests include community and restorative justice, public policy, juvenile justice, and programme evaluation.

George Pavlich is a Professor of Sociology at the University of Alberta, Canada. He has authored several articles and books, including *Justice Fragmented: Mediating Community Disputes Under Postmodern Conditions* (Routledge, 1996), and *Critique and Radical Discourses on Crime* (Ashgate, 2000). He is currently writing a book-length critique of restorative justice.

Daniel W. Van Ness is Executive Director of the International Center for Justice and Reconciliation, the restorative justice advocacy arm of an association of NGOs in 95 countries known as Prison Fellowship International. He has written many articles on legal aspects of restorative justice, and authored, with Karen Heetderks Strong, *Restoring Justice* (Anderson, 2002, 2nd edn).

Lode Walgrave is a Professor of Criminology at the Katholieke Universiteit Leuven (Belgium), and chair of the International Network for Research on Restorative Justice for Juveniles. He has published several articles and book chapters on the issue of restorative justice and the law, and edited, with Gordon Bazemore, *Restorative Juvenile Justice: Repairing the Harm of Youth Crime* (Criminal Justice Press, 1999). His most recent book is (in Dutch) *In View of Restoration* (Leuven University Press, 2000).

Ido Weijers is Professor at the Department of Education at the University of Utrecht. He has published several articles on juvenile justice, punishment and education, and has completed a book (in Dutch) *Guilt and Shame: A Pedagogical Perspective on Juvenile Justice* (Bohn Stafleu, 2000). With Antony Duff, he is co-editor of *Punishing Juveniles: Principle and Critique* (Hart, forthcoming). Ido Weijers is research director of an evaluation programme of five restorative justice projects in the Netherlands.

Foreword

This book is based on papers which it was originally planned to present in their draft form as keynote presentations at the Fifth International Conference on Restorative Justice in Leuven (Belgium), 16–19 September 2001. The conference was organised by the International Network for Research on Restorative Justice for Juveniles. The events of 11 September 2001, however, prevented some colleagues from coming to the conference and presenting their papers. Fortunately, we had other opportunities to comment on and discuss the drafts. The result is a volume with chapters of very high quality, presenting sometimes opposing and even provocative, but always thought-provoking, views and standpoints on a topic which is now becoming a central issue in the development of restorative justice.

I am grateful to the authors of the chapters. They all immediately accepted invitations to contribute, made many suggestions which have considerably improved the final result, responded very positively to comments on their own drafts, and completed their revisions on schedule. I would, however, like to thank them especially for the support and the many pleasant and stimulating exchanges we have had over the last few years, especially under the auspices of the International Network for Research on Restorative Justice for Juveniles. Let that continue.

As usual, the secretarial staff of Criminology-K.U. Leuven, and especially Andrea Ons, have provided highly efficient support which I have been very fortunate to be able to count on.

Finally, it has been very rewarding to work with Brian Willan of Willan Publishing. His attentive and supportive follow-up of the project has been an encouragement, and has helped to produce a better book.

Thanks to all.

Lode Walgrave
Leuven, 5 September 2002

Introduction

by Lode Walgrave

'The best reform of penal law consists of its replacement, not by a better penal law, but by something better.' This quotation of Radbruch by Tulkens (1993: 493) illustrates very well the *basso continuo* of this book. Based on empirical and socio-ethical arguments, it is believed that restorative justice can point to the path towards 'something better' than penal law. It remains, however, uncertain how far doing justice through restoration will in the future really replace the current punitive predominance in the response to crime. It will depend on many conditions, including changes in the socio-cultural and societal environment, the improvement of restorative practices, the development of coherent normative theoretical reflection on restorative justice, and finding a balanced relation between restorative justice and the law in a constitutional democratic state. This volume is focused mainly on the latter topic.

In its pure version (as in McCold 2000), restorative justice is an ideal of doing justice in an ideal of society. It promotes voluntary consultation and negotiation in mutual respect, leading to understanding, reparation and reconciliation, healing even, supported by caring communities, in protecting societies. Such deliberative processes actually do take place, but they are not the mainstream response to crime. The opportunities for reparation are mostly reduced, dependent on the benevolence of criminal justice agents, and the legal context often hampers real restoration. Most restorative practices are currently implemented in systems which are grounded on another philosophical foundation, that is to say the 'apriorism' that crime must be punished or that the (juvenile) criminal must be treated. So far, most restorative practices seem to be located on a sort of 'island' in a traditional system, where, as a favour, the traditional apriorisms were exceptionally not implemented, or at least modified. These islands were like 'reservations' of experimentation, tolerated because they were considered to be not harmful to the 'real' justice business, or protected by the personal involvement of enlightened criminal justice actors. As long as they were in their experimental form, restorative practices might afford some *flou artistique* with regard to legal safeguards, because they were reduced in scope and were considered to be carried out by prominent scholars whose personal moral authority seemed to guarantee that serious violations of participants' legal rights would be avoided.

Restorative justice now seems gradually to be leaving its research and development phase. Official international organizations like the United Nations and the Council of Europe issue declarations and recommendations which advise the member countries to include so far as possible opportunities for restorative actions in their legislation (Van Ness *et al.* 2001; European Forum for Victim–Offender Mediation and Restorative Justice 2000). Many countries increasingly provide legal opportunities for practices with respect to repairing harm caused by crime to individual victims and victimized communities (Miers 2001).[1] Restorative justice is a key issue in all debates on reform in criminal justice, especially in juvenile justice.

These developments emphasize the urgency of considering how to place restorative justice within an adequate legal framework. First, because it will facilitate the spread of restorative justice practice into the institutional response to crime, and, second, because it will provide an opportunity to check the appropriateness of existing legal dispositions for implementing restorative practices properly. Without neglecting the communitarian and restorativist dream, we must look for ways to implement possibilities for restoration as far as possible in the real world. Legal formalism must not intrude upon the restorative process, but the process must take place in a legalized context.

This reflection brings an intrinsic tension to the surface. The participatory philosophy of restorative justice, which aims at a maximum possible openness to informal dialogue and process, is difficult to combine with the need for formalization and legalization. The concrete terms of the debate are partly different in the Anglo–Saxon based common law countries and in the countries with centralized legal systems on the

European continent, but the basic issues are the same: how to juxtapose informal processes with formal procedures, how to rely on communities while living in organized states, how to combine creativity and the richness of the bottom-up approach with the clarity and strictness of the top-down approach, how to balance a priority for voluntariness and compliance with possible coercion. If the paradigm status of restorative justice is to be taken seriously, pretending that restorative justice does offer another option for doing justice after a crime has occurred, we cannot just reproduce the same legal safeguards of the punitive systems. Due process, legality, equality, right of defence, presumption of innocence and proportionality may be irrelevant or may need to be experienced in a different form. Maybe other legal principles need to be constructed in a manner more appropriate for the restorative perspective.

Restorative justice literature on these questions is not abundant. Understandably, in fact, the vast majority of publications to date have positioned restorative justice as another approach to crime, described the different concrete models, and tried to establish whether restorative practices 'do work', for what kind of cases and under what conditions. Now that it is generally accepted that 'it does work', that its renovating appeal is deeper and its scope larger than just a few techniques, and that attempts are made to insert restorative practices into mainstream systems of responding to crime, the relation between the traditional options for doing justice and the restorative option must be explored thoroughly. Sceptics do not believe that restorative justice can ever be combined with proper legal standards, and therefore keep it at the margins of the mainstream of the social response to crime (Ashworth 1993; Feld 1999; von Hirsch 1998). Among restorative justice proponents different positions are held by so-called 'diversionists', 'maximalists' and 'purists'.

The debate is now gradually getting into its stride, as is witnessed by several recent publications and projects (Braithwaite 2002a; von Hirsch *et al*. 2002a; Van Ness 2002). This volume is conceived to enhance the debate. It intentionally presents a collection of different and sometimes opposite views on the ethical foundations of restorative justice, the relation between restorative responses and punishment, the possibility of including rehabilitative aims in restorative justice, the interaction of community and the state in relation to positioning restorative justice, and possible foundations for a restorative justice system. The contributions do not represent mainstream restorative writing, but offer new and often controversial positions. The book is structured under several sub-topics.

First, the ethical bottom layer of restorative justice is explored. Does restorative justice serve other values than those of punitive or rehabilitative systems? In Chapter 1, George Pavlich warns against trying to develop new general maxims, because that would in fact lead to another form of ethical imperialism. He promotes the value of not promoting general values, and advances 'hospitality', as a great opportunity for a true bottom-up approach in restorative justice. In Chapter 2, Hans Bouttelier, in contrast, observes that societies are looking for a minimal moral consensus, which he believes is found in the 'victimalization' of our moral values. We are not bound by common values, but by common rejection of evil. That is, in Boutellier's opinion, the sociological explanation of restorative justice's breakthrough in recent decades.

How does restorative justice relate to the other two basic intervention models? Chapter 3, by Gordon Bazemore and Sandra O'Brien, makes clear that restorative justice does not stand in opposition to the rehabilitation of offenders. On the contrary, within the restorative justice process there is ample space for rehabilitating the offender, a proposition based on both empirical and theoretical arguments. Ido Weijers, in Chapter 4, takes the more traditional pedagogic standpoint, and explores family group conferences according to their educative potential. Chapter 5 is about restoration and punishment. Antony Duff looks at restorative processes from a retributivist standpoint. In his view, criminal mediation has intrinsic retributive potential, because the communicational setting will bring the offender to repent, which is an appropriate purpose, and promotes his willingness to repair the wrong committed.

In Chapter 6, Adam Crawford sets the scene for the debate on how to reconcile restorative justice and the law. Whereas many adherents of this justice option have advanced the community as a crucial stakeholder, and not the state, Crawford makes it clear that this opposition is untenable. A constructive relation must be sought between the participatory philosophy of restorative justice and the ruling safeguarding role of the state. Daniel Van Ness's Chapter 7 puts the ideal restorative justice approach into a perspective of less ideal responses. Adhering to fully restorative models only would indeed paralyse possible interaction between the fully restorative processes and the more formalized context which is needed for legalization. Accepting that restorativeness can exist at different levels of application opens opportunities for extending the principles beyond the ideal 'national park' practices.

In Chapter 8, John Braithwaite develops his view on how procedural rules in the responsive state would be different from the traditional approach to procedures and safeguards. He especially challenges the proportionality principle, and relies on the sense of responsibility of active citizens. Restorative justice needs to be contextual, driven by the value of freedom as non-domination or dominion. Jim Dignan, in Chapter 9, then describes a model which concretizes what has been put forward by Van

Ness and Braithwaite. He demonstrates convincingly that it is possible to conceive a system which would be maximally oriented towards restoration, while at the same time respecting the principles of a constitutional democratic state.

In Chapter 10, I set out my own position on why a systemic response to crime should be oriented primarily towards restoration, and how such a system could look. This vision is largely inspired by the preceding chapters. Not that they all confirm what I advance, but rather they have obliged me to correct, or to explain better, what I think to be important.

Note

1. Though it is not always really conducted according to restorative justice philosophy. A few of the policy makers and less informed practitioners often see restorative practices as isolated techniques to be inserted as additional opportunities into the traditional rehabilitative or punitive justice systems.

Chapter I

Towards an ethics of restorative justice

George Pavlich

Introduction

Over the past two decades, restorative justice programmes have pro-
liferated vastly into the conflict management arenas of many western
contexts. Although usually envisaged as an alternative to retributive
criminal justice institutions, restorative justice is notoriously difficult to
define.[1] Even so, most protagonists portray it as a hospitable, non-
alienating, victim-centred and community-orientated way to resolve
conflicts.[2] Its processes are guided by values respectful of all parties to a
dispute. It aims to empower victims, communities, offenders and families
to repair the effects of a harmful event, using effective 'repentance rituals'
to restore community life. Justice is thus understood as restoring harms
and hurt, reflecting a commitment to such normative values as individual
empowerment, responsibility, peace, community strength, respect, compassion, agreement and so on.[3]

Calculating justice in this fashion raises a question to which the
following chapter is directed: how might the ethics of restorative justice be
formulated under the historical conditions facing us nowadays?[4] For
some, a response to this question requires overarching, universal and
founded moral principles. Apart from distinguishing restorative from
retributive, guilt-based justice, such principles are designed to guard
against the excesses of a proverbial lynch-mob, kangaroo court, justice.

This explains, perhaps, why restorative justice is often predicated on different authoritative 'foundations': religion (e.g. Hadley 2001; Consedine 1995); philosophy (e.g. Hadley 2001; Cooley 1999; Zehr and Mika 1997); evaluation data (e.g. Umbreit 2001; Bonta *et al.* 1998); emancipatory social science (e.g. Morris 2000; Bush and Folger 1994); communitarian ideals (e.g. Bazemore and Schiff 2001; Walgrave 2000; McElrea 1994); political and social theory (e.g. Strang and Braithwaite 2001; Braithwaite 2000); peacemaking (Sullivan *et al.* 1998); and so on.

Without denying the many penetrating insights of these discourses, one might ponder whether the quest for unshakeable foundations is doomed from the outset, especially given the uncertainty at the heart of contemporary moral thinking (e.g. see Pavlich 2000; Bauman 1992, 1997; Lyotard 1984; Smart 1993). Can ethics, and more specifically notions of justice, ever achieve such formidable ambitions? Discussions of justice over the past few decades suggest not. For instance, Walzer (1983) has persuasively challenged the quest for universal principles by pointing to increasingly incommensurable spheres of justice that operate independently of one another. MacIntyre (1988) ponders further whether it is even possible to demarcate such spheres, given the lack of agreement on how to decide between competing images and definitions of justice (hence the title to his book, *Whose Justice? Which Rationality?*). Against MacIntyre's seeming despair, Young (1990) celebrates the concomitant diversity and difference as a triumph over the constraints of universal approaches to justice. Then there are various deconstructive formulations, such as Lyotard and Thebaud (1979) and Derrida (1992), for whom there is no such thing as justice *per se*, amenable to singular definition. I shall return to the latter idea, but these various debates underscore the essentially contested nature of justice, and underscore an inability to establish the bases of a universal justice in ethical arenas saturated with uncertainty.

Under the (postmodern?) conditions before us now, it may be apposite to refuse a blackmail that commands us to come up with well-founded universal principles or else be condemned as unethical, immoral or just plain irrational. This supremely arrogant demand is perhaps the major impediment to developing a different language of ethics appropriate to our times (e.g. Bauman 1993). Living under blood-encrusted residues of (modern) dreams pursued in the name of absolute moral maxims – the holocaust, apartheid, large scale warfare, the Gulag archipelago, ongoing ethnic conflicts, etc. – provides reason enough to question the assertion that such principles can provide guarantees against evil, terror or danger. As Bauman puts it,

The foolproof – universal and unshakeably founded – ethical code will never be found; having singed our fingers once too often, we know now what we did not know then, when we embarked on this journey of exploration: that a non-aporetic, non-ambivalent morality, an ethics that is universal and 'objectively founded', is a practical impossibility; perhaps also an *oxymoron*, a contradiction in terms (1993: 10).

Facing up to that stark realization puts a unique onus on ethical discussions, and reinforces the contours of the rather different ethos in which we now make moral claims. This offers unique opportunities, including restorative justice's quest to go beyond the 'coercive normative regulation' licensed by modern justice, and to search for an alternative grammar of ethics (Bauman 1993: 3–4).

With this in mind, this chapter explores a different language through which the ethics of restorative justice in an uncertain ethos may be articulated. It begins with an analysis of a growing disjunction between the (modern) pursuit of certain ethical principles in (postmodern) contexts that increasingly recognize their obdurately uncertain promises. This assessment provides several openings for re-conceptualization of the ethics of restorative justice. Drawing on Derrida (1999, 2000) and Derrida and Dufourmantelle (2000), I proffer restorative ethics as hospitality. Here, ethics is framed through specific cases of hospitality in which subjects imagine new ways to be with others. This vision of restorative ethics does not claim to be universalizable, nor does it assume that ethical subjects are natural or fixed (as say, victim, offender, etc.). It accepts that the language, together with the subjects, of ethics is produced through responses generated when a 'host' welcomes – opens up to – a 'guest'. The final sections of the chapter describe some features of this ethics before examining its implications for restorative justice.

Ethics, universality and uncertainty

In his assessment of current conditions, Bauman (1992, 1993, 1995, 1997) describes the postmodern as modernity reaching a self-critical, self-effacing and 'self-dismantling' moment. This ethos is, for him, saturated with an 'ambient' uncertainty, no longer accepting that progressive (rational, etc.) social action can be guaranteed through absolute and universal ethical foundations. Without certainty on the validity of over-arching social ends, or processes for determining these, universal moral maxims to guide action cannot be firmly established. In the ensuing ethos, people go about the business of moral life as though nothing had changed, evoking a modern grammar of ethics whose translucent splendour has faded. Ethical subjects enunciate moral statements as though there were a common *telos*, or a general belief in the intrinsic value of universal maxims. So, despite vastly different normative approaches to restorative justice, one regularly witnesses people speaking and acting as though there were some underlying consensus.

These, however, become especially problematic in situations where religious, philosophical, scientific, administrative, technical, sociological, etc., frameworks offer competing and disparate ethical precepts without agreed-upon ways to decide between them. As Bauman astutely notes, clashes between such precepts expose the ultimately unfounded, open-ended character of ethical debate and indicates the imperiousness of attempting to universalize a given set of ethical precepts over others. Recognizing uncertainty admits a fundamental groundlessness to ethical life, with paradoxical results:

> Of one thing we can be sure: whatever morality there is or there may be in a society which has admitted its groundlessness, lack of purpose and the abyss bridged by just a brittle gangplank of convention – can be only an ethically unfounded morality. As such, it is and will be uncontrollable and unpredictable (Bauman 1995: 18).

Silhouetted against the fervent pursuit of universal maxims, the admission of groundlessness produces a peculiar, if disingenuous, vision of our ethical life.

Transposed into the context of restorative justice discourses, this situation plays itself out thus: universal moral maxims and formal pro-cedures are touted as if they were incontrovertible, generally accepted and universally valid. Arguing that justice necessarily revolves around universal maxims like 'individual empowerment is a key to restorative justice', 'restoring harm is necessary to assure justice', or 'strong com-munities are required for just outcomes' implies very specific moral orientations and licenses specific practices, like 'conferences'. At the same time, the sheer diversity of restorative maxims, and the lack of a sure way to decide between competing values (e.g. restoration versus trans-formation, maximalist versus minimalist alternation, etc.), leads to a plural clamour of moral voices without any signs of abate. In the end we come back to MacIntyre's unresolved question: *Whose Justice? Which Rationality?* The seeming impossibility of this ethical context need not licence despair, or an abandonment of ethics. On the contrary, as Young (1990) and Derrida (1992) suggest, once we accept no apodictic foundations of justice, then other possible formulations present themselves. Working out of such openings, the present analysis seeks a new language for addressing restorative justice's ethics.

Re-assessing restorative ethics

How could the above noted possibility generate an alternative conception of ethics within restorative justice discourses? First, one might start with the realization, troubling though it may seem, that no ethical system can be generalized across contexts without imperial and often violent aspirations (see Bauman 1993: 12). At the same time, however, this does not mean that one is thereby committed to a paralysing form of moral relativism, to a position that 'anything goes'. Rather, this means that:

> There is no ethics in general. There are only – eventually – ethics of processes by which we treat the possibilities of a situation (Badiou 2001: 16).

So, ethics might be linked to different, non-generalizing possibilities that critically imagine, through local processes, new ways to be with others. This ethical imagination would be involved with new concepts, truths and regimes of association. A restorative ethics could be understood as the critical work performed when subjects gather to name injustice or harm, and address promises of just patterns of being with others that are yet to come. This entails complex negotiations between different subjects' ideas of future being, imagined through local (restorative) processes. Negotiations that open up to the future lie at the heart of ethics – not the pure implementation of a universal justice envisaged through past abstractions.

If this is so, then one might question restorative justice practices that operate in the name of supposedly universal principles of harm, or absolute conceptions of general community interests. For instance, defining restorative justice as a way to redress harm in the community assumes that 'harm', 'redress' and 'community' are incontrovertible concepts capable of building principled foundations. In the process, ethical work is reduced to narrow questions. Who has harmed whom? What sort of victim has been produced through the harm? Which community interests have been transgressed? What reparation is needed to restore balance and a community order? (see Pavlich 2001).

Such questions do not actively seek out ways to envisage entirely new forms of social life much beyond those that have brought subjects together in the first place. They also effectively disable ethical searches not centred on values of community interest, victimization, reparation, etc., as conceived within present horizons. The danger of totalitarianism looms large when justice is reduced to programmatic questions that imply the simple application of necessary, absolute maxims to given situations. When principles reign supreme, calling for the elimination of harm in the name of a predefined community interest, there is little opportunity to imagine other conceptions of harm, or indeed new collective patterns. Moreover, moral values like 'community interest' might be treated as if they were incontrovertible, but their definitions are by no means transparent, absolute or universally agreed upon. Treating them as if they were so disallows fundamental critique directed to the principles/concepts themselves. In the absence of guarantees, or a general framework of ethics applicable to all situations, every context demands that ethical work be carried out specifically – appealing no doubt to wider perceptions, but without assuming that these are universalizable, or necessarily better than any others.

Secondly, a fundamental ambiguity surrounds ethical subjects. Human subjects are, as Bauman (1993: 10) usefully notes, neither inherently good nor bad. Following Levinas and others, he notes that the ethical self does not even exist as an entity prior to being involved in specific types of ethical practice (Bauman 1999). The subject is not simply a natural, pre-given entity (as enshrined in human rights) capable of suffering (as a victim) and encountering the world of others. Instead, the subject is, or rather comes to be, through the very process of ethically determining specific courses of moral action. Thus, '...moral responsibility – being for the Other before one can be with the Other – is the first reality of the self, a starting point rather than a product of society' (Bauman 1993: 13).

If this is so then, Badiou (2001: 8) may signal an important concern: contemporary ethics has been reduced to discussions about the protection of human rights. This 'immense return to Kant', and 'natural law', reduces the language of ethics to ontology,[5] to discussions premised on the problematic assumption that the natural subject's true ethical essence can be fixed in absolute rights. Thus,

> according to the way it is generally used today, the term 'ethics' relates above all to the domain of human rights, 'the rights of man'... We are supposed to assume the existence of a universally recognizable human subject possessing 'rights' that are in some sense natural: the right to live, to avoid abusive treatment... These

rights are held to be self-evident and the result of a wide consensus. 'Ethics' is a matter of busying ourselves with these rights, of making sure that they are respected (Badiou 2001: 4).

These rights take various forms beyond legal domains (e.g. patients, consumer, health, disability, student, etc.), and find particular expression in restorative justice; namely, through calculations that focus on victim rights.[6] Defining the ethics of restorative justice in terms of victimization patterns (the victim of harm, the offender as victim, the family member as victim, the victimized community, etc.), reduces ethics to ontology;[7] in the process, moral choices about which sorts of victimization are addressed (as opposed to silenced), or even ought to be addressed, are dressed up as necessities determined by the supposed 'nature' of human subjects.

This move effectively disables ethics as a discourse directed toward the contingency of collective life, engaged with the unpredictable, open and never-ending flows of being-with-others. If ethics is anything, it cannot be the slave of any determinate ontology;[8] ethics emerges precisely because what it is to be human is undecided, contingent and radically indeterminate. By virtue of the contingency, freedom and flexibility of situations in which subjects may be identified and act, ethics becomes possible. To assert a fixed, natural moral subject is therefore to discard ethics, to elevate the dictates of a predetermined ontology. By contrast, conceptualizing the undetermined self, the open subject, created through moral responses to others is pivotal to ethical discourse.

Thirdly, in view of the above observations, the language of ethics involves an element of mystery not encompassed by any rational precepts; in Bauman's parlance, it is 'incurably *aporetic*' (1993: 11). That is,

> Few choices ... are unambiguously good. The majority of moral choices are made between contradictory impulses ... The moral self moves, feels and acts in the context of ambivalence and is shot through with uncertainty ... uncertainty is bound to accompany the condition of the moral self forever (1993: 11–12).

As such, it is an aporetic, fundamentally contestable, discourse born out of undecided and undetermined moments of being. When ethical frameworks disable the undecidable (by claiming to be necessary, unambiguous or certain) there lies totalitarian thinking in the making. This thinking invariably involves disastrous situations in which ethical choices, always encompassed by radical uncertainty, masquerade as blind necessity. The legacies of these blights of recent history might valuably etch themselves in our collective memories, warning of dire consequences when asserting a determined being and so eliminating ethics.

My main point is this: ethics requires a distinctive and autochthonous language – it is never fully engaged through the languages of meta-physics, ontology, physics, empiricism, human rights, victimhood, natural law and so on. Indeed, many such languages deny the flow of human contingency, the always undecided movement of the yet-to-come, of the ultimately undecidable facets of life in which subjects are nevertheless called upon to decide and be responsible for the decisions made, the incalculable horizons of future being with others calculated here and now. The very impossibility of this situation renders ethics possible: the demand to calculate the incalculable, to decide upon matters which are ultimately undecidable, to justify in contexts that are not amenable to absolute justification, determination or subjective stability.

In the meantime, current ethical horizons often seek to perpetuate themselves on the momentum of conventions whose privilege once stood magnanimously over modern moral orders, but which increasing appear as quaint anachronisms. The remainder of this chapter attempts to open up to an ethical grammar beyond one that seeks universal maxims to guide and define restorative justice contexts. In particular, it tries to formulate a restorative ethics as a way of imagining how to be with others through the welcome provided by various contexts of hospitality.

Restorative justice and ethics as hospitality

> Insofar as hospitality has to do with the *ethos*, that is, the residence, one's home, the familiar place of dwelling, inasmuch as it is a manner of being there, the manner in which we relate to ourselves and to others (as our own or as foreigners), ethics is hospitality; ethics is thoroughly coextensive with the experience of hospitality. But for this very reason, and because being at home with oneself (…the other within oneself) supposes a reception or inclusion of the other which one seeks to appropriate, control and master according to different modalities of violence, there is a history of hospitality, and always-possible perversion of the law of hospitality … and of the laws which come to limit and condition it in its inscription as a law (Derrida 2001: 16–17).

At base, restorative justice aspires to a justice hospitable and meaningful to those involved in a harmful event (individual and collective). This stands in contrast to the variously described inhospitality, even hostility, of the adversarial courtroom's version of criminal justice and its attempts to prove guilt against general laws, its coercive consequences, etc. With the spirit of alternation in mind, one could imagine an ethics of restorative justice as hospitality. Hospitality involves a welcoming of those before the threshold of the place where a host receives. It is directed towards an amorphous other; the welcome is always extended to others, and so implies an ethics that imagines and negotiates various ways of being with others.

Just as a host welcomes guests, strangers, foreigners, refugees and so on, receiving them at dwellings, residences, universities, societies, nations and any other number of institutions, so restorative justice's family group conferences (community mediations, victim–offender reconciliations, etc.) offer situational forms of hospitality (e.g. the mediator welcomes disputants and extends hospitality conditioned by the rules of a given mediation, the family group conference coordinator explains the pro- cedural rules of the conference, thereby defining the sort of hospitality one can expect when participating in the process, etc.). Understood as hospitality, therefore, the ethical impetus of restorative justice need not involve formulating ahistorical, universal moral maxims, specifying how these should be applied in all contexts, or ensuring fidelity to definitional principles of restorative justice.

Conceptualizing ethics thus involves a degree of nominalism, for it is only through particular instances of hospitality that ethical subjects are negotiated. This said, how should we understand hospitality?[9] Etymo- logically, hospitality derives from the Latin *hospitale* connoting 'of a guest' (Ayto 1993: 287), and from *hospitare*, 'to receive as a guest' (Skeat 1993: 209). This place of reception constitutes the welcome, where the other (foreigner, guest, stranger, etc.) is received into one's home, event, nation, etc. Ethics takes shape through the how of this welcome, the manner in which the unformed content of a given instance of hospitality plays out. The contingency of hospitality delineates ethics and its uncertain, undecided, negotiations of how to be with others.

Hospitality, however, is self-contradictory and never fully attainable.[10] It is never possible to host without constraint, for to do so would be to yield hospitality to some other arena (asceticism, sainthood?); at the same time, to host with constraint is to limit the seemingly unrestrained welcome that attaches to western preconceptions of hospitality. Thus,

> Hospitality is a self-contradictory concept and experience which can only self-destruct ... put otherwise, produce itself as impossible, only be possible on the condition of its impossibility ... or protect itself from itself, auto-immunize itself in some way, which is to say,

deconstruct itself – precisely – in being put into practice (Derrida 2000: 5).

Hospitality (and its welcome) therefore never exists as such – it is always to come, of the future. The host is plagued by inhospitable motivations – selfishness, greed, control, manipulation etc. – and so does not measure up to unconditional hospitality. S/he imagines future occasions that would improve upon the hospitality of a past event. This paradoxical encounter between infinite preconceptions and finite instances of being a host makes hospitality (and its associated ethics) possible.

This paradox makes clear that we cannot know hospitality absolutely. To start with, hospitality does not lend itself to 'objective knowledge' – we may have a 'pre-comprehension' of the concept, yet this pre-comprehension resists stable definition (i.e. it is 'before', pre-, knowledge). Furthermore, hospitality does not exist through time – it is an 'intentional experience' and as such it is not so much a being as an ethical imperative (Derrida 2000: 5). That is, the experience is a temporally fleeting moment, a vague prescription (how should I be hospitable?) not a discoverable entity. In addition, hospitality is never present in the sense that it is 'not yet' – since one is never a perfect host, s/he always defers to future possibilities to be a better host. That is, if the host can never be a perfect host without giving up the required mastery of place where guests are received, '...hospitality can only ever take place beyond hospitality, in deciding to let it come, overcoming the hospitality that paralyses itself on the threshold which it is' (Derrida 2000: 14).

The paradox is re-enacted through the etymology of the term 'host' which contains traces of its opposite (see Ayto 1993: 287). The word derives from the Indo-European *ghostis* (stranger), the Greek *xenos* (guest, stranger – as in 'xenophobia') and the Latin *hostis* (stranger, enemy – as in 'hostility'). The welcoming host who invites the stranger retains power and mastery (*pets, potis, potes*) over the place of reception. S/he bears traces of the hostile warrior who approaches the stranger as enemy (*hostilis*). But as master of the house, the host welcomes, receives and opens to the other. As such,

> The *hospes* is someone who has the power to host someone, so that neither the alterity (*hostis*) of the stranger, nor the power (*potentia*) of the host is annulled by the hospitality (Caputo and Derrida 1997: 110).

Situated between mastery and conviviality, hospitality is conditioned through the undecided place where the host invites, welcomes and meets the other.

This understanding raises several issues regarding the 'host' and 'guest' as ethical subjects. For one, they do not meet each other as pre-existing subjects or determined entities. Rather ethical subjects are developed through the welcome, the 'hospitality of the other'; the subject *is* in a strong sense a response to the other ('...there is no first yes, the yes is already a response ... it is necessary to begin by responding.' Derrida 1999: 24). The hosting subject is thus response to the guest and so hostage to the others' primordial calls to respond; s/he is continuous response(s) to the other who is welcomed. At the same time, the guest is received as a specific subject, 'victim', 'offender', 'community representative', etc.

In all cases, the welcome is a moment of excess; it exceeds the capacity of any subject in a finite context. The responsively created host welcomes, knowing that any given instance is never completely hospitable and that s/he is the creation of local performances of the welcome. As such, ethical subjects are always profoundly responsible for each other and to the traces of otherness to which given responses are addressed. This call of the other is both infinite and constitutive of the finite subject. The subject is thus nothing other than response to traces of otherness, addressed from within a (welcoming) context. As Derrida puts it,

> The other is in me before me: the ego (even the collective ego) implies alterity as its own condition. There is no 'I' that ethically makes room for the other, but rather an 'I' that is structured by the alterity within it, an 'I' that is itself in a state of self-deconstruction, dislocation (2001: 84).

Umberto Eco underscores the point: ethics is about being with others, and the subject is born out of the ethical response in which the other calls upon the subject to respond. Quite literally then, the 'other is in us':

> This is not a vague sentimental propensity, but rather a basic condition. As we are told by the most secular of the social sciences, it is the other, his gaze, that defines us and determines us. Just as we couldn't live without eating or sleeping, we cannot understand who we are without the gaze and reaction of the other. Even those who kill, rape, rob, and violate do so in exceptional moments, and the rest of the time beg love, respect, praise from others. And even from those they humiliate, they seek recognition in the form of fear and submission... We might die or go insane if we lived in a community in which everyone had systematically decided never to look at us and to behave as if we didn't exist (Eco and Martini 1997: 94).

As such, the subject of restorative justice who is cast as victim, as bearer of rights or suffering or evil, as offender, etc., is not an absolute entity; it takes shape through complex ethical contexts and with others.

Moreover, to the extent that the other is an unnamable dimension of any self (for future forms of the self can never be predicted or limited by the horizons of the present), a given subject's responsibility to the other is infinite.[11] This infinite responsibility is encountered obliquely and mostly apprehended outside reason-based discourse. It is a pre-apprehension that – as Levinas (1998: chapter 7) argues – is glimpsed through the 'face', or rather through traces of otherness encountered through an un-specifiable 'face' beyond clear perception. Memories of this face structure our recognition of being-in-a-world-with-others. And therein lie the auspices of ethics together with the infinite responsibility that enables any finite ethical self to be.[12] Both host and guest are constituted by specific instances of the welcome. There is no independent host or guest: their identities emerge from within places where hospitality is extended.

These comments on hospitality suggest an ethics that could open restorative justice practices up to possibilities that are simply not available so long as conventional ethical calculations of human rights, harm, com-munity interest, or victim rights, absolute ethical frameworks or universal maxims are assumed. What are some implications of this ethics as hospitality for restorative justice?

An ethics of restorative justice: imagining future being with others

If the ethics of restorative justice is conceived as hospitality, then the various ways in which participants are welcomed to finite restorative processes are especially consequential.[13] If restorative justice welcomes in ways alternative to criminal justice institutions, then it works under different auspices from the law-based, universalizing, retributive, adversarial calculations of criminal justice. Its ethics need not defer to universal principles, natural subjects, or to the idea that ethical dilemmas of justice can ultimately be settled through absolute courtroom judgments. Such an ethics implies specific images of justice, ethical subjects and ways of framing moral discourse.

Is restorative justice universalizable?

Understanding ethics as hospitality refers us to local instances of the welcome where attempts are made to open up to others. The ethical arena at hand is neither uniform nor teleological. It is a self-contradictory horizon of thought/practice coextensive with various welcomes extended, and the creation of finite ethical subjects with infinite aspirations and responsibilities. Returning to an idea previously noted, this means that justice is best understood as an incalculable, undeconstructable promise imagined in finite contexts (Lyotard and Thebaud 1979; Derrida 1992; Pavlich 2000, 1996a). Its promise is infinite – it never arrives. Its power lies in the enticing lure variously held out through promises of what might be, what might become. Justice's appeal is especially enticing to subjects who define their plight as unjust, and who seek changes, new life, in the name of justice. But the incalculability of justice in no way annuls our responsibility to imagine just patterns of being with others in context. This is a fundamental responsibility of being with others, of any ethical self's being (that is, quite literally, I am constituted through the other).

Ethics imagines multiple promises of justice through absent promises sent forth, again and again, calculated in local encounters with others. There are no guarantees, and no universal justice absolves us of the responsibility to challenge totalitarian programmes that claim to be necessary. This responsibility assumes that no justice – restorative, criminal or any other – is ever beyond potentially disastrous outcomes. More precisely, no calculation of justice can escape the horrific tragedies of totalitarian closure, of allowing closed systems of thought to reign supreme. We ought to remember that many of the greatest political excesses have propelled themselves under mantles of absolute justice. The force of justice, if anything, weighs in against totalitarian thinking that universalizes itself as necessary. It always keeps the way open for new calculations. Preserving such openings, encouraging cultures of critique that beckon to new signs of life, could be ethics' abiding aspiration (Pavlich, 2000). No amount of willing – even if through pretences of universal, necessary, or progressive moral maxims – can evade the ubiquitous totalitarian potential of any system of ethics.

In this light, restorative justice should continuously calculate justice, for the promise of justice is never captured through given calculations. Justice is ultimately incalculable from finite spaces, but this in no way diminishes continuous aspirations towards justice; it may even make more urgent the need to keep calculating justice. Harm, victimhood, and the call to heal broken relationships are not intrinsically ethical – they are political creations that claim to serve a given calculation of justice. Ethics as hospitality demands ongoing attention to the form and effects of restorative justice's calculations. A hospitable restorative justice will keep discussing and challenging the ways in which it professes to welcome, deferring to the promise of a future justice and imagining new ways to be with others.

Who are the ethical subjects of restorative justice?

Restorative justice encounters are instituted, put into play, at moments of invitation and welcome. The parties to the welcome at, say, family group conferences, are invited to accept roles demanded by its brand of 'restorative' justice. In general, this means avoiding adversarial processes that pit ethical subjects against one another before judges, prosecutors and defence attorneys/advocates. In addition, calculations of restorative justice do not focus on determining whether a specific law has been broken, or who is guilty of transgression, etc. Agents of restorative justice (field officers, referees, mediators) welcome 'victims', 'offenders', 'family members', 'social workers' etc., inviting each to tell the truth about themselves in relation to specified events. The hosting subject welcomes all according to rules of a restorative justice process (mediation, conciliation, conferences, etc.), and obliges participants (in order to continue with the process) to accept specified freedoms and constraints.

The outcome, situational though it may be, is a complex series of implicit and explicit negotiations that produces specific ethical subjects – hosts, guests and 'others'. These ethical subjects are, as noted, not primordial to the ethical encounter. There are no absolute victims, offenders, etc. No absolutely shaped, inviolable, ethical subject meets the welcome, places its stamp upon it; instead, subjects become present at the instant of the encounter. Ethical subjects are thus created by, and creatures of, local welcoming procedures. Could restorative justice's welcome be viewed as an opportunity to create new subjects and patterns of association, perhaps beyond isolated individuals in communities? After all, the events that bring people to restorative justice have in some way emerged from, and/or shattered, the sinews of their previous ways of being with others.

Perhaps restorative justice could be viewed as a dissociation and deconstruction of subject identities for those who are named as recipient or doer of unjust, wrong, unacceptable, harmful etc. behaviour. The deconstruction of identities involved in having subjects face each other (at say, family group conferences), may be seen as a preface to imagining new patterns of existence with others. No doubt, subjects as host/guests approach the threshold of restorative justice institutions with memories of otherness, the imperceptible 'faces', through which they have emerged as particular kinds of selves. The other in the I, created through past ethical encounters, is carried over, and meets the threshold of a particular restorative justice's welcome. What is brought in from the past, traces of previous relations with others, will bear on the ways in which subjects of a given restorative justice session call and respond to the welcome. Their responses will constitute what eventually emerges as the subjects of a given instance of restorative justice. This is as much the case for the referee as host, who is also hostage to the scene, as it is for guests who must contemplate the events that have variously led them to restorative justice.

In light of the above, one might raise an issue about the ways that many restorative justice practices narrow the scope of subject formation by demanding participants to play the roles of 'victim', 'offender', 'family member' and to focus exclusively on a given 'harm', 'community transgression', 'crime' and so on. This form of welcome radically limits ethics, and the promise of justice, because it requires subjects to appropriate 'justice' through individual conciliation, healing, atonement, redemption or repentance. By contrast, ethics as hospitality demands that we do not calculate justice by presuming subjects with predetermined natures who live in fixed communal patterns. The encounter between host (e.g. referees) and guests (victims, families, members of the 'community', and offender) could also create spaces for the negotiation of new ethical terrains, for subjects, identities and collective lives yet to be conceived.

Crucial here are the ways in which negotiations of subject identity occur – there are no absolutes, no certainties, no guarantees.[14] All that there is, is the welcome; the ethical voices that this releases in finite contexts bear an infinite responsibility to future forms of the welcome, to future ways of being with others promised by an incalculable justice. This image of restorative ethics endorses the idea that different circumstances, calculations of otherness and hospitality can elicit diverse sorts of ethical subjects in search of justice.

What guarantees does restorative ethics conceived as hospitality provide?

In short, none; but this is not exclusive to its ethics. No doubt the question raises a worry often directed to postmodern formulations: if ethics does not involve developing a secure ground (universal principles, absolute visions of justice, etc.) then how can we identify, let alone avert, disastrous political programmes derived from unethical precepts? The question is an important one whose shadow remains long after its modern auspices have faded into the uncertainties of our times (Bauman 1993). We have already noted that despite the assurances ascribed to the role of universal moral maxims (or maybe even because of the delusion involved in thinking ethics could ever be absolute) blood has flowed around and through the seams of human order. Wars have raged more furiously than ever, imperial weapons have expunged so many lives and, to repeat, let us not forget the blueprints behind the Gulags, the holocaust, apartheid, etc. In the shadows of such disasters it may be apposite to state the point bluntly: maxims cannot guarantee justice any more than they necessarily work against totalitarian injustice.

Recognising these limits again suggests the 'incurably *aporetic*' character of ethics. It may also be seen as refusing the blackmail of a politics that requires one to speak ethically as if a universal *telos* reigned supreme. This refusal could reclaim ethics as an undecidable terrain of thinking; ethical decisions are made in restorative practices without the comfort of secure foundations, and outside of necessary political programs. That is, 'decisions must be made and responsibility, as we say, taken, without the assurance of an ontological foundation' (Derrida 1999: 21). The values of restorative justice cannot be projected as incontrovertible guiding lights for political processes. Equally, because ethical decisions always involve a leap outside the context of what is presently possible, they are never politically necessary.[15] Our ethical responsibilities are contingently structured but infinite. Hence, ethics should resist any attempts to close politics off through totalitarian programmes – this is a key responsibility.

With this complex responsibility in mind, restorative ethics as hospitality is at its heart ambiguous and *aporetic*. Unknowable and self-contradicting hospitality provides a space where subjects created through a restorative welcome must calculate justice without any certainty, or sure blueprints. The only weapon against totalitarian political programmes is this: cultivate undecidable spaces that exhort subjects to calculate – continuously – infinite promises of justice from within finite circumstances. This is the difficult and never-ending work of ethics that cannot be abandoned for quick fixes, universal guidelines or mandatory maxims. A hospitable restorative ethics strives for something else: to nurture the promise of justice that imagines new ways of existing with others.

Apertures

The force, power and promise of this restorative justice ethics lies here: it never actually exists, is never fully there in a given instance. Restorative ethics – reflections on how to imagine new ways of being with others – is linked to infinite promises of justice that beckon as alternatives to what is. The ethical imagination is particularly relevant at moments when subjects declare an injustice and yearn for transformed futures. Such imaginings are contemplated within the finite limits through which we live our lives, and breathe life into restorative justice's ethics as hospitality. This ethics persistently involves a welcome to otherness, to a future, as yet not possible. It does not yield mastery over the place where gatherings take place without asserting itself as universally necessary. Such are the aporetic auspices of postmodern ethics, and therein lies an opening, an aperture, for glimpsing an ethical language of restorative justice that refuses to be blackmailed by universal maxims. There is, no doubt, an ironic justice in refusing the imperialism of a universalized ethics.

Notes

1. There is, however, considerable debate on the degree to which restorative justice does or should offer a 'maximalist' alternative to retributive justice (see Walgrave 2000), and whether there are important continuities between criminal justice and restorative practices (see Daly 2000).
2. See, for instance, Zehr (1990), Van Ness and Strong (1997), and Sullivan *et al.* (1998).
3. For example, Braithwaite (1998, 1999, 2000), Bazemore (1998), Harris (1998), Walgrave (1995, 1998, 1999), Galloway and Hudson (1996), Mika (1995) and Zehr (1995).
4. Surveying the wide-ranging field, Strang and Braithwaite point out that, 'Restorative justice is conceived in the literature in two different ways. One is a process conception, the other a values conception' (2001: 1). As this chapter addresses an ethics of restorative justice, it will largely engage the 'values conception', and particularly the question of how such values may be articulated under current conditions.
5. Badiou contests the view that this conception of ethics is a self-evident fact of life on the grounds that it is inconsistent with the 'perfectly obvious' reality which, '…is characterized in fact by the unrestrained pursuit of self-interest, the disappearance or extreme fragility of emancipatory politics, the multi-plication of "ethnic" conflicts, and the universality of unbridled competition' (2001: 10).
6. See, for example, Umbreit (2001, 1994), Bazemore (1998), etc.
7. For Badiou, subjects are potentially much more than victims, and casting them as such in order to deal with a given situation denies fundamental aspects of their existence with others, beyond their being objective bearers of suffering. Also, focusing on victims centres ethical discussion on evil, thus eliminating discussions of the good and a broad-based discussion of a 'positive vision of possibilities'. For him, human subjectivity is 'sustained by the incalculable and the un-possessed' (2001: 14), by non-being: 'To forbid him to imagine the Good, to work towards the realization of unknown possibilities, to think what might be in terms that break radically with what is, is quite simply to forbid him humanity as such' (2001: 14).
8. Levinas makes the same point thus: 'Ethics, here, does not supplement a preceding existential base; the very node of the subjective is knotted in ethics understood as responsibility' (1998: 95).
9. To help grapple with this question, I shall draw on Derrida's various analyses of the concept (see 1999, 2000, 2001 and Derrida and Dufourmantelle 2000).
10. See Derrida and Dufourmantelle (2000: 77–83).

11. Following Levinas, Derrida insists that this is crucial: 'If responsibility were not infinite, if every time that I have to take an ethical or political decision with regard to the other… those were not infinite, then I would not be able to engage myself in an infinite debt with regard to the singularity. I owe myself infinitely to each and every singularity. If responsibility were not infinite, you could not have moral political problems. There are only moral and political problems, and everything that follows from this, from the moment that responsibility is not limitable' (1999: 86).

12. Let us recall, ethics as hospitality involves a continuous, if always finite, opening up to the infinite: 'hospitality is infinite or it is not at all; it is granted upon the welcoming of the idea of infinity, and thus of the unconditional…' (Derrida 1999: 48)

13. Although I use the term 'welcome' for the sake of avoiding the cumbersome welcome(s), I take for granted – and indeed consistently with what has already been said about the ambiguity of restorative processes – that there are multiple forms of this welcome that claim the name of restorative justice.

14. Here Foucault's work on ethics becomes directly relevant. He speaks of a 'ethical work' in which selves are constituted by working on themselves against moral codes (see Foucault, 1984, 1994). I have elsewhere indicated the value of this conception for community mediation (Pavlich 1996b). That analysis is directly applicable to the sort of ethical work that particular hosts/ guests conduct in welcoming, and responding to, traces of the other.

15. This creates a useful 'distance' between ethics and politics, between values and processes, which Derrida reflects on thus: 'Without silence, without the hiatus, which is not the absence of rules but the necessity of a leap at the moment of the ethical, political, or juridical decision, we could simply unfold knowledge into a program or course of action. Nothing could make us more irresponsible; nothing could be more totalitarian' (1999: 117).

Chapter 2

Victimalization and restorative justice: moral backgrounds and political consequences

Hans Boutellier

In this chapter I would like to raise two questions. The first question is how the emergence of restorative justice can be understood within its social, moral and cultural context. What has happened in western societies that the restorative justice movement increasingly finds fertile soil for its initiatives? The second question is what this explanation tells us about the consequences for the future of restorative justice. It is important that the restorative justice movement understands its own emergence. If you know where you come from, you might better understand where you are heading.

Using the words restorative justice I would like to refer to the definition of Bazemore and Walgrave (1999b: 48): 'every action that is primarily oriented towards doing justice by restoring the harm that has been caused by a crime'. In their view this harm transcends the victim; it includes the environment, the community, society as a whole and even the offender himself. In order to add a little to the understanding of restorative justice I need to cover some broad issues. The first deals with the characteristics of contemporary morality; the second issue is the development of the criminal justice system in recent decades.

Crime as a moral problem

Reflecting on crime and justice we can use several perspectives, which all have their own legitimacy. The first perspective is related to the rule of (criminal) law: crime is defined by criminal law and refers to the framework of criminal justice: prosecution, criminal trial and sentencing. Although in the theory and practice of punishment various goals are distinguished, retribution is the backbone of this perspective on crime and justice. According to the definition of criminal law 'a wrong' has been done, and penance by inflicting pain is required to compensate the violation of law.

The second perspective is a social one in which crime is understood as an effect of social (and psychological) conditions. It was the main perspective of the penal–welfarist criminology which dominated the twentieth century (Garland 2001); its aim is to determine the causes of deprivation which lead to criminal behaviour. There are several sorts of deprivation: psychological and physical neglect, poverty, bad living conditions and so on. The hope of the social perspective is the rehabilitation of the criminal offender. From a wider social perspective efforts are made to improve the social conditions of the (potential) offenders.

As a third perspective I would like to add a moral one, which in my view has now become more and more important. When I entered the field of criminology two decades ago, I was surprised that morality was not a subject of research and understanding at all. Trained as a social psychologist in the tradition of positivism I expected to find a moral perspective in criminology, but in none of the criminological textbooks did I find the word morality in the indexes. Morality seemed to be an off-word, used by priests and theologians, but not by criminologists. A moral perspective was chosen only by the occasional right-wing criminologist such as James Q. Wilson.

In my view things have changed, however. It is increasingly relevant to understand crime as a moral matter, or maybe better, primarily as a matter of cultural and historical ideas about good and evil. A criminal act is a violation of a norm which is – rightly or not – objectified and defined by criminal law. Crime derives its significance from our moral beliefs, understandings and institutions. It is related to our intuitions about good and evil and criminal acts take place within this normative context. From a moral perspective we can learn about the motives, attitudes and beliefs which surround the criminal act and the reactions of the public. A moral perspective is necessary to understand the 'crime complex' of today's societies.

Summarizing these three perspectives one could say that crime is defined by criminal law, caused by social factors and acquires its significance from the moral context. It is this moral context which in my view has determined the emergence of restorative justice. To put this somewhat schematically: as the law perspective is connected to retribution and the penal–welfarist perspective to rehabilitation, so is the moral perspective related to restorative justice. Although moral premises are part and parcel of every response to crime, it is characteristic of restorative justice, because the moral – or ethical – perspective is dominant in the very idea of restoration.

Restorative justice defines, more or less explicitly, crime as a moral act for which the offender – as a moral subject – is responsible and account-able. Although the criminal act is defined by law, and is caused by social factors, the offender is addressed as a moral subject who has harmed another person, group or even society. It is expected from the offender that he understands what he has done and restores or compensates the harm done to the victim and to the community. What is hoped for is a moral agreement between the people concerned in the restorative process: reparation, an apology, moral reflection, expression of regret, or reconciliation.

A moral view on crime is not new, of course. Durkheim has understood crime as an infringement of the unity of the *conscience collective* of the moral community (Durkheim, 1893). In his view criminal procedure must be seen as 'a celebration of morality'. The community confirms its moral conditions by punishing the offence against these conditions. The moral culpability of the offender is presupposed, but the recognition of his culpability by himself is not necessary. In the daily practice of the courtrooms the moral inclusion of the offender is seldomly realized (Garland 1990).

Moreover, the moral community of Durkheim's days no longer exists. 'The community' as defined by Tönnies as an obvious 'sameness' has become a problem. According to Bauman (2001b) the community is something which we might long for, but which can no longer be realized in contemporary individualized, multi-ethnic societies. This has con-sequences for the way offending is understood and judged; restorative justice re-invents, so to say, the moral character of crime, but it does so in a new form.

Victimalization

If we understand crime as a moral act, it is necessary to get some grip on the morality of our times. There is a lot to say about this subject, but as a point of departure we can say that the moral conditions of today's western societies have dramatically changed. I would like to diagnose the morality of our times in two propositions. Many authors agree upon the first of these: morality has been fragmentized and privatized. During the last three decades of the twentieth century we shifted from an institutional ethic of duty to an individualistic ethic of self-fulfilment.

Giddens (1990) in this respect speaks of the identity- or self-politics which are characteristic of 'late modernity'. Constructing and developing a self is the major assignment of our times. We are no longer supported by strong moral traditions, institutions and expectations. We are – in the words of MacIntyre (1983) – 'unencumbered selves', who have to cope with an intuitive, emotivist morality – what MacIntyre regrets. In the words of Lyotard (1979), we are not united any more by 'grand narratives', grand ideals or political ideologies. 'Postmodern' civilisation has gradually undermined the unity of religion or ideology.

Our beliefs and ideas on how to live a good life are individualized. Everyone can (or has to) design and manage his own life project. Every human subject can choose any God he likes, and he may even think that he is God himself (not uncommon in our narcisistic era). But we have to be more precise here; there is another side to this, which relates to the second proposition on the morality of our times. While our consensus on the good life is privatized, our common moral understanding focuses on 'evil'. It is 'bad behaviour' which triggers the need for moral consensus.

'Communality' in public morality is found in what we reject. And what we reject most in liberal, secular societies is cruelty: suffering, humiliation and victimhood (Shklar, 1984). As the American philosopher Richard Rorty (1989) has stated, the central moral question of our times is: 'Are you suffering?' In an individualized culture the main evil is 'harm done to individuals'. We recognize here 'the harm principle' which was formulated by John Stuart Mill in the nineteenth century: our freedom is limited by the freedom of others. No harm may be done by violation of other people's physical or psychological domain. This liberal point of view was hidden behind the political and confessional philosophies of life in the twentieth century.

Now these 'grand narratives' have been broken down, cruelty, suffering and humiliation are the vices of liberal society. It is not that everyone is guided by the rejection of these vices, but they have become the keywords in our common moral language and have a primary position in our individual accountability and deliberations. For that reason the victim has become the main character of our times. I propose the use of the word 'victimalization' to describe the essence of today's morality, victimalization defined as the processes by which – on an individual level

– suffering is defined as victimization, and – on a cultural level – morality is defined as agreement on victimization (Boutellier, 2000).

It stands between victimization (becoming a victim) and criminalization (defining deviant behaviour as crime), and describes the victim as a sociological category. Nowadays morality is no longer an integrated, institutionalized taken-for-granted matter of ideas and ideals. Morality is no more and no less than the sum of fragmented answers to questions of life, with which every individual has to cope ('existentialism' as a social fact).

We find our common moral grounds in the rejection of evil and cruelty. It is not that we always agree on the subject of who is suffering or who is treated in a humiliating way. But our common moral vocabulary is found at the negative pole of moral communication. That is why the victim has become the main moral agent of postmodern culture. Restorative justice can be seen as a very special moral response to this cultural process of victimalization.

The safety problem and criminal justice

Crime is defined by criminal law, and a criminal act triggers a penal system of investigation, prosecution and sentencing. But over the last decades the victim has become the focal point in the morality of contemporary culture; the criminal justice system is more and more in need of a response to this victimalized morality. How can we understand the emergence of restorative justice from this institutional point of view? To answer that question we need to have a closer look at the safety problem.

Safety has become one of the main topics of our era. In today's societies it has become, so to say, a number one issue. Concentrating on the crime problem, I would like to stipulate three reasons for the dominance of the safety issue – the increase in crime, the growing sensitivity to crime and the increased interest of the state in reducing crime. From the 1960s onwards crime was rising steeply in most western countries. In the Netherlands, for example, in 2000 the recorded crime rate (1.3 million) was ten times that of 1960 (130,000). Related to the increase of the population there was a sixfold growth in crime rates in about forty years (Huls *et al.* 2001). According to Dutch victim surveys, 25 to 30 per cent of citizens become a victim of crime each year.

During the 1990s there was in some countries some stabilization or even a decrease in crime. However, in European countries violent crime, especially among youngsters, was still rising. Although there has always been a lot of criminological debate on the issue of increase in crime, there can be no doubt that the population in general became more and more 'victimized'. This increase in crime influenced, of course, public opinion on crime. The safety problem became a number one issue because of the growing amount of crime in the first place.

A second reason why the safety problem has become such a big issue in contemporary western cultures is the increase in sensitivity to crime. The rise in crime rates might be partly related to a growing attention and sensitivity to criminal behaviour. More attention to certain crimes, or to crime in general, may have influenced the activity of the police in recording crime. But more important is that citizens have become more sensitive as potential victims of crime. The mass media in particular played an important role in generating an increase in the fear that one might become a victim of crime. This fear is – due to the crime rates – understandable for certain people in certain places. But there seems to be a 'paradox of fear' making the least victim-prone people the most frightened ones (older women).

In addition there seems to be a tendency to criminalize more types of behaviour because they no longer fit with our understanding of civilization (rape in marriage and domestic violence for example). Rising crime figures and victimalization of morality go very well together and they have led to a growing attention to the safety problem. This public attention is of course very important for the state. If we realize how the rise of nation-states was entangled with guarantees of safety (internal and external; Van Creveld 1999), we understand why politicians are so obsessed by the safety issue. Safety is one of the main pillars of the legitimation of the power of the state – and this is the third reason why the safety problem has become a number one issue.

If citizens no longer trust the state any more to bring about a reasonable state of social order in an adequate way, its institutions are really in trouble. We remember the Dutroux case in Belgium which led to mass demonstrations and a political crisis (Walgrave and Rihoux 1997). I do not want to go into detail here; it suffices to stress that the increase in crime, in the sensitivity toward crime and the importance of the safety issue for the state, together put enormous pressure on the criminal justice system. It results in an ever-growing demand for criminal justice. The victimalized morality forms a breeding ground for an anxious and worried population, for desperate politicians and for a criminal justice system seeking a credible response.

The criminal justice paradox

In most western countries the growing demand for criminal justice interventions has led to an enormous growth of the criminal justice system: more police, more prosecutors, more sentencing, more prisons. It has also led to an interesting diversification of penal sentences and measures. It is important to realize, however, that the growing demand for criminal justice is accompanied by distrust in its supply. In spite of the growth of the criminal justice system, there is still a growing demand for more. It seems that there is a never-ending demand for what essentially will remain in limited and poor supply. I would like to elaborate this argument on three levels: quantitative, qualitative and theoretical.

Quantitatively I would like to use again the crime figures of the Netherlands (Huls *et al.* 2001). In 1999 there were 4.8 million offences according to the victim survey of that year (offences against business and retail outlets, fraud and victimless crimes are not included). About 35 per cent of these offences were recorded by the police (1.3 million); about one fifth were forwarded to the prosecutor's office (the clearance rate was 15 per cent). In about 190,000 cases some kind of punishment was delivered, 25,000 offenders were annually sent into custody. In spite of the growth of the criminal justice system (for example: from 4,000 to 12,500 prison cells in fifteen years) less than 15 per cent of the crimes recorded by the police resulted in sanctions under the criminal justice system.

This means that the criminal justice system – quantitativily – has a very limited coverage with respect to the total number of crimes against citizens. This picture becomes even more confusing if we compare these figures to those of 1960. In that year there were about 130,000 crimes recorded by the police, of which more than 50 per cent were cleared up, while 60 per cent of these ended in punishment. In those years about 45 per cent of the recorded crimes were punished by the criminal justice system. The demand for penal intervention is increasing, while its actual instrumental impact is decreasing!

There seems to be a comparable paradox in a qualitative sense. It is common knowledge that prisons are good schools for bad behaviour. Estimates on recidivism range from 40 to 70 per cent. In general sentencing comes too late (too much time between the start of a criminal career and the first correction) and sentencing is too slow (too much time between the offence(s) and the execution of the sentence). What is intended to be a moral judgement and an (implicit) hope for improvement turns out to be a measure of exclusion and defiance. Garland (1990: 80) speaks of the tragic quality of punishment: it causes the opposite of what it intends, social exclusion instead of moral inclusion.

The third reason for the existence of a criminal justice paradox is a theoretical one, or perhaps a dogmatical one. Historically, criminal law is codified in most western countries as an ultimate remedium. It has never been understood and developed as a system which is intended to play a dominant role in constructing social order. It is individually oriented, with important guarantees against its misuse by a powerful state. The constitutional embeddedness of criminal law generates tensions between political and public demands and the inherent requirements of prudence in the use of criminal law and sentencing.

In conclusion: there seems to be an ever-growing demand for what is meant to be an ultimate remedium. Besides the growth of criminal justice institutions, this has serious effects on the 'culture of crime', or in the words of David Garland (2001), the crime complex. These effects are ambivalent in their directions: they range from tougher policies and sentences to a search for tailor-made sanctions and different methods of dealing with crime. In my opinion we can observe two major consequences of the paradoxical tension between supply and demand in the criminal justice field: on the one hand there is a growing rationalization of the criminal justice systems, while on the other we can observe a growing moralization in the ways the safety problems are approached.

Like other governmental areas the criminal justice system is influenced by processes of managerialism and marketization. The citizen (as a victim or a potential victim) is seen as client, sentencing as a product, the different stages of the criminal process are organized like a chain, and punishment is judged in terms of effects and consequences. This rationalization of the criminal justice process has – in Weberian terms – to be understood as *Zweckrationalität*, which received a radical impulse in the neoliberal eighties and nineties of the last century. In relation to the limited coverage by the criminal justice system of the crime problem, its representatives seem to utter something like this: 'although it is not very much, at least we try to make the best of it.' In that respect there also seems to be a tendency toward harsher sentencing.

Next to this rationalization process however, another development can be observed, which I would like to call the moralization of the safety problem. This tendency is not so much focused on the enforcement of criminal law as such, but on the maintenance or revitalization of values and norms which lie behind criminal law. For this tendency I can refer to some recent adaptations of the criminal justice system, like the introduction of community service, victim schemes and made-to-measure sanctions. But moralization can also be seen in several initiatives and programmes in the sphere of crime prevention and community safety.

In the US, for example, the prevention strategy Communities that Care

(CtC) was developed by the criminologists Hawkins and Catalano (Hawkins 1999). This strategy aims to redesign the work of community development, especially local youth policy, in such a way that it can effectively tackle problems of crime, violence, substance abuse and some others. CtC is an example of the way in which the prevention of norm violations inspire the social policy of communities. The strategy is oriented toward stimulating 'healthy behaviour' by attacking 'risk factors' like 'bad family management' and stimulating protective factors like 'school attendance'. Although the CtC strategy can be seen as a form of social technology, its essence is an (unproblemized) normative redesign of social policy, which aims to prevent and reduce criminal behaviour.

Another example is the development of so-called 'community justice' or 'neighbourhood prosecution'. These initiatives aim to adapt the criminal justice system to local safety problems. The constructive powers (schools, community centres, churches and so on) are supported by a problem-oriented criminal justice system in order to realize a more integrated approach to safety problems of the community. In more and more urban contexts preventative partnerships of the police, justice and local organizations are developing. In general we can observe a growing entanglement of social and criminal justice policy (Boutellier 2001).

The aforementioned pressure on the system and the resulting paradox of much demand for an ultimate remedium has created space for innovations and alternatives to traditional ways of dealing with crime. In this space for problem- and context-oriented approaches to the safety problems of local community there is a growing need for norm-establishing projects in which offenders, victims and the community are involved (Mannozzi 2000). Against this background it is understandable that restorative justice schemes, like mediation or group conferencing, are seen as viable alternatives to law and order politics. In this respect restorative justice is – nothing more and nothing less than – an attempt to cope with the problems of crime, victimization and norm-violation in a new moral and cultural context.

Political consequences

In a morally divided, plural society, criminal law forms a solid ground, by defining cruel and harmful acts as moral wrongs. I do fully agree with Antony Duff (in this book) where he states that criminal law defines 'public wrongs'. I do not do so because I believe these wrongs are naturally defined or God-given, but because they have been throughout the ages slowly engraved in the legal system. Criminal law has a long and strong tradition of coding, recoding and institutionalizing of reactions and interventions with respect to morally unacceptable behaviour. Even if crime is understood as a 'social construction', we must admit that it is a very strong construction and that there are good reasons for this – the rejection of victimization for example. Criminal law has – in other words – a very important moral significance in 'pluriform culture'.

At the same time we recognize that the instrumental meaning of the criminal justice system is actually very limited. Quantitatively, qualitatively and dogmatically the criminal justice system cannot meet the extreme expectations of politicians and the public. Because the 'supply' of the criminal justice system is so limited and ineffective, it tends to give direction to normative community building strategies. It does so not in an instrumental way but as a normative institution which defines 'public wrongs'. In several countries one can see a growing entanglement of social policy and criminal justice into a community safety policy.

Whether this must be judged as a desirable development or not depends on our political views. Several authors (Goris 2001; Wacquant 2001) are critical on this point. Gilling (2001), for example, believes there is the risk – at least in the UK – that notwithstanding the social rhetoric on community safety, social policy threatens to become co-opted from a criminal justice point of view. This could lead to a policy of inequality and exclusion. 'So, in the UK, community safety shows little sign of bringing about the socialisation or welfarisation of criminal justice' (Gilling 2001: 398). The restorative justice movement however, which in my view must be understood as part of the same development, makes it possible to deal with the safety problem in a more social way.

Although a critical assessment of community safety is needed in terms of social exclusion, the introduction of restorative ideas in this area does offer a positive element. At least three arguments need to be considered. Firstly, the nature and volume of crime and lack of safety form a serious and real problem for citizens. In theoretical criminology the reality of citizen's experiences with crime are overlooked too easily. The Left Realists had already addressed the issue of the greater chance of victimization for the less privileged in the 1980s, but this reality has not been drawn significantly into the critical criminological analyses. Most attention is devoted to the possible punitive or exclusionary state measures, which bypasses the urgency of the crime problem.

The fact that crime has become an everyday – not wished for – experience, brings with it a sense of urgency which cannot be neglected. The lack of safety in the public domain is a direct threat to the wellbeing of all citizens, also (or maybe especially) to those who are – socially speaking – underprivileged. This brings me to a second argument. Many social institutions and welfare organizations are hindered by safety problems. In some areas the safety issue is such a dominant factor that it prevents institutions from performing their core business. In schools, welfare organizations, social security agencies and public transport in problem areas, crime and problems of lack of safety are dominant problems. Better cooperation with the police and criminal justice agencies can help these institutions to regain space to conduct their essential tasks.

Finally, an argument that has to be drawn into a critical discussion of the development of community safety is that it can be an alternative to a more dangerous option, the shift from a welfare state to a penal state. The security problem has high stakes because it is directly attached to the legitimacy of the state. When citizens lose their trust in the protective functioning of the state this can be a real threat to the social functioning of the state. The development of community safety offers possibilities for the democratization of safety policy by the empowerment of citizens and social institutions. The growth of restorative justice schemes must be understood as part of this development – whether you like it or not. In my view restorative justice is an attempt to add a morally inspired response to the scale of interventions which the criminal justice system so poorly delivers.

Against this background I would like to draw the following conclusions. It seems of minor relevance to look at restorative justice as a countermovement in opposition to the criminal justice system. The relative success of the restorative justice movement must be explained by the victimalization of morality and the safety problem of the twenty-first century. It does have better points of departure than do the criminal justice procedures for restoring harm and suffering, for moral reflection and for the social reintegration of both victim and offender. In that respect restorative justice seems to be able to deal with the safety problem in a more desirable way. The viability of restorative justice will depend on this legitimation as a peacemaking procedure in an era of high crime rates and safety problems.

In this respect restorative justice, as a morally and socially inspired answer to safety problems, should be developed in close cooperation with the criminal justice authorities. The criminal justice system is desperately seeking new answers and procedures which can mitigate the pressure on its institutions. Restorative justice derives its significance from the moralizing of the criminal event in order to overcome the poor moral impact of criminal justice procedures; that is its most convincing argument. It does address the offender and the victim as moral subjects and not as legal subjects, and might be a more effective response to social conflicts, criminal events and safety problems.

I realize that this is quite an instrumental view on the development of restorative justice. Positioning restorative justice as an answer to today's safety problems is not very common in the literature. I have done this on purpose. On the one hand I see objective, historical reasons for defining restorative justice as another response to the crime problem, because it fits very well with today's, strongly divided, morality. At the same time we know from other alternatives – the victim movement, alternative sanctions and crime prevention – that the only way to arrive at a strong position is in being recognized as a relevant device for the problems of the traditional institutions.

Restorative justice means an opportunity to deal with crime and evil in a more subtle way: near the subjects, their motives, their narratives and their understanding of themselves and others; with a better view on the context of the problem; and a better understanding of the possibilities of repairing the harm done and the integration and inclusion of the offender and the victim. An instrumental use of this opportunity seems to me to be a much more challenging perspective than sticking to the idea of having discovered another utopian world.

Chapter 3

The quest for a restorative model of rehabilitation: theory-for-practice and practice-for-theory

Gordon Bazemore and Sandra O'Brien

Introduction

Restorative justice often appears to offer an awkward fit with current juvenile justice policy because it is not clearly connected with widely accepted policy goals. To bring restorative justice into the mainstream, it is therefore important to develop policies and practices that address these virtually universal system goals without sacrificing restorative justice principles in doing so (Umbreit 1999; Bazemore 2000). One such universal goal is promoting offender rehabilitation.

From the beginning of the restorative justice movement, popular literature, policy statements and practitioner guides have been directly connected with offender outcomes including reduced recidivism and rehabilitation (e.g. Schneider 1991; McDonald *et al.* 1995). Research and scholarly literature, on the other hand, deemphasizes this focus and, for good reason, often gives priority to victim needs (Umbreit 1999), even in discussions of offender concerns (Bazemore 1998; Toews and Zehr 2001). For their part, victim advocates present valid criticisms of restorative justice, arguing that there remains a strong offender bias in much restorative practice that at times treats victims as an afterthought (Achilles and Zehr 2001). Practitioners, with the exception of those who work specifically in victim services (Young 1995), are arguably even more likely to lean toward pursuit of offender-oriented objectives, in part because policymakers fund programmes largely based on the promise of reduced recidivism. In fact, a recent survey of restorative conferencing practitioners in the US (Schiff *et al.* 2002) suggests that rehabilitation and other related offender outcomes receive high priority, though most respondents also expressed strong support for victim and community-oriented visions and outcomes.

Restorative justice is, however, not simply or primarily about offender rehabilitation, and it cannot, as some have suggested, be classified simply as 'a new correctional paradigm' (Levrant *et al.* 1999). The core idea and overarching principle of restorative justice, that doing justice requires repairing the harm of crime (Bazemore and Walgrave 1999), should place restorative justice clearly in the category of victim-focused intervention (Achilles and Zehr 2001), though such intervention is clearly three-dimensional in its agenda to seek multiple and collective outcomes for three stakeholders. But while the effort to repair harm is not primarily about rehabilitation, or other offender outcomes, reparation – in all its forms and meanings – can however, lead to such outcomes (Braithwaite 1999). Moreover, we will suggest that the reparative task is essential to reintegration.[1] On the one hand, we agree with some restorative justice advocates that practitioners who try to 'sell' restorative justice practices primarily as an effective new approach to rehabilitation are in Dignan's words 'barking up the wrong tree' (Dignan 1999). On the other hand however, we do so not because we question the appropriateness or potential effectiveness of using restorative practices to change the behaviour of offenders (see also Braithwaite 1999: 69). Rather, we do so because presenting restorative justice as primarily aimed at reducing recidivism is inappropriate because it is fundamentally inconsistent with the normative theory – or values and principles – restorative justice advocates claim to support.

It is simply too early to make the determination about the overall effectiveness of restorative justice in reducing recidivism based on a handful of studies limited primarily to one intervention. However, despite any systematic effort to develop restorative justice ideas as a rehabilitation paradigm, we believe that restorative justice has shown that it has much to offer – especially by virtue of recent breakthroughs and advances in practice in the past five years. Indeed, we and others (e.g. Braithwaite 2001) have in previous work argued that there is great untapped potential in the application of core restorative values and principles to treatment and rehabilitation. We remain optimistic about this prospect given some important changes in thinking and practice about what this would mean.

The primary focus of this chapter is on what is needed to make such changes. Generally, whether viewed as a rehabilitative model with restorative components, or a restorative model of rehabilitation, the important question remains what essential features make an approach to rehabilitation 'restorative'. More practically stated, what is it that a restorative framework and practice contributes to offender rehabilitation that a traditional treatment model does not. We have argued on a number of occasions that the 'restorativeness' of any model of offender reintegration must be grounded in the core principles that constitute a normative theory of restorative justice (e.g. Bazemore and Walgrave 1999; Bazemore 2001). Specifically, based on a critique of the insularity and individualizing tendencies of most current treatment/rehabilitative models, we proposed that the idea of repairing harm implies a collective approach to offender reintegration that begins with a core focus on rebuilding or strengthening relationships damaged by crime, or building new relationships (Bazemore 1999; Bazemore *et al.* 2000; see also Toews and Zehr 2001; Braithwaite 2001).

We have suggested in past work that a restorative model of rehabilitation, as an alternative to the traditional clinical focus on psychological adjustment, would have four essential, but related, features. First, such a relational rehabilitation is fundamentally a naturalistic approach that unlike some other models does not always assume the necessity (or value) of formal intervention. Rather, a more organic process of informal support and social control informs a view of the rehabilitation and desistance process that emphasizes the community role in offender transformation and increased reliance on the role of citizens as 'natural helpers' rather than, or in addition to, juvenile justice professionals. Second, such a model cannot be offender-focused, but in all cases must account for the practical and symbolic role of all primary stakeholders in restorative justice: victim, community, offender and system professionals. When these other stakeholders are not 'in the picture' in a proactive and positive or potentially positive way, the role of intervention is geared around bringing them into the rehabilitative process. Third, removing the barriers between the now compartmentalized juvenile justice system functions should promote a more seamless and resonant relationship between those interventions concerned primarily with offender treatment, risk management and public safety, sanctioning, victim support and prevention. The basis for such convergence would be the idea of repair and relationship building as core outcomes of intervention related to each of these functions. Consistent with the emphasis of this volume on the legal/jurisprudential components of restorative justice, decompartmentalizing justice functions in this way would also mean that a restorative theory and process of 'justice' would become a central feature of a restorative rehabilitation model. Hence, in this merger of justice functions within a restorative framework, we believe we will in turn address at least provisionally two questions of vital concern to scholars focused on the legalistic components of the restorative model: what is the crucial difference between the restorative and traditional models of rehabilitation; and to what extent do these differences represent a satisfactory answer to juridical criticisms of rehabilitative models in general? Finally, as an added benefit, we have argued that a restorative framework for rehabilitation should also be linked through the concept and practice of relationship building to a more socio-ecological or community-level focus (Bazemore 2001; Bazemore and Erbe 2002). Here, networks of relationships built up over time as a by-product of restorative responses at the neighbourhood level have the potential to build *social capital* (Putnam 2000; Rose and Clear 1988) in the form of new and enhanced forms of informal social control and social support (Cullen 1994).

What we and others have failed to do so far is propose and test alternative theories of desistance and reintegration consistent with restorative principles. Such theories, theories-in-use or synthesizing concepts should provide some basis for intervention logic models and intervention theory (Weiss 1997). As suggested by the title of this chapter, a premise of this effort is that we can learn much about such theories from existing practice. To do so, this chapter draws upon qualitative findings from exploratory research on restorative conferencing (Bazemore and Schiff, forthcoming) to illustrate alternative mechanisms through which restorative processes may impact offender transformation. Recognizing that restorative theories of rehabilitation should apply equally to a range of restorative practices, we use the restorative conference as a case study to illustrate how these theories operate as practitioners apply restorative principles in prioritizing specific outcomes in the decision-making process of conferencing programmes.[2]

The value of this exercise is to suggest research questions and propositions for testing the relative importance of intermediate outcomes such as shame, relationship building, social support, and completing reparative obligations in influencing the behaviour of offenders. The urgency about this is that without some priorities for intervention based on empirical findings of impact, practitioners may continue to focus on one or another or combine various theories in unproductive, or even counterproductive, ways. First, in the section that follows, we consider what is known about the impact of restorative practices on offender transformation, and the lack of understanding about why such change might occur. We then briefly review the naturalistic model of restorative, or relational, rehabilitation, and indicate how this can guide our efforts to develop systemic rather than programmatic approaches to intervention grounded in restorative principles.

Restorative practice and a theory of rehabilitation

Regardless of how much theorists, policymakers, and practitioners seek to move restorative justice toward an essential focus on victim needs – and we have argued that this is also essential to its survival – the fact remains that restorative interventions do have implications for offender change.

Comments on empirical data

Certainly, there is now a substantial body of evidence that restorative practices can have a significant impact on recidivism (Schneider 1990; Umbreit 1999; Pennell and Burford 2000). In an important sense this impact is not overwhelming. Critics are correct in their conclusions that restorative justice research has not yielded conclusive evidence that restorative practices reduce recidivism (Dignan 1999; Levrant et al. 1999). This conclusion, however, is misleading when taken to mean, as it often is, that empirical research has demonstrated the ineffectiveness of restorative justice practices in reducing recidivism.

The critics of course present the 'glass is half-empty' side of a debate based on limited evidence. The 'half-full' side would remind us that the same lack of conclusive evidence for effectiveness can be said to character-ize most other juvenile justice programmes. Though some programmes yield comparatively impressive results, the effective treatment program-mes in the current juvenile justice market seem to remain the exception rather than the rule. What is more important to note about restorative justice practice is that no known studies of restorative justice suggest that restorative practices increase recidivism (Walgrave 1999). The same unfortunately cannot be said to be true of scores of popular sanctioning programmes and treatment models that have been clearly shown to make matters worse. Such a finding of neutral, but not harmful, impact in itself would be sufficient for those who argue that benefits of restorative justice practice other than reducing recidivism provide sufficient justification for its use. However, most studies, in fact, indicate some positive impact despite generally (though not uniquely) weak designs and statistical controls (Schneider 1991; Schiff 1999; Umbreit 1999; Braitwaite 1999a; Bazemore et al. 2000; O'Brien et al. 2002).

In another important sense, the limited impact of restorative interventions at this comparatively early stage of both programme development and evaluation may be considered surprisingly strong and robust when viewed in context. Specifically, we have suggested that no one should expect dramatic rehabilitative impacts from short-term conferencing encounters when these are contrasted with long-term, multi-modal treatment programmes whose sole purpose is reducing offender recidivism (Bazemore *et al.* 2000; Bazemore 2001). One may question why anyone should expect a single half-hour meeting between victim and offender, or one experience providing community service or participating in a peacemaking circle to have any significant impact on recidivism – and raising the question in this way implies that restorative justice proponents are naive to say the least (Levrant *et al.* 1999). However, restorative justice practitioners are not naive, and we do not know any who expect one-time conferencing encounters alone to produce much in the way of long-term effects on offence behaviour.

It is therefore quite surprising that such short-term encounters on the whole, and based on the evidence to date, indeed appear to be more impactful than many treatment programmes (Umbreit 1999; Sherman 2000). In their small meta-analysis of some 20 victim–offender mediation programmes, for example, Umbreit and his colleagues found an average of 32 per cent reduction in recidivism (Umbreit 1998). Though these effects do not measure up to those associated with the most effective, high-end, multi-modal treatment programmes (Andrews *et al.* 1990), these short-term restorative programmes perform significantly better than most other long-term treatment programmes in common use.[3]

For those who wish to see the more comprehensive comparisons with multi-modal treatment programmes, some adjustments are necessary to create something that resembles a level playing field. Most importantly, restorative justice must be conceptualized as more than a programme, and its normative theory as one which suggests causal propositions about how offenders get better, how at-risk youth avoid initial or further involvement in crime, and about how communities mobilize to repair harm and resolve conflict peacefully (e.g. Van Ness and Strong 1997; Braithwaite 1999). Yet, unlike evaluations of multi-modal treatment programmes, the overall impact of restorative programme components (e.g. participating in a restorative conference, completing community service, attending a victim impact session) has not been studied in evaluations that view these components collectively as part of a holistic rehabilitation approach (Bazemore *et al.* 2000). It is also possible, therefore, that programmatic interventions universally accepted as restorative practices – e.g. victim–offender mediation, conferencing – should be viewed not as primary rehabilitative interventions as some have implied (Levrant *et al*. 1999), but rather as steps or components in a broader model of restorative reintegration (Bazemore 2001; Braithwaite 2001).

Though such holistic, restorative approaches are currently difficult to find and document in the real world, they are not difficult to envision. Moreover, they have certainly been operationalized in practice in some cases. For example, imagine a young offender who attends a victim impact panel or victim sensitivity class, then completes a successful family group conference, then works with neighborhood adults on a meaningful community service project as part of the agreement emerging from the conference, then is tutored and offered a job by a support person in the conference, pays restitution to the victim from wages earned in the job, writes a letter of apology to victims, gets follow up calls from other conference participants to check in with him on his school attendance and other obligations.[4] We are suggesting, of course, that restorative practices need to be conceptualized as an ongoing series of experiences some of which are programmatic, or at least spurred by a programmatic encounter such as a conference, but most of which are more organic. In doing so, we move beyond the narrow focus on professional interventions and programme evaluation in order to facilitate making meaningful comparisons between multi-modal treatment approaches and comprehensive reintegrative approaches informed by restorative justice principles.[5]

In the meantime, restorative justice advocates and researchers have some explaining to do. What is to be explained is not the failure of restorative justice, but why these short-term conferencing and other practices have any impact at all. In other words, currently we can simply speculate that a restorative conferencing programme has one of several possible impacts depending on its focus, and then most likely 'sets up' other important subsequent encounters and intervention – in much the same way that a thorough and accurate professional assessment is said to do in the effective treatment literature (Andrews *et al.* 1990). What is in doubt, or up for debate, is the mechanism(s) by which restorative practices, individually or as part of a package of interventions, might impact the future behaviour of offenders.

A lack of clarity about intervention objectives, however, has required that much evaluation proceed in a kind of theoretical vacuum. Typically, studies examine recidivism and other traditional outcomes with little indication from programmes as to why or how these outcomes should result from such interventions. In addition, there has been a great deal of ambiguity about standards for assessing the 'restorativeness' of interventions (McCold 2000; Bazemore 2001; Presser and Van Voorhis 2002). Extant claims of success in the literature may have little to do with restorative justice *per se* and more to do with other intervention characteristics. There are doubts for example, about whether positive impacts on recidivism in victim–offender mediation and some family group conferencing studies – which presume impacts through the vehicle of satisfaction or sense of fairness – may in fact simply operate through procedural justice rather than restorative justice logics, or through other processes that are more consistent with theories other than restorative justice (e.g. labelling theory, control theory or even deterrence). Of equal importance is the fact that we cannot say with any certainty in a given programme evaluation whether restorative justice has indeed failed to deliver (Immarigeon 1999; Levrant *et al.* 1999), or some other intervention is implicated in programme failure.

Turning to the practices of restorative justice in the conferencing context, we find multiple and at times competing propositions and multiple restorative theories-in-use that may be viewed as compatible and/or competing explanations. The 'bad news' about the emerging group of theories in use in restorative conferencing is that many are loosely formulated, not always internally consistent, or clearly aligned with restorative principles of intervention. (This is, of course, not a situation unique to restorative justice.) The 'good news' is that the theories are for the most part compatible, and can be viewed as components of a larger whole in the normative theory of restorative justice. While different theories may create conflicts in practice just as efforts to balance the three core principles of restorative justice (Van Ness and Strong 1997) create conflicts in a complex practice context (Bazemore and Earle 2002), for researchers this creates opportunities for testing the relative importance of intermediate outcomes, such as shame, social support, dialogue, completing reparative obligations, etc. on long-term healing.

While some research based on normative data (see Sampson and Laub 1993) and some traditional and emerging criminological theories are highly consistent with restorative justice in a general sense and are supportive in a *post hoc* sense, it seems more appropriate to begin to develop intervention theories that would allow for more specific tests of restorative practice. The most appropriate way to do this is to turn directly to the normative theory of restorative justice – that is, to the core values and principles. Ideally, we might want then to move beyond existing practices to propose a variety of principle-based processes and interventions that would be expected over time to decrease the likelihood of offence behaviour. Short of this, we can turn to the practices of restorative justice to see what can be learned from field experience about intervention theories that appear to inform practitioners in attempts to align interventions and outcomes. We do so in the section that follows, which proposes several theories-in-use based on core principles of restorative justice. Before turning to this, we present an example of a restorative model of the cycle of rehabilitation that provides an example of a naturalistic approach to desistance based on the core concept of the informal social relationship, with the restorative process and reparative process as a first step in the cycle.

A relational theory in a cyclical rehabilitation process

In contrast to the more linear, 'receptacle model' of rehabilitation where the professional counsels the relatively passive offender into avoiding future crime, Figure 3.1 suggests a more naturalistic, cyclical model of reform and reintegration. As one of us has suggested in previous work (Bazemore 1999; Bazemore *et al.* 2000), the social relationship, in conjunction with opportunities to repair harm and thereby earn one's redemption, is the catalyst that provides the necessary context both for ongoing social support and asset building. New assets, in turn, lead to more support and connections, and hence to stronger relationships, a greater repertoire of skills, and still more connections (and the opportunities these provide) through a cyclical process. In this non-recursive model, anticipated feedback loops between skill-building, service to others as an opportunity to contribute to the common good, relationship building, access to positive roles and offender adjustment are associated with a gradual reduction in criminal behaviour. This decline in criminal activity continues until at some point the life space of the offender is

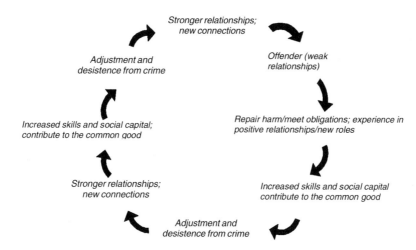

Figure 3.1. Restorative/relational model.

simply too committed to conventional lines of action to make offending an attractive or practically feasible prospect.

In this model, because relationship building is more complex than simply creating new intervention programmes, we have argued elsewhere for the development of new models of reintegration and rehabilitation based essentially on strengthening offender competencies, and building connections between offenders, law-abiding adults, and socializing institutions (Bazemore 1998, 2000). A primary agenda of this theory is to emphasize the fundamental role of informal processes missing from much of the correctional and effective treatment literature. Specifically, what is most clear from this depiction is the role of the community that we believe stands in sharp contrast to treatment models in which the theory of intervention is dependent upon the offender's response to professional intervention. We have more fully elaborated this role at the social ecological or community level utilizing an underlying theory of social capital/human capital in which the social relationship is also the primary vehicle for engaging broader forces of formal and informal community social support and social control. This in turn, provides the affective or emotive components of offender attachment to conventional groups as well as the basis for instrumental commitment to conventional behaviour through experiences in roles that provide opportunities for offenders to demonstrate their potential value as resources to communities. An intervention model aimed at maximizing this attachment and commit-ment must focus on the creation of new institutional roles, as well as informal and quasi-formal support networks for building connections to facilitate reintegration and integration of offenders (Polk and Kobrin 1972). The core feature of this general theory is the positive, pro-social relationship between young offenders and caring adults and community groups that provides the basis for informal support and social control. Though primarily informal in nature, this relationship is presumed to provide the basis for meeting both instrumental and affective needs, as when the offender is supported by an employer (in an instrumental relationship) who helps him connect to other pro-social groups such as recreational or civic groups (in affective relationships).

While Figure 3.1 does not specify the role of vital cognitive processes that some have referred to as 're-storying,' we view such processes as essential in the complete transformation process offenders are believed to experience as they gradually desist from involvement in crime (Maruna 2001; Toews and Zehr 2001). In our model, however, we suggest that these processes emerge experientially. Specifically, as the diagram suggests, it is the experience in new roles, and the expectations and support that go with social relationships in these roles, that spur the cognitive changes associated with the offender's 'new story' and with the legitimate public identity associated with the new role (Maruna 2001).[6] In other words, as one community reintegration practitioner puts it: 'it is easier to act one's way into better thinking than think one's way into better acting'.

The following are general propositions that appear to flow from this depiction of the rehabilitation/reintegration process in more or less sequential form.

Proposition One: offenders who come together in a restorative process with supportive adults and/or peers and victims are more likely to acknowledge and accept responsibility to make amends;

Proposition Two: offenders who complete their obligation to make amends essentially 'earn their redemption' and are more likely to gain support than those who do not;

Proposition Three: offenders in relationships of support have access to roles that commit them to conforming behaviour, and offenders in such roles will be less likely to reoffend;

Proposition Four: when offenders in relationships of support based on earned redemption and linked to productive roles reoffend, offenses will be more minor and more likely to continue to receive support of the community.

Though this is not a linear model, we suggest that different theoretical orientations may suggest different temporal ordering. The normative theory of exchange as it applies to making amends or earning one's redemption, however, we suggest would come first as a necessary first step in building or rebuilding the relationship. On the other hand, a theory of social support may suggest that support is necessary prior to making amends.

There are, of course, several important missing components in the proposed approach. First, missing from this general model and these propositions, are guiding theories of intervention that form the basis for alternative hypotheses about how various interventions produce intermediate outcomes and how the latter lead to long-term offender desistance from crime and reintegration. For example, while we have focused on the social relationship as a model of social support, we have said little about repair in its other senses such as the act of reparation of material damage that may be seen as essential to community and victim acceptance of the offender as worthy of reintegration. Second, while we have challenged the premise of the static 'receptacle model' of most treatment and outlined a more nonlinear model of sequential gains and perhaps relapse on the bumpy road to offender rehabilitation (Maruna 2001; see also Braithwaite and Mugford 1994), we have said little specifically about the role of restorative processes – especially restorative decision-making or conferencing process in this model. Third, we have said relatively little about the professional role that remains essential in a restorative model (see Van Ness and Strong 1997, discussion of the principle of community/government role transformation, and Bazemore and Walgrave 1999), but takes a different form in a restorative model. In the remainder of this chapter, we outline four theories, and intermediate outcomes and practice associated with them as they apply in one restorative practice context, restorative conferencing programmes. Following each theory, we suggest propositions that may be tested in subsequent evaluations of restorative conferencing.

Normative theory, restorative principles and the path to intervention theory

Restorative practices are essentially different ways of 'doing justice' by seeking to repair the harm of crime (Van Ness and Strong 1997; Bazemore and Walgrave 1999). Because repair is a difficult prospect in the absence of the active involvement of those most affected by the crime, proponents of restorative justice promote informal decision-making, or conferencing to include victim, offender and community in developing a reparative plan. Restorative practice is, in turn, grounded in a commitment to change system roles and relationships and to empower communities to address the needs of victim, offender and community as primary 'stakeholders' in the justice process. Together these ideals have been articulated as three core principles (Van Ness and Strong 1997) that together provide a normative theory, an overall vision for restorative justice and an agenda for systemic reform in juvenile justice (Bazemore and Walgrave 1999). These core principles provide the basis for determining the 'restorativeness' of intervention and therefore, in evaluating restorative programmes and interventions for gauging the integrity and strength of the intervention.

Three principles for restorative justice

Principle One: repairing harm – justice requires that we work to heal victims, offenders and communities that have been injured by crime (Van Ness and Strong 1997).

The first and most important 'big idea' of the restorative perspective is that justice requires healing of victims, offenders and communities that have been injured by crime or other harmful behaviour. Restorative justice responses to intervention therefore begin with a focus on identifying the damage to victims and communities that has resulted from the actions of offenders. Repairing harm is in the most general sense the ultimate goal sought in all restorative justice practice.

Principle Two: stakeholder involvement – victims, offenders and communities should have the opportunity for active involvement in the justice process as early and as fully as possible (Van Ness and Strong 1997).

Because harm cannot be understood in a vacuum, repair cannot be achieved in the absence of input from those most affected by the crime. The second core principle of restorative justice therefore follows logically from the principal of repair which implies that the extent and quality of repair is largely dependent on the quality and extent of stakeholder involvement. While Principle Two defines the process by which three primary stakeholders are engaged in decisions about how to achieve this goal, the primary goal of stakeholder involvement is to get conference participants to 'own' and take responsibility for the decision-making process.

Principle Three: transformation in community and government roles and relationship – we must rethink the relative roles and responsibilities of government and community. In promoting justice, government is responsible for preserving a just order, and community for establishing a just peace (Van Ness and Strong 1997).

The third 'big idea' in restorative justice stems from the conviction that there are limits on the role of government in the response to crime and trouble, and the parallel view that communities have an essential role to play in this response. Hence, if we wish to focus on repairing the harm of crime by utilizing a decision-making process that provides a primary role for victim, offender and others in this process, we must restructure the role of justice professionals and the justice system to ensure that communities play a major role. Principle Three defines the structural configuration required to allow for such engagement in the reparative effort within the justice system and community context. There are two related primary goals associated with the principle of government/community role transformation: (1) changing the role of criminal justice professionals and the mission of justice systems and agencies to support community ownership of the restorative process and (2) increasing the capacity of citizens and community groups to address the harm of youth crime.

Linking core principles for restorative intervention

An overall intervention theory of restorative conferencing may be expressed as a proposition that practices aimed at healing or reparation of harms to individual and collective stakeholders, rather than professionally-driven practices aimed at achieving other objectives, will lead to safer, more peaceful and more just communities. There are, however, in addition, specific theories of practice associated with primary goals linked to each of the three principles, and to intermediate outcomes associated with each goal.

In the discussion which follows, we describe the practical task of restorative conferencing as a context or decision-making 'space' for achieving outcomes associated with intervention theories, that in turn define 'focal concerns' that may be at times highly compatible or in conflict. This conflict may be seen in comparing the orientations of various conferencing programme models (e.g. family group conferencing, victim–offender mediation), in the contrast between specific conferencing programmes, and in comparing incidents of individual conferencing encounters or events.

In other work (Bazemore and Schiff, forthcoming), we have suggested that there are potentially nine sets of dimensions that define intermediate outcomes linked to the principle of repair, stakeholder involvement and community/government role transformation respectively (see Appendices I–III for a summary of all nine dimensions and intermediate outcomes associated with each core principle). In the remainder of the chapter itself, we briefly describe intermediate outcomes of restorative conferencing associated with the principles of repair and stakeholder involvement and then discuss four emerging intervention theories, conferencing practices directed toward these outcomes, and the linkage between these and offender reintegration.

Repairing harm: theories and intermediate outcomes

The normative theory of restorative justice is linked to a more naturalistic attitude toward crime and the offender. According to recent citizen surveys, the obligation to address harm and damage in the aftermath of crime is widely supported by the general public (Pranis and Umbreit 1992; Schwartz 1992; Moon *et al.* 2000). The overarching, long-term goal of a restorative justice process is both individual and collective healing of those impacted by crime.

Various dimensions of such a process and intermediate outcomes associated with these dimensions are focused on specific types of harm related to the impact of the crime(s) being considered in the process. Crime may result in material and emotional damage to individuals – victims, offenders and the family and acquaintances of both. It also may be linked to past harms that have occurred in the community, such as patterns of child abuse, substance abuse and domestic violence that may currently or in the past have impacted offenders and victims. Between these individual and collective harms, crime damages the interpersonal relationships of victim and offender. Participants in a restorative encounter may wish to address one or more of these harms as they relate directly to the current incident, or as they indicate a larger need for collective healing in the aftermath of the incident for the well-being of future victims and offenders (Ross 1996, 2000).[7]

Appendix I describes intermediate outcomes that may be said to reflect these three dimensions of repair focused on material and emotional harm to individuals and communities, harm to relationships and past harms. Because past harm is less intentionally and less frequently pursued in most conferencing models (and is less immediately relevant to offender reintegration), we focus on the first two forms of harm in this discussion. The general task of a restorative conference is to focus on repairing one or more of these types of harm. However, we briefly describe how the specific agenda of the conference may vary depending upon the type of harm that is the primary focus of attention in a given incident and the philosophical/ theoretical commitment of programme staff to one of two intervention theories. These theories, earned redemption and social support, attempt to link two intermediate outcomes – making amends and relationship building – to long-term goals, in this case offender reintegration.

Amends, reciprocity and the theory of earned redemption

Intermediate outcomes
The intermediate outcome associated with the dimension of making amends is about repair in its most literal and practical sense as 'cleaning up one's mess', or making atonement in the form of compensation, or repair of emotional or material damages following acknowledgement of responsibility for harm (Van Ness and Strong 2001; Karp 2001). Making amends is typically the most common component of the reparative agreement negotiated at the conclusion of the conference. Amends as an objective may be to some extent addressed by events in the conference itself, e.g. an apology by the offender (Umbreit 1999), and/or in the follow-up period. In the latter case, amends constitutes the meeting of an obligation that may take the form of concrete reparation in the form of restitution, service to victims, apologies, community service or a promise of behaviour change (Van Ness and Strong 2001).

Repair in the form of making amends appears to build upon a virtually universal sense of the need to address imbalance, and to reinforce norms of fairness and reciprocity. Even critics of restorative justice acknowledge that norms of fairness and reciprocity work against the idea that someone who has hurt another citizen should receive help or service without making amends for what has been damaged (e.g. Levrant *et al.* 1999). However, by moving 'away from the principle of entitlement to the principle of social exchange' (Levrant *et al.* 1999: 22), restorative justice practices seek to engage the community and victim side of the justice equation. This side has been missing from offender-focused 'best practice' treatment models (e.g. Andrews *et al.* 1990), as well as from intervention based on deterrence, just desserts, or other justice philosophies.

Theory and practice: earned redemption and the task of the conference
How does the conferencing process meet the objective of making amends? Regarding the intermediate objective of amends, the task of the restorative conference is to ensure that these reparative obligations are addressed as an outcome of the conference. Conferencing programmes are therefore restorative to the extent that they seek first to achieve these objectives, rather than other outcomes (e.g. those associated with offender treatment or punishment).

Making amends requires that the conference first assess and agree upon the material and emotional harm to be addressed in a reparative agreement. This objective will be executed in the conferencing process when participants are able to directly connect the obligation to repair with this harm and articulate this in the conferencing agreement or contract (Karp 2001). Though the quality of the reparative agreement is an essential predictor of the quality of and extent of the amends to follow, the 'storytelling' phase of the conference that allows victims and other participants to say how they were affected by the crime is a vital prerequisite. This phase of the conference is a time for active listening to ensure that participants understand the nature of the harm and the offender's acknowledgement of his/her responsibility in creating this harm. Though acceptance of responsibility is something established in a general way prior to the conference, our qualitative research suggests that more subtle, yet deeper ownership of responsibility for the crime is often experienced only after the offender hears a thorough account of the harm. In some programmes, the focus on repair begins in the preparation phase of the conference. Some conferencing practitioners report spending time in the preconference meeting getting the victim and offender thinking about what they would like to see in an agreement to repair harm. Others, however, operate from a different theory of the purpose of the conference;

specifically, those focused more on the dialogue itself as a way of allowing the victim and offender to chart their own course tend to guard against the overemphasis on the agreement as the central goal of the conference (Umbreit 1999). The 'settlement-driven' approach creates problems for amends when it encourages participants to pass over the harm story and the reactions to it. However, a not uncommon failure in some open-ended dialogue programmes is a tendency to be unclear about goals of the conference even in the introduction (Bazemore and Schiff, forthcoming).

A problem in developing the agreement itself is in ensuring meaningful input from young offenders, who too often are passive participants in the conference. In some programmes practitioners seem comfortable with simply telling the offender what his obligations will be. Such programmes provide an extreme example of minimizing stakeholder input, and are not unlike arbitration and other similar dispute resolution models that claim no grounding in restorative principles. In situations where they have minimal input, offenders may object, or acquiesce, but in neither case are they given the opportunity to 'own' the obligation. In other conferences, facilitators seem to try to maximize the chance that the offender will provide thoughtful input into the process of crafting an obligation to be approved by the group. A practitioner in a unique model of 'community conferencing', for example, first asks offender and victim what they would like to see as part of the agreement. After frequently getting little input from the offender, she then asks the larger group of community members and supporters of victim and offender what they would like to see. Then, as she explains it:

> ...[in] the brainstorming period, we get all the ideas from the group, then say to the offender, 'What will you do? At this point, they essentially self-sentence – they have a chance to claim it [and they have] won the choice around repair. Then we say to the victim, 'Will that satisfy you?' ...There is some group negotiation after that.

Finally, a practical issue about the discretion of conferencing participants in the agreement phase may have an essential theoretical implication. In some jurisdictions, conferences at best share jurisdiction with the court or other system entity in determining either the amount of restitution and community service, the schedule, or the nature of the service or other obligation. This of course weakens the mandate and emotional power of the input of victims, offenders, and other citizens. In the worst case, the power of the conference is emasculated, and the process may even be viewed as simply a way to add punishment to what the court has already ordered – with obvious implications for the offenders' sense of fairness and perhaps ability to accomplish excessive requirements in a reasonable period of time.

Based on these considerations, propositions about the ability of the conference to ensure that the process is able to ensure that the offender makes amends include, but are not limited to:

(1) when the purpose of the conference is clearly presented as to repair the harm (vs. open dialogue or discussion of other issues), amends will be more likely to result;

(2) when participants are made ready for, but do not rush to, the question of how to repair the harm, amends will be more likely;

(3) when victims and community members are allowed to present the complete story of the harm and the group focuses on addressing victim needs as well as offender needs, amends will be more likely;

(4) when conferences give the community primary input into agreements, and limit system input into offender obligations, amends will be more likely.

A summary of this section is presented in Table 3.1.

Table 3.1. Restorative conferencing and repair: theories, intermediate outcomes and intervention priorities

Theory	Intermediate outcomes	Conference intervention priorities
Earned redemption	Making amends	Ensure that offender accepts responsibility for harm and for repairing material and emotional harm to victims and communities and that a plan is developed for such repair

Long-term impact: connecting amends to desistence and reintegration

Why and how does the process of making amends influence the future behaviour of the offender? What is the link to recidivism and reintegration? Making amends as a primary outcome is, as suggested previously, generally associated with exchange theory approaches that suggest that human cooperation and civil discourse is grounded in expectations of reciprocity (Molm and Cook 1995). Practitioners have used these assumptions in restorative intervention as a specific rationale for requiring action on the part of the offender as a type of practical demonstration of positive intent, or 'good faith' (Maloney 1998). Grounded in exchange theory assumptions, the intervention theory of earned redemption posits that the offender who demonstrates what he/she professes by acknowledging responsibility for the wrong, and then actively working to make things right, has taken a first step on the road to reintegration (Bazemore 1998; Maloney 1998).

By contrast, community members and victims will be less likely to accept offenders who have not demonstrated such good faith. Hence, the failure to make things right becomes a barrier to offender reintegration – as well as to victim healing and community peace. Specifically, as Toews and Zehr (2001) have argued, victim and community vindication requires reciprocity in order to allow those harmed by crime to feel that they are not somehow at fault for the harm done to them. The failure to reciprocate may therefore weaken the esteem of victims and victimized communities, who then feel a need to vindicate themselves by replacing one harm with another. Vindicating victims and communities by transferring shame back to the offender through punishment merely repeats the cycle of harm. However, the need for reciprocity that appears to be imbedded in human psyches and cultures (see Miller 1993) can also be met by denouncing wrongs, establishing responsibility for them and allowing the offender to make amends.

Making amends and the theory of earned redemption is focused primarily on the community and victim side of the equation by addressing the needs of those ultimately responsible for accepting and reintegrating the offender. Meeting one's obligation to victims, as Braithwaite (2001) has observed, also has important implications for offender cognitive change. Such change is believed to occur because the experience of 'giving back' by helping others (including those not directly victimized by the offence in question) provides the offender with a sense of value and competency. Now in a positive 'helping' role (Reisman 1962; Bazemore 1999), the offender herself may begin a cognitive 're-storying' process of developing a new identity inconsistent with offending by crafting what has been described by one reintegration researcher as a 'redemption narrative' (Maruna 2001).

Making amends alone seems unlikely to lead to long-term reduction in recidivism. Though the social exchange theory of earned redemption would suggest that community support is indeed dependent upon these efforts by the offender to 'put things right', the process itself must offer both support and opportunity for such amends for the offender to meet these reparative obligations. As suggested earlier in Figure 1, the sequence is something like the following: the offender acknowledges responsibility in a safe and supportive environment; the community provides additional support; the offender meets his obligation and makes amends; more support and opportunity is provided; offending decreases. Finally, we note from our qualitative study that reparative agreements may at times read like a 'laundry list' of requirements and obligations for the offender that may not be easily connected by the offender to the harm he/she has caused (O'Brien *et al*. 2002). By contrast, it is clear that reparation agreements seem richer, more doable, less onerous, and ultimately more meaningful and impactful when other conference participants are assigned roles in repairing the harm. For example, family, community members and victims may assist with community service requirements, provide transportation or jobs for earning restitution funds, etc. We can therefore suggest three general propositions that form the basis for empirical examination of the theory of amends as it relates to the long-term behaviour of the offender.

Proposition One: when the roles of conference participants other than the offender in completing the reparative agreement are made clear, making amends will be more meaningful, and more likely to impact future behaviour.

Proposition Two: offenders who accept responsibility and meet their obligations in the aftermath of the crime will receive greater support from the community for their reintegration.

Proposition Three: offenders who accept responsibility and meet obligations to repair harm will experience cognitive changes supportive of desistence from crime.

Relationship-building and the theory of social support

Intermediate outcomes
Relationship building is also frequently discussed as an important objective of conferences (Braithwaite and Parker 1999; Braithwaite 2001; Bazemore 2001) (see Appendix I), specifically with regard to relationships damaged by crime. Though a number of conferencing programmes in our qualitative study said they viewed relationship building as an important goal (Bazemore and Schiff, forthcoming), its status as an observable and measurable outcome may be viewed as quite nebulous. However, some practitioners argue that they can gauge success in achieving relational outcomes using rather simple formulas such as this one suggested by Kay Pranis in which effectiveness is measured by the extent to which a specific conferencing encounter or conferencing programme has: (1) created new positive relationships or strengthened existing ones; (2) created informal

support systems (Pranis and Bazemore 2001). In the conferencing setting, relationship-building may be initiated by an informal connection between the offender and another conference participant. As suggested in the normative theory presented in Figure 3.1, the long-term goal is to establish long-term connections that lead to other relationships that provide instrumental and affective support.

Theory and practice: social support and the task of the conference

How does the conference build relationships? The focus of the conference regarding the relationship-building outcome is on connecting or re-connecting, as appropriate: victim and offender, offender and community, and/or victim and community. The task of rebuilding or building new relationships in the conferencing process and its aftermath requires critical examination of the extent to which the process is able to mobilize and call forth social support and in fact make necessary connections between sup-porters, offenders and victims (Braithwaite and Mugford 1994; see Bazemore 2001).

Addressing harm to relationships may be strategized in preparation for conferences by seeking to ensure that those most closely connected to the offender and victim are part of the encounter. In addition, others that may need to be connected as resource persons are strategically identified and brought to the table. The possibilities for relationship-building seem more likely as the number of conference participants increases, but these prospects may be diminished when the number of participants creates an unmanageable situation, or when participants are not clear about their role in the process. In our qualitative study of conferencing, we find two competing intervention theories that suggest different rationales for inclusion of conferencing participants other than victim, offender and facilitator (most victim–offender mediation programmes included other participants only at the request of victim and offender, or actively discouraged other participants). One theory, consistent with that ex-pressed in training materials on family group conferencing and the theory of reintegrative shaming (McDonald and Moore 2001), recommends limiting other participants to intimates of offender and victim. From this perspective, it is argued that only those already close to the offender in some way can make a difference in his transformation. From another perspective, more community-oriented practitioners offer rationales and theories-in-use suggesting that there is value in including other com-munity members. When asked why she would consider bringing in community members unknown to the offender or victim, the director of a 'community conferencing' programme, a variation of family group conferencing, explained that:

We are hoping for one outcome – the offender will recognize them as offering a broader connection to the community … they get a certain kind of feedback from this: 'Look how many people care about me'. In the beginning, [in choosing participants] we stuck to who was impacted directly, but learned how valuable it was to have [broader] community – who have some distance from the offender – bring a different perspective.

Citing more practical justifications, she argues that, in any case, 'it is rare for the juvenile to (identify and) bring his own support group'. Validation of this view came from a number of practitioners who discussed the struggle to get the offender to identify supporters, thus leading by default to reliance on the 'voice-of-the-broader community'. In general, conferencing practitioners, regardless of their preference, argue that participants should not be present for the sake of having 'community representation', but should have a role to play in the conference either by virtue of their connection to victim and offender, or by virtue of the voices and experiences they represent or resources (e.g. employment or educational connections) they can provide.

Propositions pertinent to the process of building relationships and support include but are not limited to:

(1) the more participants in the conference, the greater the likelihood that social support will emerge and relationship building will occur;

(2) the greater the extent to which participants who are either important in the lives of the offender, or bring special resources to the agenda, the greater the likelihood that social support will emerge and relationship building will occur;

(3) when participants are assigned a specific role to work with the offender and others in carrying out and monitoring the reparative agreement, relationship building and social support is more likely.

Long-term impact: connecting social support to desistance and reintegration

Relationship-building is grounded in the general theory of social support and more specific theory of relational rehabilitation in which the social relationship with other pro-social individuals and groups is a primary factor in desistance from crime (Cullen 1994; Bazemore *et al.* 2001). The linkage between these informal social relationships and the future behaviour of offenders is through the support and guidance of community members and groups who provide access to opportunities for productive activities. Such activities provide opportunities for skill building and commitment to the common good. Community members function as natural helpers, and the groups they may represent provide both affective and instrumental informal support, as well as guardianship and reinforcement of law-abiding behaviour (Bazemore *et al.* 2001). As 'community guides' (McKnight 1995), they act as bridge and buffer between the offender and the community by smoothing the way for the development of additional connections between the offender, law-abiding citizens and legitimate institutions (Sullivan 1989; Maruna 2001). More instrumentally, such connections provide them with a legitimate identity and a 'link' to conventional community-based commitments and opportunities (Polk and Kobrin 1972; Bazemore *et al.* 2000), as well as responsibilities and obligations (Cullen 1994: 543).

A summary of this section is presented in Table 3.2.

Table 3.2. Restorative conferencing and repair: theories, intermediate outcomes and intervention priorities

Theory	Intermediate outcomes	Conference intervention priorities
Social support	Building/rebuilding relationships	Ensure that offender strengthens ties to law-abiding adults and positive community groups and/or makes new positive connections

Programme models
Though the dimensions of making amends and relationship building are not mutually exclusive, conferencing programmes and models may vary in part based on the emphasis given to each dimension. For example, as will be reflected in some of the discourse of practitioners presented in subsequent sections, some programmes may also have stronger ideological commitment to the goal of making amends for direct harm, while others may focus more attention on repairing relationships.

Stakeholder involvement: theories and outcomes

Though some harm can be repaired in court and formal settings, the primary purpose of conferencing is to provide a more 'user-friendly' forum for informal decision-making that gives consideration to the needs of victim, offender and community, and their roles in this process. Its primary, practical value is in allowing those harmed to articulate how the crime has affected them in a way that should allow for more effective and meaningful repair. Stakeholder involvement in decision-making is, however, more complex than providing a mechanism to facilitate completion of the reparative agreement.

More than the other two core principles, stakeholder involvement is about the process of a conference. The task of the conference with regard to the principle of stakeholder involvement is to ensure that the quality of decision-making conforms to a maximum degree with the standards suggested by the process dimensions of inclusion, communication and role-taking (Van Ness and Strong 2001). While inherently linked to repair, the process and its quality is viewed as important in its own right and is first concerned with the overarching goal of getting stakeholders to take responsibility for addressing what should be done in the aftermath of the crime.

What obligations or intervention outcomes are sought for the conferencing encounter? Current practice suggests four pertinent intermediate objectives of the conferencing process that as dimensions of stakeholder involvement/ownership may themselves influence long-term healing (see Appendix II). As intermediate objectives of the conferencing process, these outcomes may themselves influence long-term healing, as well as effect more immediate and concrete completion of reparative obligations to make amends, rebuild relationships, or address past harms. We discuss two such intervention theories below.[8]

Respectful disapproval and the theory of reintegrative shaming

Intermediate outcomes

Some conferencing programmes wish to ensure that the offender experiences shame in the form of disapproval from those with whom he/she has personal relationships. This supportive, or 'reintegrative' shame is intended to distinguish the offence from the offender by emphasizing the positive aspects of the latter, while expressing disapproval of the former. Participants in the conference, and especially intimates of the offender, also express disappointment that this young person could have done such a thing.

Because the offender is assumed to have by-passed the emotion of shame that is expected to arise naturally by virtue of confrontation with the harm of his/her crime, conference participants may seek to ensure that the offender experiences shame as a result of hearing about how his/her behaviour has effected others. In doing so, they seek too achieve what McDonald and Moore (2001) refer to as the larger goal of 'building conscience' as gauged by emotional indicators of shame, remorse, and then possibly, expressions of empathy.[9]

Theory and practice: reintegrative shaming and the task of the conference
How do restorative conferences address outcomes associated with reintegrative shame? First, the conference facilitator must ensure that the
process is not focused on outcomes associated with humiliation on the one
hand, or a sole concern with the offender's needs on the other. To do so, the
conference facilitator may solicit and/or encourage participants to make
positive comments about the offender as a person, while ensuring that
victims and others are allowed to clearly articulate the harm caused by the
behaviour and the group's disapproval of it. Conferences grounded in the
theory of reintegrative shaming seek also to encourage expression of
emotion on the part of the offender as an indication of his understanding
of this disapproval and sense of regret and/or remorse as a result. The
facilitator may also pay special attention to emotional signs of shame or
remorse in order to steer the group to act positively on these signs toward
transformation (McDonald and Moore 2001).

While some practitioners have placed emphasis on the 'shaming'
features of the theory, more recently other restorative justice advocates
have expressed concerns about the negative implications of shame – when
the term is used as a verb (see Toews and Zehr 2001). These practitioners
give far more emphasis to the role of social support (see Cullen 1994 for
commentary on the connection between these theories) and the
importance of a general, firm but supportive presentation of how the
offender's behaviour has affected others as suggested below. As
Braithwaite and Roche (2001: 72) observe:

> The testimony of the victims and the apologies (when they occur,
> as they often do) are sufficient to accomplish the necessary shaming
> of the evil of violence. But there can never be enough citizens active
> in the reintegration part of reintegrative shaming.

Given this understanding of the goal of the conference regarding outcomes associated with reintegrative shaming, we may state the following
propositions about the likelihood of achieving these outcomes in the
conferencing encounter:

(1) reintegrative shaming is more likely to occur when the victim's voice
    is heard, and when ample time for harm discussion is allowed;

(2) reintegrative shaming is more likely to occur when those whose
    opinions matter to the offender are present in the conference;

(3) reintegrative shaming is more likely to occur when those whose
    opinions matter to the offender express disapproval respectfully.

This section is summarized in Table 3.3.

Table 3.3. Theories of intervention and intermediate outcomes: stakeholder involvement

Reintegrative shaming	Offender experience of shame, remorse; emotional indicators of empathy, shame, remorse	Ensure that support persons are present and respectively express disapproval and support

Long-term impact: connecting social support to desistance and reintegration

The theory of reintegrative shaming gives emphasis to the importance of offenders experiencing social disapproval from those whose opinions matter to them. From this perspective, shame is a natural, healthy emotion that may motivate all of us to either positive or negative action (Nathanson 1992). Such expressed disapproval as a denunciation of the behaviour in question by friends and family, rather than judges or other criminal justice professionals, is the external source of shame believed to decrease the likelihood of recidivism as the would-be reoffender is deterred by concern about disgrace and loss of status and affection, rather than by the threat of punishment (McDonald and Moore 2001). The mechanism for positive impact on the offender, is moreover, not the 'stigmatizing shame' that occurs in the formal justice context (and is applauded by some advocates of retributive justice), but a reintegrative disapproval that gives equal emphasis to caring, approving behaviour (Retizinger and Scheff 1996) and denounces harmful behaviour while providing support for the person.

Braithwaite (1999a) has more recently suggested that the essential claims of reintegrative shaming theory are that 'tolerance of crime makes things worse; stigmatization, or disrespectful outcasting shame of crime, makes things worse still; while ... disapproval within a continuum of respect for the offender ... terminated by rituals of forgiveness, makes things better'. Hence, an intervention theory focused on assertive and demonstrative 'empathetic engagement' of all stakeholders who matter to the offender and victim is a relational one, rather than one based solely on shame or any individual psychology of motivation. In such a relational theory, the 'collective quality of the resolve' provides the source of motivation to begin the difficult task of stopping or reducing the harmful behaviour in question (Braithwaite 2001: 230). Shame that may occur through the essential act of denouncing the offence and confronting offender and the community with the harm it has caused, though an essential characteristic of reintegrative shaming theory, is therefore but one step in a sequential three-stage process of collective transformation.

Such a process, which as Braithwaite (2001: 228) suggests, actually begins with 'the experience of love as a key ingredient', includes empathy (that for the offender may even be associated with the experience of shame), provides for 'redemption rituals' that assist with 'motivational transformation', and, finally, offers offenders the opportunity for 'earned redemption' (Bazemore 1998).

Propositions related to the theory of reintegrative shaming that connect respectful disapproval of the offender, coupled with support, with long-term offender reintegration outcomes include:

(1) reintegrative shame is more likely to impact reoffending and desistance when the offender is concerned that loss of status and affection will result from continuation of such behaviour;

(2) reintegrative shame is more likely to occur when the offender has understood the harm caused and can articulate and express his feelings about this;

(3) reintegrative shame is more likely to impact reoffending and desistance when it is clear that the behaviour is not to be tolerated;

(4) reintegrative shame is more likely to impact reoffending and desistence when the offender experiences empathetic engagement and support and a collective resolve to stop the harmful behaviour;

(5) reintegrative shame is more likely to impact reoffending when expressions of support for the offender do not minimize, and generally follow, the discussion of harm and disapproval of the behaviour.

Mutual transformation and the theory of common ground

Traditional juvenile justice responses separate the parties in crime and conflict, and assume that their interests are mutually exclusive. The idea of 'finding common ground' or collective transformation (Stuart 1996; Moore and McDonald 2000) is based on the assumption that the best solutions for each individual stakeholder (e.g. the offender) cannot be achieved without consideration for the needs and interests of the other two (e.g. victim and community). The promise of a restorative justice process is the possibility of finding 'common ground' between victim, offender and community by giving consideration to the roles and needs of each stakeholder (Stuart 1996). Because conflict and distrust in current, formal justice decision-making may result from an over-emphasis on the needs and risks presented by the offender (Bazemore and Umbreit 2001; Achilles and Zehr

2001), the most important challenge in restorative justice decision-making is the search for a balance of stakeholder needs, and stakeholder voices in the decision-making process.

Intermediate outcomes

Conferencing programmes may therefore also seek a somewhat distinctive kind of process outcome that takes the form of a collective transformation in two or more stakeholders. The lingering harm addressed in such cases is the barrier created by the actions of the offender to the interaction and dialogue needed to develop a meaningful and mutually satisfying resolution. Such a resolution would take the form of affirmative efforts to repair damage to the victim, families and everyone else in part by resolving the conflict itself. The harm is addressed in part by the extent to which the conferencing process leads to shared ownership of the problem among conferencing participants (Moore and McDonald 2000), increased understanding between the relative positions of victim, offender and others, and various signs of success in the transformation of the conflict (see Moore and McDonald 2000).

Often achieved through commitment to a consensus decision-making process, seen in its most elaborated form in peacemaking circles (Stuart 2001), common ground as an intermediate outcome of restorative conferencing is more than a simple reparative agreement. It is viewed as vital to the future well-being of victim, offender and the relevant community, and the ongoing relationship between all three.

Theory and practice: common ground and the task of the conference

The collective transformation that can occur as victim, offender and their supporters find common ground, or at least gain a basic understanding of the other's position, may be a direct result of how conference dialogue is managed. Such management would involve making space for active listening on the part of participants and for clear and uninterrupted storytelling by victim and offender, and then efforts to ensure that there is mutual understanding among conference participants of what has been said. To achieve objectives associated with finding common ground, conferences must, among other things, allow for interchanges between victim and offender at strategic points in the conference, especially in response to each participant's respective story of the incident and the expression of feelings about the incident. Though observers have sometimes described such collective insight and transformation as 'magic', some facilitators suggest that moments of silence, a sense of when to build on 'bridging comments', mutual acknowledgement of the validity each other's stories, and a sense of movement through a key phase in the conference, provide guidance in making the finding of common ground concrete.

Though this theory has broad application to a variety of conflicts, including those associated with violent crimes (Stuart 2001; Umbreit 1999), it seems to be put into practice most often in the response to incidents involving ongoing disputes in which the harm to be addressed involves a series of incidents resulting from an unresolved conflict. In school conferencing, for example, victim and offender may change roles in such cases over a period of time, and the goal of conferencing in such contexts is for both parties to learn skills of conflict resolution and build the practice and reinforcement of such skills into the agreement to influence future behaviour. Examples we observed of such reinforcement in school conferencing processes in our study include requiring offenders (and victims, when there is an ongoing dispute) to teach conflict resolution skills to others, recruitment of peers to support victim and offender and monitor their agreement, referral to more formal conflict resolution training, and (most interesting and important) recruiting offenders and victims as resource persons to assist in crafting agreements in future conferences.

Open input from a variety of participants is viewed as absolutely critical in conferences that seek common ground as an intermediate objective. Facilitators often listen for transition comments by participants other than victim and offender, and efforts to reframe conflict. Facilitators and others may seek to build on small areas of agreement between victim and offender, even when there is much disagreement and remaining anger. It is often these other participants that bring victim and offender along toward shared ownership of the conflict and commitment to future peaceful resolution needed to move to the next phase. Points of transition are sought strategically, and care is taken not to push agreement when no common ground has been established. Agreements must reflect shared understanding without stretching, or pushing either side too far.

Propositions related to the objective of reaching common ground in the conference setting may include the following.

(1) The objective of common ground is more likely to be achieved in the conference when the facilitator and others build upon small points of common understanding after careful listening to victim and offender stories and necessary exchange and clarification regarding these stories.

(2) The objective of common ground is more likely to be achieved in the conference when peers and/or supporters are encouraged to reframe and reinforce areas of common understanding.

(3) The objective of common ground is more likely to be achieved in the conference if the facilitator does not move toward agreement until there are signs from the group of some shared ownership of the conflict and collective commitment to its resolution.

Long-term impact:common ground and the connection to desistance and reintegration
A theory of common ground for the victim may mean coming to terms with the offence and the reasons behind it – even to the point of developing some empathy for an offender who may find herself in difficult family situations or other challenging life circumstances. Supporters and other community members in conferences may similarly find shared agreement even with those they initially doubted – e.g. supporters of the offender might empathize and/or concur with the victim on some issues (and vice versa for victim supporters in the case of the offender). Similarly, a neutral community member may find a 'small plot' of common ground in the form of a connection with either offender or victim which provides enough leverage to turn a difficult conference around – even in the case where victim and offender have little or no basis for shared understanding (see Figure 3.2) – and in addition, provides the necessary link needed to reinforce commitments made in the conference in the future.

For the offender, a theory of common ground would suggest that such understanding might lead to a reduction in offence behaviour as the offender gains at least the foundation for empathy. Empathy is theorized to create a cognitive resistance to reoffending by creating a sense of causing harm to another that may prevent future harm in this form. Indeed, this important connection is borne out in empirical research, which suggests that restorative conferences produce greater empathy in offenders than do courts (Ahmed *et al.* 2001, cited in Braithwaite 2001) and that empathy seems to be a primary ingredient in successful conferences (Maxwell and Morris 1999). Regarding offender reintegration, the experience in finding common ground through a respectful deliberative process may provide insights for avoiding resolution of conflict in destructive ways in the future. If nurtured, followed up and reinforced with other opportunities to demonstrate and practise these new skills, these common ground outcomes may be influential in future conflict resolution for the offender. However, in this theory also, it is not simply the increase in offender empathy that leads to positive outcomes for the offender, but rather using Braithwaite's term, the 'collective resolve' of the group that reinforces commitments made in the conference and supports the offender in efforts to avoid destructive decisions in the future.

Propositions relevant to the linkage between the experience of finding common ground with others in the conference are as follows.

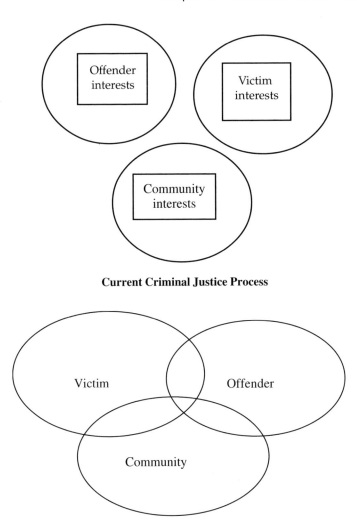

Current Criminal Justice Process

Restorative Justice Process

Figure 3.2. Stakeholder interests and common ground: objectives of alternative decision-making processes.

Proposition 1: offenders who have the experience of gaining a shared understanding of the harm they have caused and of the views of others will become more empathetic and therefore more likely to avoid confrontations and encounters that lead to crime in the future;

Proposition 2: offenders who have opportunities to give active input into the agreement are more likely to honour these agreements and more likely to avoid confrontations and encounters that lead to crime in the future;

Proposition 3: offenders who have opportunities for reinforcement of the experience of finding common ground and to practise skills in conflict resolution/transformation will be more likely to avoid confrontations and encounters that lead to crime in the future;

Proposition 4: offenders who have support from conference participants which reinforces commitment to agreements will be more likely to avoid confrontations and encounters that lead to crime in the future.

Conclusion

In conclusion, we return to the primary jurisprudential questions raised earlier about the differences between the restorative agenda for offender rehabilitation/reintegration. The crucial difference is that in our approach to rehabilitation is precisely that offender rehabilitation is not the primary agenda when it is subsumed within the broader restorative framework. In doing so, we suggest that rehabilitation is thereby both subordinated to, and driven by, restorative principles. It is thus pursued organically as part of the overall effort to repair harm by involving stakeholders in decision-making and transforming the role and relationships between justice systems and the communities they serve.

Ironically, this distinction may not only provide the critical break with the traditional treatment model, but also offer the key to the success of restorative rehabilitation. As Braithwaite (2001) has suggested, restorative processes may help to rehabilitate offenders precisely because this cannot be their primary intent. Rather, 'getting motivated to help others', may be one important factor in helping offenders 'get on top of their own problems' (p. 241). This incorporation of rehabilitation within the principle-based intervention agenda of restorative justice is in our view a limiting factor that helps to safeguard against the abuses of the traditional treatment model. While it should never minimize concern that restorative practices will avoid all legal problems encountered in the traditional treatment enterprise, it should provide some reassurance. The difference that makes the difference in the restorative approach to intervention is that such intervention is never simply about the offender. While they make intervention more complex, the collective nature of restorative responses provides the ultimate checks against abuses. The collective focus as operationalized through some of the intervention theories discussed here is the vehicle for also accomplishing the primary goal addressed here: better theory, for better practice, for better research, for still better theory and practice.

APPENDIX I   Restorative Conferencing Dimensions: harm and Intermediate Outcomes of Repair

(1) *Making amends.*
Harm to be repaired: material or emotional damage.
Objective: offender acknowledgement of responsibility and choice in the decision to commit the offence; fixing what is broken/damaged by the crime, or 'making things right'.

(2) *Addressing past harms.*
Harm to be repaired: systemic prior or ongoing damage to one or more stakeholders that limits their own healing and that of other community members.
Objective: acknowledging and attempting to redress past collective harms that may have impacted victims, offenders and communities.

(3) *Relationship building.*
Harm to be repaired: damage to relationships caused by the crime.
Objective: strengthening, rebuilding or building victim, offender and community connections.

APPENDIX II   Restorative Conferencing Dimensions: harm and Intermediate Outcomes of Stakeholder Involvement

(1) *Stakeholder satisfaction.*
Harm to be repaired: defined by individual victims and other stakeholders in the conference, and may be highly intangible and difficult to articulate (e.g. feelings of helplessness, estrangement, loss of control).
Objective: meeting the needs of the victim, offender and their supporters as indicated by various measures of positive feelings about the conference.

(2) *Supporting safety, order and security.*
Harm to be repaired: sense of security of victim, offender, family and community.

Objective: reassuring victims, offenders and supporters of future safety (as indicated by reduced fear), and development of plans to provide support for victims and risk management to decrease likelihood of offender recidivism.

(3) *Common ground.*

Harm to be repaired: relationships caused by a failure to appreciate the situation and thought process of other participants.

Objective: finding one or more points of agreement or mutual interest around the incident or increasing understanding of the position of others in the process.

(4) *Reintegrative shaming*

Harm to be repaired: Absence of recognition on the part of the offender of the impact of his behaviour on victims due in part to the lack of opportunity to hear this from intimates in a respectful way.

Objective: ensuring that the offender experiences the emotion of shame as a result of hearing from those whose opinions matter to her about the harm caused to others as a result of her behaviour.

APPENDIX III   Restorative Conferencing Dimensions: harm and Intermediate Outcomes of Transformation in Community/Government Role

(1) *Changing system and organizational mandates and mission.*

Harm to be repaired: historical expansion of system responsibility for social control, sanctioning, and social support tasks, and for decision-making about these.

Objective: changing the vision and mission of criminal and juvenile justice agencies and systems to a leadership function aimed at empowering community leadership and citizen ownership of the response to youth crime.

(2) *Changing professional roles.*

Harm to be repaired: the professionalization of tasks and roles in a way that undercuts community initiative, devalues citizen competencies, and denies possibilities to nurture and develop new problem-solving skills.

Objective: changing the work of the criminal justice professional from 'expert' service provider to supporter of community and citizen-driven restorative responses.

(3) *Collective efficacy.*

Harm to be repaired: the historical loss of community skills in conflict resolution, social control, informal sanctioning, and social support.

Objective: strengthening the capacity of neighbourhoods, schools, parochial organizations, and other community groups to respond effectively to crime.

(4) *Norm Affirmation.*

Harm to be repaired: the breach of community trust and the weakening of shared behavioural norms and values in the aftermath of the offence.

Objective: community and victim expression of harm and disapproval of the violation of standards of conduct as indicated by participant expression of these standards and their importance.

Notes

1. In attempting to explain the strong connection between completing restitution and recidivism documented in one national study (Schneider 1991), Schneider suggests that the mechanism at work was a kind of 'good citizenship effect' in which young offenders completing these obligations had a greater sense of legitimacy as someone who takes care of community obligations. It could conceivably also detract from these outcomes. Though critics have been fond of explaining the many ways this could occur, there is no known empirical support. We have also suggested that if restorative justice is to become a viable systemic approach to justice, as opposed to a programme or technique, we should expect to see 'restorative approaches' to core criminal and juvenile justice functions: sanctioning, public safety and social control, victim services, and offender rehabilitation (Walgrave and Bazemore 1999). And we do not believe that anyone would now debate that a concern with the reintegration and well-being of offenders who make it right with their victims is a primary concern of restorative justice.

2. We use the term 'conferencing' in a somewhat unconventional sense to include a range of decision-making models that seem to take four general administrative forms: victim–offender mediation/dialogue; family group conferencing; neighbourhood accountability boards; peacemaking circles (Bazemore and Umbreit 2001). Though there is wide variation within these basic models (Schiff *et al.* 2002; Bazemore and Schiff, forthcoming), the focus on restorative decision-making as operationalized in conferencing not only narrows the scope of this discussion but also, consistent with the focus of this volume, incorporates the informal side of the legal process in the intervention model. This informal side in the form of conferencing can therefore be viewed as pursuing multiple goals, including offender rehabilitation, but also 'justice' in the general sense. These theories suggest essential intermediate outcomes necessary to impact

recidivism and long-term offender change and also support decisions about use of alternative conferencing protocols that form the basis for propositions for future research.

3. Recidivism reduction effects are positive though not as strong in the case of restorative sanctions such as restitution and community service (for summaries see Bazemore *et al.* 2000; Braithwaite 1999a). Though these studies generally contrast restorative practices and programmes with other diversion- or treatment-focused programmes, the most important comparison are with other sanctions, e.g. probation, fines, boot camps. But such apples and oranges comparisons (more properly, apples and grocery stores) are inappropriate in any case. As informal decision-making processes, conferencing programmes are most appropriately compared with court and other formal and quasi-formal procedures; and when this is the test, restorative programmes win hands down (Umbreit 1999; Bazemore *et al.* 2000).

4. This example does not imply that all of the above obligations would likely by required of any offender. The point is to illustrate how various restorative justice practices could be linked based on the nature of the harm to form a holistic multi-component response. From a legalistic standpoint, one may raise questions about who ultimately decides what obligations will be required and what legal safeguards are in place to protect against disproportionality. Though the decision about obligations is generally made by the conference group by some form of consensus process, this does not mean that there cannot be oversight as well as standards about upper limits; these are in fact set by courts in some jurisdictions, and there may of course be judicial or other forms of oversight by legal advocates assigned to review cases.

5. In the interim, this leads us to think beyond extant intervention programmes to consider evaluating restorative justice impacts on offenders in terms of how restorative principles and their implications for intervention are in fact consistent with broader research agendas and funding theories of desistance and findings based on normative rather than evaluation data (Maruna 2001), and with theories of community crime rates (Braithwaite 1991). In doing so, we may also look to find empirical support for restorative justice theories. For example, empirical work on youth resiliency in the face of adverse, high risk environments, as well as data on maturational reform of serious offenders lends at least indirect support to restorative theories we will discuss later in this paper that address the vital importance of relationships and movement into new legitimate institutional roles (e.g. work and family) in desistance from crime. The collective efficacy studies also in an important sense confirm reintegrative shaming theory at a collective level, affirming Braithwaite's key point that low crime communities are those in which 'citizens do not mind their own business'.

6. Moreover, qualitative work that defines the cognitive elements of development of new identities among ex-offenders as a re-storying process suggests an experiential process that allows the offender to develop a 'redemption script' that is not necessarily connected in any way to formal intervention (Maruna 2001). As Maruna (2001) puts it, neither the 'medical model story [which]

suggests that offenders desist when they are "fixed" or corrected by psychotherapy [or the] *specific deterrence* story in which offenders get sent to jail, learn their lesson, and resign themselves never to go back' has much to do with recidivism or reform. The difference between this restorying process and the cognitive restructuring interventions now common in correctional treatment is that where the latter focus on correcting 'thinking errors' as cognitive deficits, the latter are based essentially on the restoration of relationships which allow the offender to reinterpret the past and move forward based on experiential learning associated with new roles.

7. The focus on redressing past harm raises concerns that conferences will easily begin to focus on harms that may be viewed as causing the offending rather than those that can be viewed as a consequence of it. In doing so, participants may easily slip into a traditional treatment/rehabilitative focus The difference in the relatively rare conferences that pursue this issue (typically peacemaking circles) and the traditional rehabilitative/treatment model seems to be in the ultimately collectivist focus that ultimately views past harms as seamlessly intertwined with the response to current harms, as is common most especially in Aboriginal communities (Ross 1996). The focus is on past harms is not posed as necessary to the restorative paradigm; it is simply a dimension that arises in some conferences. It is nonetheless problematic when it is not linked to the harm of the current offence.

8. Not included here is a familiar form of theory, which we have labeled 'healing dialogue', (Bazemore 1997; Bazemore and Schiff 2002). This theory is more often associated with victim healing and therefore not as straightforward in its implications for offender reintegration.

9. Though RISE is an offender-focused theory in the sense of its predictions of impact, the shame concept may resonate with victims as well with regard to the earlier mentioned notion of vindication, as in part, removal of victim shame in the absence of vindication (Zehr 2000); the tendency of adult victims to assume some culpability in cases involving juvenile offenders has been observed in juvenile justice practice.

Chapter 4

Restoration and the family: a pedagogical point of view

Ido Weijers

In this chapter I will present some pedagogical reflections on restorative justice. I will concentrate on a special form of restorative justice, family group conferencing. I will justify this focus in pedagogical terms. The chapter deals with the psychological impact, the justification and the conditions for successful family group conferencing seen from a pedagogical point of view. My central thesis is that any justifiable and any successful family group conference (FGC) presupposes a good relation between the young offender and his parents.

Although respect for the victim is one of the sources of inspiration for restorative justice, aiming for restoration cannot mean that all or even most of its attention is restricted to the victim's position. In my opinion, the offender may not and cannot be used as a tool for the goal of restoration. Anyway, using young persons who have committed a serious crime simply as a tool for restoration for their victims will be counter-productive in the end. Far from offering restoration, this kind of instrumentalism, which does not look seriously at the precarious position and role of the young offender, can offer at best some sort of material reparation of the harm done. Since it denies the complex and precarious moral and emotional expectations involving the role of the (young) offender in any restorative process, it seems unlikely that the things that are really crucial for restoration – that is recognition of personal responsibility for the wrongdoing, some sort of repentance for that wrongdoing and some convincing sort of apology – can be reached. All of these things pre-suppose an active and positive, moral and emotional involvement of the young offender which in turn presupposes that he is taken seriously, as a responsible, almost fully responsible, moral agent.

I fully agree with the idea that we badly need good state-compensation schemes for victims, completely independent of what we know about and do with the offender, as Elmar Weitekamp has said (Weitekamp 2001). I agree also with the more general idea that the position of the victim should be valued higher than is usually the case in our modern criminal law systems. Actually, we do not live in a moral culture in which the position of the victim is crucial. On the other hand, though, if we want to develop something like the systemic restorative justice model Jim Dignan, for instance, is pleading for, we definitely need a pedagogical view on the young offenders we are dealing with. I think that any hope for a systemic integration of the notion of restoration in our criminal justice systems presupposes a clear view on the meaningful involvement of the victim and of the offender, and on desirable outcomes for both parties.

A striking point in most restorative literature is that its special relevance for young offenders is often mentioned in its title, and in fact taken for granted, without taking into consideration that we have to deal with young, that is immature, offenders. This is my point of departure. From a pedagogical point of view the central aim of any reaction to serious misbehaviour of juveniles is their reflection on the bad moral con-sequences of their actions. This perspective makes the formula of the FGC in principle distinctly preferable as an educational action compared to other restoratively meant victim–offender confrontations, as I will make clear.

The question that I want to raise in this chapter is whether and when the formula of the FGC might be appropriate to achieve the aim of reflection on the moral consequences of the wrongdoing, of repentance and apology. I will lay on the table the casualness of the idea that the dialogue between victim and young offender, with active and crucial participation of the parents, will provide always for the best pedagogical reaction to juvenile offenders. Can the family (and close friends) be the moral reference point without saying? Are there not conditions to be fulfilled to be able to function as a moral reference point? I will reflect on the literature and on the few experiences we have in the Netherlands with family group conferencing up till now. I hope that this will contribute to a convincing specification of the justification of restorative justice practices for juveniles. I am fully aware that my argument is one-sided, since my focus in this chapter is purely on the impact and the appropriateness of this procedure for the young offender. Nonetheless, as I said, I think this is an important dimension in any reflection on restorative justice, also in relation to the state and the law.

My argument is built up in four steps. The first two steps in fact are preliminary remarks. My starting point is that the immaturity of young offenders implies a pedagogical task. I will specify that task first and I will make clear that I do not intend any traditional paternalism. Next, after having explained why I prefer family group conferencing as, in principle, the most promising restorative practice for young offenders, I will offer an analytical sketch of the psychological impact of this formula for the adolescent. If this analysis of the impact for the young offender is correct, my conclusion is that the application of this procedure needs specification, taking proportionality in consideration. My third step is to point to a simple but fundamental premise for the justification of restorative justice for juveniles concerning the seriousness of the wrongdoing. In my fourth and last step I will discern a factor that seems crucial from a pedagogical point of view, that is basic trust in the parent–child relationship. Only when we are sure that there is basic trust in the family can there be a sound pedagogical ground for family group conferencing. In my opinion, this is the minimum requirement that has to be fulfilled for any active involvement of the parents in a restorative dialogue between a victim and a juvenile offender.

Youth's immaturity implies a pedagogical task

My starting point and first preliminary remark is that young offenders cannot be seen as just little criminals. They are a special category which forces us to treat them in a special way. My point is that young offenders cannot be held fully responsible under the law. Criminal justice for young people will always have to take account of the dilemma that, while they are developing towards responsibility, they are also presumed to be dependent and not fully responsible. Our social policies do recognize this in so far that they do not hold us responsible as citizens who may vote, pay tax, stay away from school, marry or have sex with adults before a certain age. The notion of citizenship – which implies responsibility (in rights and duties) towards the state – is crucial here. All age boundaries in our social policies are moments where the young person becomes held to be responsible as a citizen towards the state.

This notion of citizenship has far-reaching implications for criminal law and the state's reaction towards juvenile delinquency. It means first of all that a minimum requirement for a criminal justice approach should be that the young offender must be able to realize that the wrong he has done is not only a misdemeanour in his personal world – that is against his family, teachers and friends. For any criminal law reaction that holds the young person responsible for his wrongdoing, the starting point has to be that the young person must be able to fully realize the social importance and consequences of that wrongdoing. He must be able to realize that this importance and these consequences do not only concern his victim(s), but also his loved ones, and his personal future and identity.

The relevant period for juvenile justice is adolescence, that is roughly the ages of twelve to eighteen. Developmental studies concerning this period tell us the following: there is no other period of human development characterized by more rapid and dramatic changes in physical, intellectual, emotional and social capabilities; this is a period of tremendous malleability, during which experiences in the family, peer group, school and other settings have a great deal of influence over the course of development; at the same time it is an important formative period, which implies that many adolescent experiences have a tremendous cumulative impact (Grisso and Schwartz 2000).

Relating these findings to delinquency and to criminal justice reactions to juvenile offending, the main questions concern two things: first, their culpability; and second; their competence to actively participate in any kind of criminal proceedings (Steinberg and Schwartz 2000). As to their culpability, it is relevant that adolescents from age fourteen or fifteen generally may have the necessary tools to engage in adult-like logical reasoning while lacking the experience that is available to older individuals. Compared to adults, young people are less future-oriented, less risk-averse, less able to control impulses and far more susceptible to the influence of others (Steinberg and Cauffman 1996; Scott *et al.* 1995)

As to their procedural capabilities, research finds not only that youths younger than fourteen are clearly incompetent to stand trial, because they simply cannot fully understand what is going on, nor fully appreciate its implications, nor make psychosocially mature judgements (Woolard *et al.* 1996). It is found also that, especially among young offenders, many continue to develop very slowly and will achieve their adult capacities at a rather late age, near to their late teens (Grisso 2000). A special point of concern is the immaturity of the young defendant concerning his supposed ability to perceive the long-term consequences of his actions in the adjudicative process (Steinberg and Cauffman 1996). It is not these different cognitive and psychosocial capacities on their own, though, that are crucial. Their relevance must be seen in the context of the actual procedures. Much more than for adults, children's and adolescent's real competence in criminal law procedures, like all their capabilities, is context-sensitive and interactive (Eggermont 1994; Masten and Coatsworth 1998).

Reviewing these findings from psychological research, my conclusion is that, to enable young offenders to fully participate and demonstrate their maximum competence in criminal proceedings, they need to be helped by specific supporting procedures, rituals, questions and explanations, and to be assisted by people who develop something like a 'professional friendship', or special 'professional concern' (Buss 2000). We certainly should hold young offenders responsible for their wrongdoing, albeit a 'diminished responsibility' (Zimring 2000), but in addressing them we need to offer them as much supportive context as possible to help them to become as responsible as possible.

I am not pleading for a traditional rehabilitative reaction, which implied that the relation with the concrete offence and its actual consequences was deliberately lost. The traditional rehabilitative attitude, with its characteristic refusal to look backwards and its exclusive future-orientation on 'the best interest' of the young offender, blocked the view on the question of the young person's responsibility (Weijers 1999). On the contrary, I am pleading for a new pedagogical perspective on reacting to serious juvenile crime, in which the appeal to the young offender's personal responsibility for his wrongdoing, that is for the consequences of that wrongdoing, is at the centre of attention. It is my starting point that the immaturity of the young offender implies that any reaction to his misbehaviour has first of all to be to help the young person to fully understand the social and moral implications of what he has done. This means that in our reaction we have to teach him both that we expect him to take full responsibility for his actions and what taking that full responsibility means. So the immaturity of the young offender charges us with a pedagogical task.

What does this task imply? It implies that we have to engage in a process of moral communication in which we have to make clear to him the consequences of his wrongdoing. That is, we have to make clear, first, what his offence means for his victim and for his victim's loved ones. It implies also that we must try to help him to understand what it means for his own environment and his own loved ones, the people he cares about, his family, his close friends, his teachers, his coaches etc. We also have to help him reflect on what that wrongdoing implies for himself as a moral person, for his future, his dreams, his idea of the person he wants to become, and for his future as a citizen, as a fully responsible and socially participating member of our society (Weijers 2000, 2002). We have to confront the adolescent offender with all these different consequential dimensions to help him to recognize that he should not have done what he did and to repent it. And in the end, our pedagogical task implies that we have to help him to find ways to show his regret and to apologize.

The psychological impact of a family group conference

If we agree with what has been advanced in this first step, we may conclude that, from a pedagogical point of view, restorative justice in general and family group conferencing in particular has a strong reason for reacting to serious misbehaviour of adolescent offenders. Indeed, restorative justice gives ample opportunity for an appeal to the moral self-reflection of the young offender, and offers him a chance to show regret and to apologize. Family group conferencing, though, seems to have some clear and simple pedagogical advantages in comparison to other restorative strategies, since this arrangement may help to make clear to him the wider moral and emotional impact of his wrongdoing. In principle, the presence of the parents (or other family members whom the adolescent cares about) may bring it home to him that it is not only the victim who experiences the bad consequences of his actions, but that something similar applies to his loved ones, the people he cares for and who care for him. In addition, their active involvement may also facilitate the adolescent's recognition of what his wrongdoing implies for himself as a moral person.

This essentially pedagogical insight is sustained by the outcomes of criminological research. Looking at meta-evaluations of prevention initiatives for adolescent offenders, we always see the same picture: very few, disappointingly few, programmes have credible evaluations. Several widely used and well-evaluated intervention strategies have been found even to increase delinquency in the long run! (McCord et al. 2001; Lundman 2001). Many such programmes rest on drawing young misbehaving adolescents together, a practice that seems to reinforce their antisocial behaviours. Restorative justice initiators should take due note of this point. But my conclusion here is that the most effective crime prevention programmes address a range of difficulties. There is one particular aspect that I want to stress: one crucial dimension for effective prevention seems to be the active involvement of the parents. For that reason we may suppose that, in principle, victim–offender dialogues will be most promising and effective when the young offender's parents are involved.

So we may conclude that restorative justice in general has a strong purpose in giving ample opportunity for an appeal on the moral self-reflection of the young offender and for offering chances to repent and apologize. We may also conclude that the involvement of the family seems

73

to promise the most effective restorative strategy both for self-reflection, repentance and apology, and for talking about ways to prevent recurrence of this type of misbehaviour. However, looking carefully at this strategy we have to ask whether family group conferencing might not have a weak point, when we look at the likely psychological impact of the procedure. My second preliminary remark is concerned with this question.

Studying reports of FGC sessions and observing them, as I have done now for some time, makes immediately clear for any experienced peda-gogical observer that complicated psychological and emotional processes do occur here. Without doubt, these psychological processes are not coincidences; they are implied deliberately and exactly aimed at by the formula of the FGC. Typical of this restorative strategy is the combination of two dialogues: a dialogue between the offender and the victim on the one hand, and a dialogue between the offender and his family on the other hand. The involvement of the family and other important persons from the young offender's world goes much further than appreciating both the position of the young offender and the pain of the victim. An FGC aims, first of all, to make an emotional and moral appeal to the young offender, presupposing his capability to experience and to express feelings of empathy, regret, remorse, guilt and shame in this family context. (On the appeal to these feelings and their possibly positive and negative effects see Taylor, Morris and Olthof in Weijers and Duff 2002.) The motive for the involvement of the family is that this morally meaningful and emotionally 'heavy' context might bring about a special susceptibility for the moral and emotional impact of the offence in the adolescent offender. The crux of the formula, as it has been expressed by many proponents of this strategy, is the hope of a catharsis, in which an emotional mask or armour might fall off (see for instance Braithwaite and Mugford 1994).

Understandable though this idea may be from the perspective of finding an effective instrument for prevention of recidivism, we must look critically at the psychological implications of this approach. We must try and weigh the impact of it to be able to justify the approach, first of all in terms of its proportionality in relation to the offence. I agree with Antony Duff, who states in this volume that restorative justice processes are not alternatives to punitive 'pain delivery' but are in themselves ways of trying to induce the appropriate kind of pain (Duff 2001, 2002). We should not only describe and analyse what procedures and what feelings are productive on the surface of the process. We need also information about the outcomes in the long run. But at the same time we need a fundamental reflection on what kind of emotional and moral appeal to the adolescent may be justified, that is, what kind of painful burden of censure, repentance and apology may be considered as proportionate to the burden of the offence, how much of that painful burden and under what conditions it may be justified. We should think about and discuss explicit and principled boundaries for the implementation of the formula as such and for the roles of the participants, the offender, the victim, the family and the mediator. It is my intention to contribute to this discussion in the rest of this chapter.

A serious offence and a disturbing record

To start with, I think, from a strictly pedagogical perspective, that there is one overall premise for the justification of family group conferencing: there may be no doubt about the seriousness of the wrongdoing. The FGC as a dialogue between victim and offender, implying an active role for the offender's parents, is a heavy moral and emotional medicine, too heavy for instance for the child that has been arrested once for sneaking some sweets from the supermarket. The enforcement of this medicine can be justified only when there is absolutely no doubt about its proportionality to the moral and emotional weight of the offence.

For different reasons, having to do at least partly with its embedding in an older rehabilitative tradition and partly from the fear of blunders, most experiments in the Netherlands are concerned with minor offences. That implies that this whole ritual, including all the labour in its preparation, is organized for offences like vandalism, theft and fighting, which could (and would normally) have been dealt with simply either by paying a small fine or doing a task for the community of 5, 10 or 20 hours. I fully admit that I leave aside here the perspective of the victim, but I think that it may be worthwhile also to take carefully into consideration the offender's perspective in itself, that is its possible productive and counterproductive outcomes for restoration. Maybe we need some extra originality here, and some additional concern about what exactly moral and emotional appeals mean and do to adolescents, and how counterproductive outcomes may be the unintended results of good and respectable intentions.

Let me make clear, to avoid misunderstanding, that I do not plead at all for soft and friendly approaches. But there are many alternatives for demonstrating and being stimulated to demonstrate one's empathy, to help the young offender to realize the consequences of his misbehaviour and to help him to show that he realizes what moral wrong he has done and to apologize for that. Pedagogically, we have to be careful to avoid a family conference becoming a 'normal' and self-evident routine. First of all, we should carefully listen to the reactions of the young offender and his parents to what we have to tell them about the moral and emotional impact of his misbehaviour. We should be aware of the counterproductive potential of too many hearings, too many words and too much well-meant attention which may easily be felt to be disproportionate to the actual moral and emotional burden of the offence or to the specific and relative part that the individual offender has had in the offence. This point is particularly relevant for adolescent offenders, since most of their misbehaviour is committed in groups. Next we have to reckon with the characteristic sensitivity of adolescents to principles of justice and in particular to proportionality, which means first of all the acknowledgement of their precise part in a collectively committed wrongful act. We should also bear in mind from a pedagogical perspective that in many cases, certainly those concerning minor offences, the first hearing itself, including some adequate suggestions for making apologies, may really be enough.

So, from a purely pedagogical point of view, the enforcement of an actual meeting with the victim in the presence of the adolescent's parents has to be seen as the outcome of a process via different preparatory meetings which in themselves may offer opportunities to come to recognition, repentance and apology. The enforcement of an actual meeting can be justified only when there is no doubt at all about the proportion of the moral and emotional burden this type of meeting implies to the weight of the offence and the adolescent's personal share and responsibility for it.

However, again from a purely pedagogical perspective, this premise concerning the seriousness of the moral wrongdoing is counterbalanced by a second premise, which is concerned with the existence of a clearly disturbing criminal record of the juvenile. To put it another way: in the case of a first offence without a record of misbehaviour at school, in the neighbourhood and/or elsewhere, only very serious moral wrongdoing justifies the arrangement of an FGC. So, being a first offender might be seen as a counter-indication for organising an FGC, unless something with really grave consequences has been done. Criminological research has found that delinquent behaviour is rare in early adolescence, increases through age sixteen and declines sharply from age seventeen onward. Most teenage males seem to engage in some delinquent conduct and in turn, desistence from this behaviour seems to be another predictable part of the maturation process. As we all know, only a very small group of young offenders will persist in a life of crime (Hirschi and Gottfredson 1983; Farrington 1986; Moffit 1993).

Since the vast majority of first offenders do not, or rarely, get into trouble with the police again, we have to be aware that the enforcement of an actual FGC runs the risk of being too strong, overdone and simply unnecessary for the adolescent offender. What is more, it will be felt as overdone and unjustified by the adolescents themselves if their mis-behaviour cannot be considered as really serious moral wrongdoing. This then is a point we can be pretty sure of: if a young offender – even if he admits his responsibility and guilt and wants to apologize (and might be willing to express that apology, for instance by writing a letter to the victim) – if this adolescent thinks an FGC would be too much, any conference will have little chance of becoming successful. And if the parents of the young offender hold the same view, there will be almost no chance at all for success.

But there may be a second motive for organising an FGC, and this is that there is a clearly disturbing criminal record of the young offender. However, given my first premise it will be clear that this second motive will not do without first reflecting on the seriousness of the actual mis-behaviour itself. We have to be able to take the concrete serious misbehaviour that has lead to the conference as really paradigmatic for serious problematic behaviour in several cases. The seriousness of the actual misbehaviour presents also a certain basic guarantee against using the victim as an instrument for the well-being of the offender in the future. This argument may prohibit cynicism and suspicion of paternalism both on the part of the victim and on the part of the young offender.

Here lies the real challenge for FGC for the pedagogue: when there is a pretty serious offence in combination with a disturbing criminal record. It is in these situations that FGC seems pre-eminently justified from a pedagogical point of view. In these circumstances there is a clear pedagogical objective for this 'heavy' strategy: to try to give the life of a misbehaving adolescent a new turn with the help of the ones he cares about.

Basic trust and social integration

But we cannot just dream of new chances and promises, we need also to look at the limits of this strategy. We have to be more specific about which situations and which conditions might justify a restorative justice reaction to juvenile offenders, and about which do not. To do that from the perspective choosen in this chapter, we will have to look at least more specifically and concretely at the world of the juvenile. Two factors in the young offenders' world seem most important to me. The first and decisive factor is a typical grounding concept in pedagogy concerning the quality of the pedagogical relationship within the family. Here the question of trust – basic trust between parents and child – is crucial. The second factor is a typical sociological concept, concerning the extent of the social embeddedness or social integration of the juvenile and his family. I will come back shortly to this last factor further in this section; however, let me elaborate now a little bit on the first factor, the concept of basic or existential trust in upbringing.

As a first step to make clear what is meant by this concept it may be helpful to distinguish between the notion of reliance and the notion of trust (Hertzberg 1988). If we think that we can rely on someone, we have reasons to do so, which implies that these reasons could also be absent, that there could be circumstances in which it would be unwise to rely on someone. In this context one can speak of putting one's trust in someone, which again implies the possibility of a refusal, that is of choice.

Characteristic for basic trust, however, is the absence of this freedom of choice. Basic trust cannot be put on someone; one lives in it. Basic trust implies that one believes in the person who is trusted. In normal up-bringing the child trusts his parents as his *raison d'être*. Whilst putting one's trust in someone is conditional and presupposes knowledge and may thus be called 'epistemic trust', basic trust is unconditional and corresponds with certainty, not with knowledge.

This 'primitive' certainty is characteristic for the basic trust in which the child normally lives towards his parents and which is given with his fundamental dependence on them. Children do what their parents want them to do basically because they trust them. They do not have reasons for their obedience. The point is that in normal upbringing they cannot *distrust* their parents. In the normal relationship between parents and child trust is never gained. It is just there as long as it is not destroyed. This fundamental vulnerability is typical of relationships within the family (Baier 1986; Smeijers 1996).

For the justification of a restorative justice approach we will always have to take into account this factor. This point is related to the point advanced above concerning the differences in addressing first offenders and young recidivists. The fact is, that with many serious and violent young (re)offenders we see a dramatic family situation where the basic trust relation within the family is severely damaged as a consequence of parental indifference, neglect or abuse.

It must be seen as a prerequisite for organizing a FGC, with its characteristic active and serious involvement of the parents in the dialogue between the young offender and the victim, that there is a normal relation of trust between the parents and the child. I do not mean of course, that within a good basic trust relationship there are no struggles or problems within the family, nor that the young offender and his parents are on good terms. Far from that. There can be – and mostly are – great problems within the families involved. Parents do not know what to do with their recidivist child and often are at an almost complete loss. Adolescent recidivists often feel frustrated by their parents, are angry at them and avoid discussing serious things with them. But a bad basic trust relation essentially has nothing to do with frustration and mis-understanding, but everything to do with indifference, fundamental neglect and/or abuse. There may be severe tensions between the adolescent and his parents, while there can be mutual trust between them at the same time. My point is, that when basic trust is absent, the active involvement of the parents would be pedagogically irresponsible towards the young person. Their active involvement in the dialogue about the consequences of the wrongdoing for the victim, for the family and close friends and for the young person him- or herself would be perverse. We have to be acute with respect to this family history.

I would suggest that, for instance, a disproportional disappointment concerning the cooperation of delinquent girls might have to do with these dramatic family situations. Many adolescent female offenders have such strong reasons to be cautious about trusting people in general that the expectation that they might be forthright and honest when confronted with any kind of group conference that includes strangers, no matter how well intentioned, may be unrealistic, as Christine Alder has made clear. But the expectation that they would be confronted and 'assisted' by exactly those people who might have damaged their basic trust is absolutely unacceptable. When we acknowledge that FGC consists of a combination of a dialogue between the offender and the victim and between the offender and his family, we need to assure that the dialogues along both lines are and remain ethically and emotionally clear and pure. Damaged basic trust relations undermine any pure and justifiable communication concerning what the adolescent has done wrong, the consequences of that wrongdoing and reflections on how to apologize for that.

Taking into account family relations seems to imply at least three things. First, any FGC approach with its crucial, active role and its emotional and moral involvement of the family first of all requires an investigation, a report about the family situation. This seems to be at least absolutely necessary in case of recidivism. Second, when the relation of trust seems to be absent, or when there are severe doubts on this point, a FGC approach must be excluded. In these cases we might better look for alternatives instead of trying to involve the family in discussing what the young person has done wrong and how to deal with it. I suggest that it should be considered whether it might be wise to arrange some other form of restorative justice in which the coordinator or the mediator (or the judge) takes a special, active educative role in the dialogue between the young offender and his victim, in a way trying to 'take over' the parental role; this needs to be done, of course, with the explicit approval of the adolescent, but again, we have to reckon with the chance that our expectations may be unrealistic.

Third, in these cases it might be better to look to building a new community for the offender, as Raymond Corrado has suggested, instead of trying to let him or her reintegrate in his or her family and neighbourhood (Corrado 2001). How could we justify trying to reintegrate and restore adolescents within their family and related moral community if these, certainly from their perspective, have damaged and betrayed their basic trust? As some authors have made clear, many adolescent offenders live peripatetic lives on the margins of their original communities. They have left home sometimes, live on the streets or with peers and companions or come home incidentally just to sleep or eat. They may have developed communities of their own and anyway associate neither their parental home nor their original community with anything benign, but rather with alienation and even hostility. They may have been victims themselves of powerful adult abuse and have good reasons to be very suspicious and cynical of moral appeals that fail to recognize their suffering (Alder 2000; Miers 2000; Crawford 2000b).

If we are sure that there is a trustful relationship between the adolescent and his parents notwithstanding severe problems within the family, an FGC focusing on the concrete wrongdoing may offer a good opportunity to help to break through these older tensions and find new patterns of getting along with each other. What is more, the factor of basic trust in itself might be a strong force in a FGC as it works on a possible negative second factor of a weak social situation. As we know, with recidivism we usually find a marginal or vulnerable socially integrated position of the young person and his or her family. In this specific situation, which we find in many family situations of young offenders in the modern city, particularly in immigrant families, the active involvement of the family in the dialogue between the young offender and the victim also may offer both the juvenile and his family new possibilities for an increase of social embeddedness within the wider social community. The FGC may offer a new possibility for the family to express their concern about the future of their problem child, which may help both the young offender and his family to express their longing for a better socially integrated life in the community.

Since in most cases of serious and persistent juvenile delinquency the experience of social marginality itself appears to be one of the negative background factors that contribute to the explanation of juvenile crime, any attempt to help lessen that experience may be helpful. The FGC with full and active commitment of the family may help first of all the juvenile with a safe pedagogical family background and an experience of social marginality. But it may not only help the young offender himself to reflect on his moral situation and to find a new way of life. The active role of the parents in the procedure, in the dialogue with the victim and his friends and supporters may also help to strengthen a more positive social experience of the family. This experience of the parents, though related to a negative cause, in turn may stimulate and help the young person to develop a more positive grip on his own life.

But on the other hand, we have to be sensible about the limits of this approach. The FGC strategy may only be successful if these conferences form part of a series of social interventions and support. In itself a conference and all its preparational activities form only a very limited intervention, which will hardly be able to turn around people's lives. Let us be sober and clear about what this strategy requires to be really successful in the long run. As I have said, all successful prevention strategies address a wide range of difficulties. The same holds for FGCs. First of all, its success seems to depend on the conditions of the conference itself: fully remorseful adolescent offenders in particular, and genuine consensus about the outcomes of the conference appear to be crucial success factors (Maxwell and Morris 2000; Daly 2002b). But longlasting positive effects simply are not possible without strong social support, without tackling structural problems that weak integrated families and adolescents confront in our modern welfare states. We had better get rid of mythical stories and tell the real story, as Kathy Daly argued recently. The inspiring starting point of FGC, though, remains its appeal to young offender's direct environment, the restorative power of the people he cares about and who care about him.

Chapter 5

Restorative punishment and punitive restoration

R. A. Duff

Introduction

My thesis can be stated quite simply. Our responses to crime should aim for 'restoration', for 'restorative justice': but the kind of restoration that criminal wrongdoing makes necessary is properly achieved through a process of retributive punishment. To put it the other way round, offenders should suffer retribution, punishment, for their crimes: but the essential purpose of such punishment should be to achieve restoration. To put it yet more simply, my slogan is 'Restoration through retribution'. That thesis sets me in opposition to advocates of restorative justice, and to those critics of restorative justice who argue for a 'just deserts' retributivism.

Both sides to this controversy are right in important respects. Advocates of restorative justice are right to insist that in our responses to, and understanding of, crime we should seek restoration, and such related aims as reparation and reconciliation; that we should not punish offenders just for the sake of making them suffer, or to deter them and others; and that our existing criminal procedures – our criminal trials, the kinds of punishment typically imposed on offenders – are ill-suited to the restorative ends that we should be pursuing. Proponents of just deserts are right to insist that punishment is the proper response to criminal wrongdoing, and that what justifies punishment is that it is deserved for that wrongdoing: it is the state's proper responsibility, and our responsibility as citizens, to bring criminal wrongdoers to suffer the punishments that they deserve.

However, both 'restorative' and 'retributive' theorists are wrong insofar as they suppose, as they often do, that we must choose between restoration and retribution as our primary aim. Thus critics of the restorative justice movement often assume that we have to choose between the 'punishment paradigm' and the 'restorative paradigm' (Ashworth 1993) – and argue that we should choose the former, since the pursuit of restorative aims is incompatible with the demands of penal justice. Advocates of restorative justice often assume that we must choose between restorative and retributive justice – and argue that we must choose the former, since punitive retribution cannot serve the aim of restoration.[1] This shared assumption is, as I will argue, mistaken. Once we understand what restoration must involve in the context of criminal wrongdoing, and what retribution can mean in the context of criminal punishment, we will see that restoration is not only compatible with retribution and punishment, but requires it.

Restorative theorists will therefore accuse me of undermining the eirenic, reconciliatory aims of restorative justice by a desire to punish, to 'deliver pain' (see Christie 1981), which is utterly at odds with those aims; proponents of punishment as 'just deserts' will accuse me of abandoning the principles of penal justice in favour of ill-defined aspirations to 'restoration' which are utterly at odds with the central demands of proportionality and penal restraint. My argument will be, however, that restorative and retributive justice are not thus opposed.

My claim is not that existing 'restorative justice' programmes are punitive (though many do have a punitive dimension); nor that our existing penal practices are generally restorative (which would be absurd). There is an obvious incompatibility between existing restorative practices and existing penal practices, and between the conceptions of 'restoration' favoured by many restorative theorists and the conceptions of punishment held by many advocates of punitive or retributive justice. I will argue, however, that once we gain a better understanding of the concepts of restoration and of punishment, we will be able to dissolve the apparent conflict between them, and to see that criminal punishment should aim at restoration, whilst restorative justice programmes should aim to impose appropriate kinds of punishment.

To make out this argument, I begin, in the next section, with the question of what 'restoration' should mean in the context of wrongdoing – of what needs to be restored and how it can be restored; apology and moral reparation will be crucial here. In the third section I apply the results of the second to the case of crime, and offer an account of the proper aims of victim–offender mediation programmes – which are often portrayed as paradigms of restorative justice: such programmes, I will argue, should be understood not as alternatives to punishment, but as paradigms of punishment, and thus as models for the criminal justice system.

Restoration and wrongdoing

Standard definitions of 'restorative justice' are, inevitably, rather vague. To say, for instance, that it is 'a process whereby parties with a stake in a specific offence collectively resolve how to deal with the aftermath of the offence and its implications for the future' (Marshall 1999: 5); or that its purpose 'is the restoration into safe communities of victims and offenders who have resolved their conflicts' (Van Ness 1993: 258): leaves open crucial questions about the significance of the 'offence' or 'conflict', and about what can count as successfully 'dealing with' the 'aftermath' or 'implications' of the offence, or 'resolving' the conflict. My main concern in this section is with the question of what kind of 'restoration' is made necessary by criminal wrongdoing: but it is worth pausing briefly to think about the implications of the basic idea of 'restoration'.

Many different kinds of thing can be 'restored'. Property which was lost or stolen can be restored, i.e. given back, to its owner; paintings which have been damaged can be restored to their pristine glory. Health which was undermined through illness can be restored – the sick can become well again. Reputations which were damaged by accusation or by slander can be restored, if the truth is established and published, which can also restore the person's standing in the community. Security – both the fact of being safe from danger and the awareness that one is thus safe[2] – can be restored after it has been undermined; the danger which threatened, or seemed to threaten, is removed, and we are re-assured of our safety. Trust which has been undermined can be restored; so too can relationships – of friendship, of love, of collegiality, of fellow citizenship – which have been damaged or weakened. What is common to all these cases is the retrieval of an original favourable condition. That original condition – of health, of security or trust, of good reputation, of friendship, for instance – is lost or removed, so that the good internal to it is lost. But that good is then regained: the condition is reinstated, the *status quo ante* is restored.

Restoration strictly speaking must thus be distinguished from such concepts as reparation and compensation. Restoration requires the re-instatement of the *status quo ante*. A harm was caused, a wrong was done, and its memory might remain: but when restoration is achieved, it is now (apart from the memory) as if the harm or wrong had never occurred.

Reparation and compensation, by contrast, seek to make up for the loss of what cannot thus be restored. Thus when property is lost or stolen, it might be restored – the owner might get back the very thing she lost. But it might not be restorable: it might have been destroyed or sold on beyond recall, in which case all that is possible is reparation or compensation rather than restoration. If the silver I inherited from my mother is stolen and melted down, my property cannot be restored; the most I can gain is a replacement, or compensation that will to some degree 'make up for' my loss.[3] Similarly, when health is lost, it might be restorable: the patient might return to as healthy a condition as she was in before illness struck. But it might not be thus restorable: she might be left permanently disabled or weakened; and the pain that she might have undergone during the illness cannot be 'restored', even if the illness is cured. This point raises a serious question about what we could even hope to restore in the context of crime or wrongdoing: we must ask what harm is done, what goods are lost or damaged, that we could even aspire to restore.

We might at first think of the material, physical or psychological effects that wrongdoing typically causes: property is lost or damaged; physical injuries are suffered; fear, anxiety and distress are caused, as may be other, more lasting kinds of psychological damage. But, first, even if some such harms do permit genuine restoration (if the victim's property or physical or psychological health can be restored), others do not: we cannot make it for the victim as if the wrong had never been done, since we cannot wipe out her suffering; we cannot make it as if she never suffered that fear, anxiety or distress. If we focus on these kinds of non-restorable harm, we must therefore think of reparation or compensation, not of restoration. (This is not to deny that reparation and compensation have an important role to play in an enterprise of restorative justice: it is simply to insist that they cannot in themselves constitute restoration – that their role should rather be seen as means to restoration.) Second, to focus on such harms as these is to ignore the fact that the victim was wronged. He did not simply lose his property, or suffer accidental damage to it – it was stolen, or maliciously destroyed or damaged; he did not simply suffer injury through natural causes or in an accident – he was attacked. Surely the harm he has suffered, what needs to be restored, must be understood in a way that includes its wrongful character.[4]

We might meet both these points by talking not (just) about the material or psychological effects of the wrongdoing on the victim, but about the relationships it damaged: between the wrongdoer and his direct victim (when there is one), between the wrongdoer and the wider communities to which he and the victim belong – communities which might be intimate and close, such as a family or a group of friends; or less intimate but still relatively local, such as a village or residential neighbourhood; or impersonally large, such as a political community whose bounds are co-extensive with those of a particular legal system.[5] Those relationships were damaged by the wrongdoer's deed, and need now to be restored. However, if we are to understand what could restore such relationships, what could even count as their restoration, we must get clear about the kind of damage they have suffered.

It might be tempting to try to describe that damage in purely factual or empirical terms: the victim, and others, are angry with the wrongdoer, or fearful or mistrustful of him, or are unwilling still to engage in their former common activities with him; the wrongdoer himself might feel ill at ease with or estranged from them. Now if we see the damage in such terms, we will naturally see 'restoration' in similarly empirical terms, as a matter of securing such changes in the attitudes and feelings of those concerned that they are no longer angry, fearful, untrusting or hostile; and we will look for techniques that might help to secure such changes. But such a perspective is quite inadequate, since it leaves out the crucial fact that the victim was wronged by the wrongdoer. We are not just dealing with an empirical breakdown in the relationship – a breakdown which, as thus described, leaves it open whether it was anyone's fault; we are dealing with a breach created in the relationship, or damage done to it, by one party's wrong-doing.[6] The wrongdoer denied or flouted the values – of mutual trust, concern and respect – by which their relationship as friends, neighbours, colleagues or fellow citizens was supposedly defined; in doing so, he damaged that relationship as a normative relationship which is partly constituted by those values.

The damage to the relationship must therefore be understood in normative, not merely in empirical, terms. There are three crucial features of this normative perspective.

First, we must understand, and appraise, the responses of those involved as responses to a wrong that was done – and as being reasonable or unreasonable, justified or unjustified, as responses to that wrong. The victim is not just angry, but indignant at the wrong he suffered; and we cannot then avoid asking whether his anger is justified. Perhaps it is excessive – the wrong was not that serious, the wrongdoer was not that culpable. Or perhaps it is too weak – he should be more indignant, more angry, than he is: for not to be angered by a wrong done to me can display a lack of self-respect (see Murphy 1988: 16–18), or a blindness to the moral quality of others' conduct. The reactions of others, and of the wrongdoer, are likewise subject to normative appraisal: we must ask not just what they in fact feel, but what they should feel; and our understanding of the damage done to their relationships is determined in crucial part by our understanding of their responses as reasonable or as unreasonable. If someone is so angry with me that he will have no more to do with me unless and until I offer him a profuse apology, our relationship has broken down: but our understanding of the character and the implications of that breach will depend on whether his anger is a justified response to some serious wrong that I did him, or an unjustified response to an imagined slight.

Second, we might sometimes want to say – and be justified in saying – that a relationship has been thus damaged even if those directly involved do not react as if it has been damaged, or do not even realize that it has been damaged. Suppose that a friend – or someone I thought was a friend – seriously betrays my trust for his own profit. Perhaps, because I do not want to have to face up to the implications of this, I try to persuade myself that the breach of trust was not that serious; or perhaps I don't even know what he has done, and so sincerely believe that our friendship is intact.[7] Others might still properly say that the friendship has been seriously damaged by his betrayal, since that betrayal was utterly inconsistent with, a complete denial of, the bonds of mutual trust and concern by which friendship is defined. If the betrayal was serious enough, others might indeed think that the friendship has been destroyed, unless the friend and I together face up to its implications and try to deal with it: whatever relationship we might maintain, that is, can no longer count as a friendship.

Third, when we ask what can restore the relationship, or repair the damage done to it, we must ask not just what will in fact make the parties feel better, or quell their anger, mistrust or fear, but what would be normatively adequate to restore it – what would make it appropriate to desist from anger, to renew trust, to restore community? Since it was the wrongdoing that damaged the relationship, it is that that must be repaired: but how can that be done? Material damage that was caused might be repaired; property that was stolen might be given back or replaced; physical injuries might be healed: but what can repair the wrong that was done?

Different relationships admit of different kinds of repair: but the obvious, paradigmatic way of repairing the normative harm wrought by wrongdoing is apology; and whilst apology can take various different forms in different relationships and contexts, and can be implicit rather than explicit, we can make some general points about the character or meaning of apologies for wrongdoing.[8] These points can be summarized as the three 'R's of apology: recognition, repentance and reconciliation. Apology expresses the wrongdoer's recognition of the wrong he has done, his repentance, and his desire for reconciliation with those whom he wronged – for the restoration of the relationships he damaged. (I am speaking here of sincere apologies; I will comment later on the problem of insincerity.)

Recognition of the wrong as a wrong is clearly an indispensable first step. It is something that is owed to the victim by others in general (whose sympathetic response to him should be structured by the recognition that he has been not just harmed, but wronged), but especially by the wrongdoer; in recognizing the wrong done to him, we recognize his moral standing as a fellow human being who demands our concern and respect (see Gaita 1991: chs. 1–4). Such recognition on the part of the wrongdoer might of course be spontaneous: she comes, perhaps at once, to see for herself the wrong she has done, and to understand its implications. But it is a painfully familiar fact about human beings that we are for a host of reasons often very slow to recognize our own wrongdoings: we often need others to persuade us to face up to what we have done. This is an important role that such responses as blame, criticism and censure play, as well as the often forcible expression of such emotions as anger and indignation: to bring a wrongdoer to recognize what she has done – a recognition that her apology then expresses.

Recognition includes understanding: to recognize the wrong I have done involves not just realizing that I did wrong, but coming to grasp the character, seriousness and implications of that wrong. It also includes or leads to repentance: for sincerely to recognize what I did as a wrong is to recognize it as something that I should not have done – which is also to repent my having done it. One who says 'Yes, I recognize that I did wrong, but so what? I'd do it again tomorrow' has not, we should say, truly recognized the wrong as a wrong; at most, he sees it as something that others call 'wrong'.[9] To repent my past wrongdoing is both to own and to disown it: I own it as mine, as something for which I must accept responsibility (and blame); but I disown it as something that I now wish I had not done, and that I repudiate (and, since repentance also involves a commitment to self-reform, as something that I will try to avoid in future). What I owe to those I have wronged, and what others may try to persuade me to if I need persuasion, is such a repentant recognition of the wrong I have done – a repentance that apology can also express. We should note too that such repentance is of its nature painful: the repentant wrongdoer cares, or has come to care, for those whom she wronged, for the values she violated; she must therefore be pained by that wrong and that violation.

An apology which expresses my repentant recognition of the wrong I have done thereby also expresses my desire, my hope, for reconciliation with those whom I wronged. At least in the case of serious wrongs, I realize that I have by my wrongdoing damaged or threatened (if not destroyed) my relationship with them – our friendship, our marriage, our relationship as neighbours or as colleagues; if that relationship is to be restored, I must seek their forgiveness through my apology.[10] For reconciliation to be complete, the other must accept my apology: it might not be possible, psychologically or morally, literally to 'forgive and forget', but the forgiving acceptance of my apology does suffice, normatively, to restore the relationship and to heal the breach.

Now apologies are supposed to be sincere, and in many contexts they have value only if they are, and are known to be, sincere. It is worth noting, however, that there can sometimes be value even in apologies that are not or might not be sincere, in formal apologies that might be to some degree a matter of ritual. Just as – or so it is said – hypocrisy is a homage that vice pays to virtue, so insincere apology can be a homage that an unrepentant wrongdoer pays to social morality: if it is not merely offered out of short-term prudence, it can express a concern to preserve the bonds of community. Furthermore, the demand that the wrongdoer apologize, even if we suspect that his apology will not be sincere, can communicate both to him and to the victim our recognition of the wrong that he did; and we can hope that the experience of apologizing might help to bring him to recognize for himself the wrong that he did.[11]

Sometimes, however, merely verbal apology might not be enough, at least for a relatively serious wrong: even a sincere verbal apology might not be adequate to the seriousness of the wrong done. It is a general, deep feature of our lives that we need to give more than merely verbal form and expression to things that matter to us, especially when that expression has a public significance. We express our gratitude for a great service done to us by a gift or, in the public realm, by a public reward or honour; we express our grief at a death through the rituals of a funeral. Such more-than-merely-verbal modes of expression have two related purposes: they make the expression more forceful to others than a merely verbal expression would have been, and they can help to focus the expresser's own attention on what needs to be expressed.

An apology can thus be strengthened, made more forceful, if it is given more than merely verbal form; and this can also help to focus the wrongdoer's attention (an attention which, as we all know from painful personal experience, is all too easily distracted) on the wrong that he did and the need to seek forgiveness and reconciliation for it. Mere words, and especially between strangers, can be too cheap – too easy to say, without any real depth of meaning; too easy to forget, without thinking about their meaning;[12] by giving apology some more material expression, we can both strengthen and express its sincerity.

If we then ask what this more than merely verbal form could be, the obvious answer is that it could consist in some kind of reparation. If the wrongdoing caused a material harm or loss that it is within the wrong-doer's power to make good, he can make reparation by making it good. If it caused no such harm, or if the wrongdoer cannot make the harm good, he must find some other way of 'making up' for what he did: some other way of making his repentant recognition of what he did forcefully clear both to the victim and to others. Depending on the context, on the nature of the wrong, and on the relationship it threatened, this might involve, for instance, undertaking some service for the victim, or for the wider com-munity; or buying the victim a thoughtful gift; or contributing time or money to a suitable charity; or agreeing to seek appropriate help to avoid repeating the wrong (someone whose addiction has led him to steal from his friends might agree to embark on a treatment programme).

We must be clear about the meaning and point of these kinds of reparation, and how they differ from reparation or compensation that aims only to repair or make up for some material harm that I have caused. If I damage or destroy your property through carelessness, it is only just that I should, if I can (and if you are not insured) pay for it to be repaired or replaced: the loss should fall on the person who culpably caused it. In this context, all that matters is that the material loss is made good, as far as that is possible. In particular, whilst I might find the reparations burdensome, it is no part of their purpose or meaning that they be burdensome: if I am so rich that the necessary payment does not impinge even briefly on my financial well-being, the payment still makes adequate reparation – as adequate as it would if I was so poor that it was really burdensome to me. By contrast, the kind of moral reparation that is needed to give an apology for wrongdoing a suitably forceful expression must be burdensome to the wrongdoer. Undertaking a task that is in no way burdensome to me (because it is something that I would have done anyway or anyway enjoy doing); or making a payment that is so small relative to my means that it constitutes no financial burden: these cannot constitute the kind of moral reparation that gives force to an apology. If, as I have suggested, mere words might not be enough to constitute a sufficiently serious apology for wrongdoing, a reparation that imposes no real burden on the wrongdoer cannot suffice either – it costs too little to add force to a verbal apology. If I am to show you (and myself) that I really do repent my wrongdoing, by offering a more than merely verbal apology, the reparation I undertake must be something burdensome – something that symbolizes the burden of moral injury that I laid on my victims and would now like (if only I could) to take on myself; the burden of wrongdoing that I laid on myself; and the burden of remorse that I now feel.[13]

I have talked so far about our informal responses to moral wrongdoing, and about what 'restoration' can amount to in that context. I have argued so far that what needs 'restoring', and what could conceivably be restored, is not so much any material harm that was caused, as the relationships that were damaged by the wrongdoing; that that damage must be understood in normative terms, as involving a flouting or denial of the normative bonds by which the relationship was defined; that it can be made good only by an apology which expresses the wrongdoer's repentant recognition of his wrongdoing and his desire for reconciliation; and that, at least in the case of serious wrongs, the apology might need to be given more forceful expression by some kind of moral reparation which must be burdensome to the wrongdoer.

I have talked in rather crude, general and abstract terms – terms which might seem quite inadequate to the subtle complexities and variations to be found in the wide range of human relationships within which wrongs may be done and repaired. If we think of the very different ways in which different kinds of wrongdoing can be understood and dealt with between, for instance, lovers; or between friends; or between colleagues; or in local neighbourhoods; or in any of the other kinds of community by which our lives are structured: it might seem simply foolish to hope to give any general account of wrongdoing and restoration that would apply to all these different kinds of case. However, first, I do not need to claim that what I have said so far applies to every kind of relationship; all I need, and do, claim is that it applies to many relationships. Second, at least some of these variations in ways of responding to wrongdoing can be seen as variations in ways of expressing or articulating the normative damage done by the wrongdoing, or in the forms that apology and reparation can take: that is to say, the basic structure that I have sketched in this section is still there, but is fleshed out in different ways.

My main concern, however, is to show how these comments about the kind of restoration that wrongdoing requires in informal, extra-legal contexts can clarify the idea of restoration in the context of crime – and make good my claim that restoration is to be achieved through retributive punishment.

Crime, mediation and punishment

The criminal law defines a wide range of 'public' wrongs. It specifies types of conduct from which citizens should refrain because they are wrongful, in terms of the (supposedly) shared values of the political community whose law it is; it claims the authority thus to declare what, as citizens, we may or may not do. The wrongs that it defines are 'public', not in the sense that they must cause some harm to the 'public' as distinct from an individual victim, but in the sense that they are matters of proper public concern.[14] In terms of its empirical effects, the violent attack perpetrated by a drunken man on his wife might cause harm only to her; and such attacks have, notoriously, sometimes been seen as 'private' affairs in which the criminal law has no proper interest – 'domestics', as they used to be called by English police who would be very reluctant to intervene in them. To claim that they constitute public wrongs which should be taken seriously by the criminal law is to claim not that they cause further, as yet unnoticed, harm to 'the public' or the community, but that they are a kind of wrong which should concern the community as a whole: we should collectively share in the wrong done to the wife as her fellow citizens, since it is a wrong that flouts the defining values of our polity; it is for us, collectively, to respond to that wrong – rather than leaving it for her to deal with it as a private matter. Similarly, to say that burglary and robbery should be crimes is to say that such wrongs should not be left as private matters between the victim and the wrongdoer, or as matters of civil law, which leaves it to the victim to sue the wrongdoer for private reparation: they are wrongs that should concern us all, as the victim's fellow citizens, and that require a collective response.

But what kind of response is appropriate? Those who think that we must choose between 'restorative' and 'retributive' justice might think that we must choose between a response – for instance, some kind of mediation process – which aims at restoration, and a response – the normal criminal process, for instance – which aims simply to punish the offender. However, my comments in the previous section on informal responses to wrongdoing should have laid the foundations for the argument, to be sketched in this section, that this is a false dichotomy.

Suppose that some kind of mediation programme is available, and that both offender and victim (violent husband and battered wife; burglar and victim) agree to take part in it.[15] What should be the aims of the mediation?

It is important, I suggest, that the mediation focus not just on the harm that was caused, but on the wrong that was done. What matters is not just that the victim has suffered certain kinds of physical injury, or loss of property, or distressing psychological states; nor just that, since it was the offender who culpably caused those harms, the cost of repairing them or of providing compensation for them should fall on him: but that he committed a serious wrong against her. It is that wrong on which the criminal law focuses (by contrast, the civil law is concerned with harms or losses, and with who should pay for them); it is on that wrong that any adequate response to the offender's crime, and to the victim, must focus; and we must therefore ask what kind of 'restoration' that wrong makes necessary.

The answer that I suggest should be obvious from the previous section. What needs to be restored, and what can in principle be restored, is the offender's normative relationship with his victim as a fellow citizen, and with his fellow citizens more generally. For the criminal law is concerned not with our more local, intimate and optional relationships as friends, as lovers, as neighbours, as colleagues, but simply with our (somewhat more abstract, detached and non-optional) relationships as fellow citizens: it defines the values and constraints which make our common life as citizens possible. What matter to the criminal law is therefore the wrongs done by one citizen to other citizens, and the damage done by those wrongs to their relationships as citizens. The offender's crime damaged his relationships both with his victim, as a fellow citizen, and with his fellow citizens more generally, by denying those values – of mutual respect and concern – that are supposed to define their civic relations, and that make civic life possible; it is that damage that must be repaired, to restore those relationships.

When such a wrong has been committed, it should be recognized: this is something that is owed to the victim, and is anyway a simple implication of taking seriously the values that the offender has violated. It should be recognized by the victim's fellow citizens, who can manifest that recognition both in their direct responses to the victim (responses of sympathy, of assistance), and in their responses to the offender: in, most obviously, the way in which they condemn or criticize him for what he has done – a kind of condemnation and criticism that is given formal expression by a criminal trial and conviction.[16] It should be recognized by the offender: he owes it to his victim to recognize the wrong he has done to her, and to his fellow citizens to recognize the way in which he has violated the public values of the polity. It is then quite appropriate that one of the initial aims of the mediation process should be, as it is often said to be, to get the offender to recognize, to understand, what he has done (and to give him a chance to explain himself to the victim).

What he should recognize is that he has culpably committed this wrong. Thus the tones in which he is addressed by others in the process (by the victim, by the mediator, by his or the victim's supporters) should be not the neutral tones of bare description, but the normative tones of censure and criticism – of blame.[17] This is not to say that those tones must be hostile, or such as to humiliate him or exclude him: although it is all too easy for censure and blame to become exercises in oppression, humiliation or exclusion, we must try to censure in a way that displays our recognition of, and concern for, the offender as a fellow citizen. But since what we must try to persuade him to recognize, or join with him in recognizing, is the wrong that he committed, we cannot but be engaged in censuring him.

And, if he comes to recognize for himself the wrong he has committed, he must censure himself: which is to say that, if he comes to recognize it as a wrong that he culpably committed and for which he is responsible, he must thereby come to a remorseful, repentant recognition of his guilt. A mediation process which is to take the wrongdoing seriously, and which aims to get the offender to recognize, to face up to, what he has done, must thus aim to induce remorse and repentance; it must aim to bring the offender to suffer the painful burden both of repentance, and of being censured by his fellow citizens.

What the offender also owes is, minimally, an apology: this is owed both to the victim and to his fellow citizens. If he has come to recognize and repent his wrong, he will want to offer such an apology: to find some way of expressing his repentant recognition and his new or renewed concern both for the victim and for his relationships with his fellow citizens. If he has not yet come to such a recognition, others can properly try to persuade him that he ought to apologize; they might indeed demand that he apologize, or – if that is within their power – require him to apologize. In making such a demand or requirement, they must of course hope that it will be, or will become, sincere: but the demand or requirement can be justified even if it is likely that the apology will not be sincere. For there can be, as I noted above, value even in ritual or formal apology; and we can hope that the experience of making even a demanded, non-voluntary apology might help bring the offender to a clearer grasp of the character and implications of what he has done. A mediation process that takes the wrongdoing seriously will thus properly aim to bring the offender to apologize to his victim, and to his fellows.

But a mere verbal apology might not, as we have seen, be enough: something more may be necessary to give manifest weight to the apology – and to help to focus the offender's own repentant attention on what he has done. That 'more' might take the form of direct reparation or compensation to the victim; or undertaking – in, as it were, the victim's name – some task or service for the wider community or for a charity; or just making a suitable donation to a charity; or perhaps agreeing to enter a programme that will address the motives and factors that led the offender to commit the wrong.[18] What is at stake here is not material reparation for material harm that was caused, but moral reparation for the wrong that was done (though the moral reparation might of course take the form of making material reparation). It must, therefore, be something that is burdensome for the offender – even if it is a burden that he welcomes, as enabling him to make reparation: for only if it is burdensome can it serve the role of giving more forceful expression to the apology that is owed.

Some restorative theorists, whilst agreeing that the making of reparations as a result of a mediation process might well in fact be burdensome, deny that they have to be burdensome: any pain or hardship that they cause is a side-effect, not part of their purpose (see Walgrave 2001a). Suppose, Lode Walgrave once asked me, that the victim would be content with the gift of a box of chocolates: should not that then suffice? Or suppose, John Braithwaite suggested, that victim and offender could be reconciled by a hug: why then insist that the offender must undertake or suffer some further burden?[19] There are two replies to such questions.

First, what matters is not simply whether the victim would be satisfied by, for instance, a box of chocolates: we must ask whether he should be so easily satisfied; and we might think that he should not – indeed, that to regard a box of chocolates as adequate moral reparation, as an adequate expression of the wrongdoer's apologetic repentance, would be to close one's eyes to the seriousness of the offence, or to denigrate oneself by implying that that is all one is worth. After all, the gift of a box of chocolates carries a familiar kind of meaning: it is the kind of thing one gives a hostess, or someone one does not know that well, or when one cannot make the effort to think of something more imaginative. It is a rather trivial gift, and to treat it as sufficient to make up for a serious wrong implies that the wrong was trivial. If we ask why that should matter, part of the answer is that we should try to dissuade the victim from thus denigrating himself; but the more forceful answer is that the offender owes an apology to his fellow citizens in general, and thus owes it to them to make a kind of reparation that will be proportionate to the seriousness of his offence.

Of course, boxes of chocolates can carry different meanings in different contexts, as can hugs; and I do not wish to claim *a priori* that neither a box of chocolates nor a hug could ever, in any context or any relationship, be an adequate expression of apology for a serious wrong. But, and this is my second reply, we are dealing here with public, not private, wrongs, and so with public, not private, reparation: we must therefore ask what could count as an adequately forceful expression of apology between citizens, and what public meaning different possible modes of reparation could have – how they could be understood by the rest of the polity. A box of chocolates or a hug, whatever private meanings they might have in particular contexts, do not, I suggest, have the right kind of public meaning.

The kind of mediation that is an appropriate response to crime (at least to serious crime) should therefore aim to bring the offender to recognize and repent the wrong she has done – which involves censuring her; and to make some suitable moral reparation for that wrong. Furthermore, whilst existing mediation programmes typically seek a reparation which is voluntary in the sense that the offender and victim both agree to it, I would argue that it is fully consistent with the aims sketched above to require the offender to make reparation if he does not agree to something suitable – in the same way as we could appropriately require a wrongdoer to apologize.[20]

What we have, then, is a process which the offender undertakes or undergoes – a process of being confronted with his wrongdoing, of being censured, of making reparation – because he has committed a crime. That process is focused on, and justified by, his wrongdoing: he is censured for that wrongdoing, he is asked to recognize and repent it, and he must apologize and make reparation for it. The process is also intended to be painful or burdensome, as we have seen. The wrongdoer should be pained by the censure of his fellow citizens: if he is not pained, their censure has failed to achieve its intended result. He should be pained by the recognition of his wrongdoing, since that should be a repentant recognition, and repentance is necessarily painful. He should be burdened, and in that sense pained, by the reparation that he has to make, since it can have the appropriate apologetic meaning only if it is burdensome. These related kinds of pain or burden are not mere side-effects of the process which – if he is lucky – might not ensue; they are integral to the aims of the process as a process of seeking restoration after a crime.

That is to say, however, that the process of what we could call criminal mediation – the kind of mediation appropriate to crime – is a punitive process; it constitutes a punishment for the offender. For it is something that is imposed on or required of her, for the crime that she committed, and it is intended to be burdensome or painful – to make her suffer for that crime. It is indeed a retributive process: for if we ask why it is appropriate that she should be thus burdened, why she should be brought to suffer, the answer is, in effect, that this is what she deserves for her crime. She deserves to suffer the censure of others, and her own remorse: for that censure and that remorse are appropriate responses to her crime. She deserves to suffer the burden of making moral reparation for what she has done: since it was her wrong, as one that she culpably committed, it is just and proper that she should bear that burden. The central retributivist slogan is that the guilty should be punished as they deserve and because that is what they deserve – that punishment should bring them to suffer what they deserve to suffer; and criminal mediation, as I have described it, is precisely a way of trying to bring them thus to suffer what they deserve.[21]

This is not to say that we do or should aim to make offenders suffer just for its own sake. What has given retributivism such a bad reputation is the impression – sometimes admittedly conveyed by retributivists themselves (see e.g. Moore 1997: ch. 4) – that the sole purpose of retributive punishment is to inflict pain on offenders: but retributivism need not mean that. On the account I have sketched here, what matters is that the offender should come to suffer the appropriate kind of pain or burden – of being censured, of remorse, of making reparation; and that appropriate pain is in part at least, insofar as it involves the remorseful recognition of wrongdoing, to be self-imposed. Furthermore, if we ask why that matters, the answer is not to be simply that the offender must suffer, or be made to suffer: her suffering is meaningful, as being intrinsically related to a repentant recognition of wrongdoing (see Tudor 2001); and it is valuable, as the appropriate way both of coming to terms with the wrong she committed and of making reparation for that wrong.

My claim that we should see criminal mediation, and the kinds of reparation to which it leads, as punishment might seem to be nothing more than a merely verbal claim which lacks substantial significance or implications – or even a philosopher's verbal trick, which need not detain those engaged in the practical enterprise of promoting restorative justice. But it is more significant than that, for two reasons.

First, it is a claim about how we should portray the proper aims of 'restorative justice', and thus of mediation programmes which seek restorative justice. The claim is that the kind of restoration that crime, as a kind of public wrongdoing, makes necessary must involve the offender in being pained or burdened – burdened by criticism, by remorse, and by the need to make apologetic reparation. If that is right, restorative justice processes are not alternatives to punitive 'pain delivery': they are themselves ways of trying to induce the appropriate kind of pain.

Second, I would go on to argue – though I cannot do so here – that we should see such processes of mediation and reparation not merely as processes that can count, in an extended or etiolated sense, as punishment, but as paradigms of what punishment ought to be. Criminal punishment should aim to bring offenders to recognize, repent and make moral reparation for their crimes, through a process of moral communication with them – a communication which includes some appropriate kinds of penal 'hard treatment'. Once an offender's guilt has been determined by a criminal trial that calls him to answer the charge of wrongdoing, his sentence would ideally be negotiated in something like a mediation process – with his direct victim if there was one, or with an official (a probation officer, for instance) as representing the victim and the wider community; and that punishment would have the aims, and the meaning, of the moral reparation that I have argued should result from criminal mediation (but it might make more central a feature which is often less prominent in mediation and reparation programmes – the need to get the offender to attend to, to think about, the wrong that he committed). Such negotiated punishments would need to be approved by a criminal court – in part to ensure that the demands of negative proportionality are satisfied: but courts would impose punishments without any such negotiation only when negotiation proved impossible or futile.

Of course, much more needs to be said to explain, develop and defend this view:[22] but I hope that in this chapter I have at least rendered plausible one of the central claims on which it depends – that the kind of 'restoration' which crime makes necessary, and which mediation and reparation programmes should aim to achieve, is to be achieved precisely through the retributive punishment of the offender. This is not to offer a justification of our existing penal practices, which are for the most part obviously neither designed nor apt to serve the properly restorative ends that punishment should, on my account, serve: it is, rather, to argue that what we should aspire to create is a system which seeks neither restoration rather than retribution, nor retribution rather than restoration, but restoration through retribution.

Notes

1. For just a few examples see Christie 1981: 11 on 'alternatives to punishment' as opposed to 'alternative punishments'; Marshall 1988: 47–8 on 'reparative' as against 'retributive' justice; Zehr 1990: 178–81 on the alternative 'lenses' of retributive and restorative justice; Walgrave 1994: 57 on 'restorative justice' as against the 'retributive and rehabilitative justice systems'; Dignan 1999: 54, 60, on the 'restorative justice approach' as against the 'retributive approach'; Braithwaite 1999a: 60 on the need to strive for 'restorative justice' rather than 'retributive justice'. For further references and apt criticism, see Daly and Immarigeon 1998: 32–34.

2. Compare Braithwaite and Pettit 1990: 60–65, on 'dominion' as involving both an assured liberty and the knowledge of that assurance. The value of assured liberty and of security depends in crucial part on our knowing that we have such liberty or security.

3. The position with property is complicated by the way in which property is often fully fungible – as far as the owner is concerned, what she owns is not so much a distinctive individual item, but a token of a type, and any token of that type would do. This is most obviously true of money: it would be absurd to deny that the money which I lost had been restored simply on the grounds that I did not get back the individual coins or notes that I lost; what matters is that I lost £100 and got £100 back. It is also to some extent true of other kinds of property, especially purely functional kinds; and to the extent that it is true, property that has been irretrievably destroyed or lost *qua* individual token can still be fully restored, *qua* type.

4. I am not suggesting that the wrong done to the victim is separate from the harm caused to him: whilst not all wrongdoings cause any identifiable harm, those that properly concern the criminal law do typically cause or threaten harm, and their character as wrongs is in part determined by that harm. My point is, rather, that we must understand the harm done by wrongdoing as *wrongful* harm, which gives it a normative character crucially distinct from that of naturally or accidentally caused harms: see further Duff 1996: 366–9.

5. Much more needs to be said about the idea of community as it figures here, especially about the idea of a political community (and about the extent to which we now have or live in such communities). I cannot pursue this point here, but see Duff 2001: chs. 2, 5.

6. Some restorative theorists are unhappy with such a focus on wrongdoing; they prefer to talk of 'conflicts' or 'troubles' rather than of 'crimes' or 'wrongdoings' (see e.g. Christie 1977, Hulsman 1986 – on which see Duff 2001: 60–64). Others, however, recognize the importance of the category of wrongdoing, and of the criminal law as defining the kinds of wrongdoing that properly concern the whole political community.

7. My claim that a friendship can be damaged even by wrongdoing that has no empirical or felt impact on its victim, is related to the familiar – if controversial – claim that one can be harmed by wrongdoing even if it has no empirical impact on one's consciousness or material well-being: someone for whom well-being and happiness depend crucially on a faithful and loving marriage is harmed, and their marriage is destroyed, by their spouse's infidelity, even if that infidelity remains concealed and unknown.

8. Apologies are not, of course, always for wrongdoing: I can apologize for some harm or inconvenience that I caused you through non-culpable inadvertence or accident; or for harm that I caused you intentionally but justifiably. But my focus here is on apologies for culpable wrongdoing.

9. If I know myself to be weak-willed, and prone to give in to temptation, I might predict that I will repeat the wrong in future, as I have so often in the past: but that prediction, if it is not to give the lie to my claim to have recognized the wrong, must be infused with pain and remorse.

10. It might of course be questionable whether the relationship can be restored; or whether I can ask that it be restored. This is not an issue that I can pursue here, nor one that can be dealt with in the same way for all kinds of relationship. On the version of it which arises in the case of crime, see Duff 2001: ch. 4.4.2.

11. I say only 'might', since it is obvious that undertaking such a required apology can have quite different effects, including a resentful anger at those who require the apology and at those to whom it is made. Much depends on the context, the tones and the spirit in which the apology is demanded.

12. Though we should not forget how hard it can be for individuals, for governments, and for other corporate bodies to apologize even when a verbal apology is all that is sought: not just because apologies might open the door to claims for compensation, but because to apologize is to admit wrongdoing.

13. To say that the reparation must be burdensome is not to say that it must be something that the wrongdoer undertakes unwillingly: I can welcome a

burden, and undertake it gladly, without its thereby ceasing to be a burden.

14. For fuller explanation of these points, see Marshall and Duff 1998; Duff 2001: ch. 2.4.

15. There are important differences between different kinds of mediation programme, which I skate over here (see Marshall and Merry 1990; Daly and Immarigeon 1998; Braithwaite 1999a; Kurki 2000): but I hope that my general claims about the proper nature of criminal mediation can still stand.

16. On the trial, as a procedure which calls a citizen to answer a charge of wrongdoing and condemns her if the charge is proved against her, see Duff 1986: ch. 4.

17. Compare Christie 1977: 9, on giving the offender an 'opportunity to receive a type of blame that it would be very difficult to neutralize'.

18. The CHANGE programme for domestically violent men is a good example: it focuses on getting them to accept responsibility both for their own violent behaviour and for finding ways to deal with it: see Scourfield and Dobash 1999.

19. They raised these questions in discussion: but see also Braithwaite 1999a: p. 20, fn. 6.

20. Compare Walgrave 2002b on 'coerced restorative sanctions'.

21. It might seem that, in my enthusiasm to portray criminal mediation as punishment, I have skated over two defining features of punishment (see e.g. Hart 1968: 4–6; Scheid 1980) – that it is *imposed* on the offender (whereas in mediation programmes the offender must agree to enter mediation and to undertake reparation) *by an authority* (whereas mediation and reparation are matters of negotiation and agreement between the parties involved). I cannot deal with these points here, but would argue that mediation and reparation could properly be required of, and in that sense imposed on, the offender; and that the process should be conducted under the aegis and supervision of the criminal courts. See further Duff 2001: 96–7, 111, 158–63.

22. I offer such an explanation, development and defence in Duff 2001.

Chapter 6

The state, community and restorative justice: heresy, nostalgia and butterfly collecting

Adam Crawford

Practical expressions of restorative justice seek to recognize that crime is more than an offence against the state. They aim to consider the impact on victims and others involved, be they family, friends, peers or members of broader networks of interdependencies. They also endeavour to explore how communities can assist in the processes of restoration and conflict resolution. Implicitly, they seek to curtail and limit the role of criminal justice professionals, preferring to empower victims, offenders, family members and others as partners in the justice process. These are the new 'stakeholders' of a revised vision of justice, which seeks to recognize and bring into play, through their active involvement, a broader conceptualization of the appropriate key actors in dispute processing and resolution. As such, restorative justice appeals to more localized normative orderings. Ideally the normative order should emerge from the extended parties themselves, rather than being imposed from above. Intrinsically, this places restorative justice in an ambiguous relationship with top-down normative orderings of the state.

This chapter comes in two parts. The first is a critique of certain dominant understandings of the state and community in much of the restorative justice literature. It suggests that there has been a tendency to assume a polarized understanding of the relationship between community and the state with regard to crime control, in which the former is seen as an intrinsic good and the latter as an essentially malign limitation upon community self-regulation. This oversimplification, I suggest, blinds restorative justice commentators to important ambiguities which structure public, as well as state, responses to crime and its control. It also clouds the implications – both the potential and pitfalls – of public participation within criminal justice.

In the second part, the chapter seeks to clarify and explore some of the reasons for community participation in restorative justice and the limitations (both practical and theoretical) upon realizing community involvement. It then goes on to consider the scope for a tense but constructive relationship between community and state norms and modes of regulation in which one serves to correct the excesses of the other. In so doing, the chapter elaborates upon the deliberative potential of restorative justice as a means of holding in tension, and engaging with, the limitations and potential of both community and state. This, it is suggested, might constitute restorative justice's primary *raison d'être* and over-arching principle.

Heresy

When asked by Lode Walgrave to contribute to this collection on the theme of 'the State, Community and Restorative Justice', it was only later that it dawned on me quite the Herculean task I had accepted. There are mountains of texts – both theoretical treatise and empirical research – on the subject of 'the state' (especially the nature of the current, 'late modern' state undergoing significant processes of restructuring), 'community' (its definition, meaning and promise) and, more recently, 'restorative justice'. However, there is very little which has sought to situate restorative justice within an understanding of both the state and community and their inter-relationships.[1] As a consequence, by way of starting point, I have chosen to return to Nils Christie's path-breaking essay 'conflicts as property' (1977). In so doing, I want to develop a sympathetic critique, focusing upon both its content and its subsequent implications for restorative justice literature today. I regard Christie's essay as important, not only because it is an excellent treatise in its own right, but also because it has come to constitute one of the most cited articles inspiring and informing restorative justice theory and practice. In fact, the article is referenced by some proponents of restorative justice as almost 'sacred text'. But like many 'sacred texts' it is too often misinterpreted or misunderstood. In many senses, it is the subsequent reception and misrepresentation of Christie's original article, which confounds its status, that is the subject of my critique.

In a piece of near heresy, at least to a restorative justice audience, I want to suggest that Christie's essay, as well as providing some essential insights into the relationship between the state, community and restorative justice,[2] suffers a number of flaws that are now to be found as commonplace in much contemporary restorative justice literature. These are that:

- it over-simplifies the historic relationship between community and state;

- it reflects an undue nostalgia for 'unregulated community self-regulation'; and

- it manifests a methodology of 'butterfly collecting'.

The theft of conflicts from victims and the public

In short, the key elements of Christie's argument – which will be familiar to many readers but warrant restating – are as follows.

- Conflict processing is an important social act. He suggests that industrialized societies suffer, not from too much internal conflict but from too little: 'We have to organize social systems so that conflicts are both nurtured and made visible' (Christie 1977: 1).

- Conflicts have been stolen, notably by the state: they 'have been taken away from the parties directly involved and thereby have either disappeared or become other people's property' (Christie 1977: 1).

- Conflicts have been stolen by professionals: 'Lawyers are particularly good at stealing conflicts' (Christie 1977: 4).

- In this theft of conflict, victims of crime have been particular losers: 'She or he is a sort of double loser; first, *vis-à-vis* the offender, but secondly and often in a more crippling manner by being denied rights to full participation in what might have been one of the most important ritual encounters in life. The victim has lost the case to the state' (Christie 1977: 3).

- He outlines and argues for a process that restores the participants' right to their own conflicts.

- In so doing, he calls for community or neighbourhood-based processes: 'one of the major ideas behind the formulation "Conflicts as Property" is that it is neighbourhood-property' (Christie 1977: 12).

• As such, forums for conflict processing should seek to involve and revitalize neighbourhoods and communities. They should be 'in tune with local values', as conflicts should be 'seen as property that ought to be shared' (Christie 1977: 11).

Understandably, Christie's arguments have come to constitute a vital springboard and legitimating discourse for the emerging mediation and subsequent restorative justice movements. Moreover, Christie's ideas were inspirational in the development of the important Mediation Boards initiative in Norway (Mørland 2000) with which he was also personally involved, notably in an evaluation capacity (Dullum and Christie 1996). Christie highlights the social importance of deliberative and inclusionary responses to crime and other harms. Where Christie's original article is at its most powerful is with regard to the social importance of civic engagement with, and participation in, dispute processing. He has some fundamentally significant things to say about the interests which exist in denying, avoiding or defining away conflict.[3] He highlights the centrality of conflict in social arrangements and the importance of public participation in conflict processing as a social activity:

conflicts represent a potential for activity, for participation. Modern criminal control systems represent one of the many cases of lost opportunities for involving citizens in tasks that are of immediate importance to them. (Christie 1977: 7)

However, the key problem has been in the way in which Christie's thesis has been interpreted as calling for the restoration of conflict to the parties themselves away from the reach of (or in contrast to) the state. This he comes close to doing in his most idealistic moments when envisioning an inclusive and victim-oriented approach with its 'extreme degree of lay orientation':

The ideal is clear; it ought to be a court of equals representing themselves. When they are able to find a solution between themselves, no judges are needed. When they are not, the judges ought also to be their equals (Christie 1977: 11).

This view is also in keeping with the wider abolitionist agenda within which Christie's work is situated (see Mathiesen 1974).

Nevertheless, careful reading of Christie's original article reminds us of the centrality that he accords to the role of legality and the state within 'restorative' processes. Even in his most idealistic moments, Christie envisages a court with judges. He cautions his readers that he is not advocating a privatization of disputes. Conflict as property 'is not private. It belongs to the system' (Christie 1977: 12). In this, the state retains a vital role balancing the interests of the different parties – notably those of the offender, victim and community. However, this emphasis has tended to be lost in the use – as authoritative reference – of Chritie's arguments (Cayley 1998). The central idea – in part incorrectly drawn from Christie – that historically the modern state has stolen conflicts from victims and the public has almost become a mantra among some restorative justice proponents and victim advocates. For example, in a recent paper Watchel and McCold (2001: 114) appropriate Christie's argument in support of a rather unsophisticated interpretation:

> The state, under the guise of caring for its citizens, steals their conflicts and hands them over to courts … Christie (1977) explains that a state monopoly on resolving conflict represents a loss for both the victim and society – a lost opportunity to deal with the anxiety and misconceptions produced by the offence and to repair civility.

However, this 'theft' actually involves a number of more complex and discrete, but related, developments.

First, it sees the state's quest for a monopoly of coercion and sovereignty over its populations.

In so doing, secondly, it involves the marginalization of the victim as a central actor in the resolution of conflicts, as the state assumes the mantle of the 'public interest'.

Thirdly, it entails the legalization of criminal procedure, ideally requiring publicly specified offences, open trial, definite safeguards, limitations with regard to evidence and the availability of review and appeal procedures, as the state assumes the role of 'power-container' in the conflicts between its citizens.

Fourthly, it sees the professionalization of the legal realm as lawyers encircle procedure and evidence with professional judgement and as the emerging criminal justice professions produced by the complex division of labour around policing, prosecution and punishment increasingly seek legitimacy in detached and rational judgement.

Fifthly, legal judgement becomes supplemented by expert decisions by an array of new specialists employing very different criteria and logic with regard to the pathology of crime (doctors, psychiatrists, social workers, probation officers and so on). These new specialists – which Christie neatly refers to as 'behaviour experts' (Christie 1977: 12) – become more concerned with questions of diagnosis and the proper administration of deviant offenders. As Garland (1985: 235) notes, the 'norms of the human sciences', which guide these new experts, 'become a kind of *raison d'état*, whose demands justify serious departure from the usual terms of the law'.

Finally, the demands of equity, universality and professionalization in administering and managing offenders herald increasing bureaucratization and standardization, which seek to efface the nature of local differences. Uniformity of response is required in place of diversity and parochial specificity.

Yet history reminds us that not only are there tensions between these logics but that none of these developments are complete or absolute. They are contested, sometimes ineffective and often produce unintended consequences. The 'theft of conflict' account conflates these processes and over-simplifies the relationship between state, law and citizens: it hides from our critical gaze the 'ironies of state and civil society' (Braithwaite and Strang 2001), imperative in locating and understanding the uneasy position of restorative justice in contemporary societies.

By contrast, Zauberman's (2000) historical analysis offers a different understanding of the victim–state nexus as a result of which the victim has become marginalized from dispute processing. The essence of the relationship between victim and criminal justice, she argues, lies in the notion of the 'state'. She shows that the very exclusion of the victim from the criminal justice process was a precondition for the existence of modern criminal justice and an expression of state sovereignty. She suggests that rather than providing a service of which victims are consumers, we need to understand criminal justice as a 'regulatory resource' to which victims may, or may not, turn. Victims, thus, need to be conceptualized as active 'users', rather than passive 'consumers', of criminal justice.

The notion of the 'theft of conflicts' denies the public an active role in the production of criminal justice policies and merely reproduces the state's presentation of itself as sovereign and monopolistic. However, the idea that 'sovereign' states alone could guarantee crime control to their subjects in a monopolistic fashion always was a myth, albeit a powerful one. More recently, we have come increasingly to recognize the 'myth of the sovereign state' as such (Garland 1996). The theft of conflict thesis privileges the role of the state as the monopolistic provider of social control.

Unfortunately, there is insufficient good (historic or contemporary) research into the regulation of conflicts within communities by non-state actors outside the shadows of the courts and police. However, this means neither that it does not occur nor that there are not some significant lessons for restorative justice to be learnt from genuinely informal conflict regulation and social control (Merry 1981; Foster 1995; Walklate and Evans

1999). Cohen (1989: 353) wisely noted that in privileging the formal state apparatus of social control we have

> bullied ourselves (and others) into thinking that social control is synonymous with state control. This is to ignore the dominant roles played by the family, gender, mass culture and the market in the regulation and control of social life ... The really difficult problem is to integrate this general notion of 'social control' with the more restricted notion of 'organised reactions' to deviance which still informs our literature.

It is worth noting that family, gender, mass culture and the market – as well as other social relations – are all structured by very different power relations which leave social control and conflict resolution to the vagaries of the abuse of power.

The 'theft of conflict' thesis confuses de-professionalization and de-centralization arguments with that of de-legalization: the idea that informal dispute resolution may be culturally and socially superior or preferable to formal legal processes. And yet, there is an ever-present need to protect against self-interest and the abuse of power. If we turn to history, we can see that throughout the last 400 years, even the most brutal of laws can be, and were, used by victims in defence against arbitrary power. The 'rule of law' emerged out of centuries of struggle – with its emphasis upon due process and individual rights – by imposing effective inhibitions upon power and the defence of the citizen from powerful claims. As the social historian E. P. Thompson (1975: 264–5) noted, 'there is a very large difference, which twentieth-century experience ought to have made clear even to the most exalted thinker, between arbitrary extra-legal power and the rule of law'. For him, due process and the 'rule of law' with their principles of equity and universality are 'an unqualified human good' (Thompson 1975: 266). He was right to direct his ire at those who would prefer to displace the discourse of law with that of 'popular' or 'informal' justice whatever the legitimizing ideology might be: 'the people', 'the masses', 'community' or 'restoration'. It strikes me that much restorative justice literature has conveniently ignored the earlier debates on the limitations of 'informal' and 'popular' justice, particularly with regard to an understanding of the relationship between the state, law and community (for example Abel 1982, Tomasic and Feeley 1982, Sarat 1988, Merry and Milner 1993).[4] History teaches us that extra-legal forms of social control, upon which restorative justice relies for much of its normative persuasion, can appear both in desirable and undesirable guises with malign as well as benign consequences.

Rather than the simplistic image of the state 'stealing' conflicts from victims and the wider public (largely as witnesses), we need to understand the more nuanced picture in which victims and the public are more actively involved in shaping criminal justice. As Garland (2001: xi) importantly has shown, the shape of crime control policies are, in part, explained in reference to 'the public's ambivalence about crime and crime control: an ambivalence that gives rise to quite divergent forms of action'.

One of the most fundamental ways in which the public actively shapes criminal justice rests in what the public does not (as well as what it does) refer to formal systems of control. Years of victimization surveys have shown us that most victims do not have recourse to criminal justice or the state. For a variety of instrumental, personal and emotional reasons, victims choose not to involve formal agents of the state. Victimization surveys suggest that some of the reasons why people do not report significant quantities of crime include fear of reprisals, the incident was considered a private matter and was dealt with by the victim and fear/dislike of the police, as well as the fact that an offence was perceived as not serious enough, the police would not be interested or could not do anything (see Kershaw *et al.* 2000). Most crimes are dealt with, put aside or managed by the public in one way or another. There are, and have been, a variety of practical adaptations to crime on the part of those affected by it. It would be wrong to assume that restorative justice programmes could or should replace such genuinely 'informal' processes.[5]

The idea that the modern state progressively stole conflicts from citizens and communities certainly chimes with the generally top-down and expert-led nature of much criminal justice policy which by-passed public debate. It is also consistent with the manner in which the organizations that made up the complex division of labour around criminal justice sought legitimacy through appeals to professionalization, specialization, bureaucratization, legality and solidaristic ideals rather than through appeals to individual victim's or parochial community's interests. This possibly reflected a degree of public disinterest in, or acceptance of, the need for a reasoned, rational and detached approach to crime. However, there are very good reasons why the public has colluded in this 'outsourcing approach' to crime control, in which the public has come to expect specialist institutions to solve most crime problems for them.[6]

The history of the contemporary state is not merely one in which the regalian state has sought to appropriate ever-greater fields of activity from civil society (as neo-liberal commentators would suggest). It is also one in which the public has come to have greater expectations of democratic institutions. Moreover, the modern state has sought to mitigate power differences (albeit not always successfully) within societies through various institutions in the name of 'public' (solidaristic) rather than private or parochial interests. The public has also come to expect greater 'freedoms' even at the cost of 'security' and 'order' (Bauman 2001a). Conversely, the contemporary growth of citizens' demands for order and security constitutes one of the major dilemmas for modern states (Crawford 2002a).

Nostalgia

Implicit in Christie's paper and explicit in other restorative justice writings (see Pranis 2000) is a romanticization of 'unregulated community self-regulation'. Alongside this is the assumption that many indigenous or pre-modern practices are or were themselves 'restorative' (Braithwaite 1999a; Weitekamp 1999). These, so the argument implies, have either been crushed by the modern state's 'theft of conflicts' or marginalized by its dominant position. Both such visions often stem from a selective reading of history, anthropological studies or contemporary commentaries. The wilful nostalgia of much restorative justice theory harks to a different age of tradition and authority, and in so doing blinds us to the complexities of community formation and social regulation. It side-steps engagement with aspects of such indigenous or pre-modern practices which, despite their cultural specificity, may be objectionable to contemporary sensibilities. It constitutes what Daly (2002b) terms an 'origin myth' of restorative justice:

> Advocates' constructions of the history of restorative justice, that is, the origin myth that a superior justice form prevailed before the imposition of retributive justice, is linked to their desire to maintain a strong oppositional contrast between restorative and retributive justice (Daly 2002b: 63).

As such, this myth has a rhetorical force. However, it collapses diversity and irons over important contradictory evidence and countervailing developments for the sake of a coherent 'story'.

The quest for community instead of (and in opposition to) the state over-idealizes as unproblematic the nature of communities' moral orders. As Cohen (1985: 117) comments: 'The iconography is that of the small rural village in pre-industrial society, in contrast to the abstract, bureaucratic, impersonal city of the contemporary technological state'. This icon-ography is explicit in Christie's account of the Tanzanian village as contrasted with the Scandinavian court. Here, there is often a slippage between 'tradition' and 'community': between 'community' as a sense of something lost and 'community' as a focus for building modern democratic institutions.

Communities are not the havens of reciprocity and mutuality, nor are they the utopias of egalitarianism, that some might wish. Rather, they are hierarchical formations, structured upon lines of differential power relations, most notably as feminists have argued, upon lines of gender, but also upon lines of ethnicity, age, class (if these social categories are not in themselves grounds for exclusion) and other personal attributes. Thus, the 'moral voice of a community' and the interests and values for which it speaks, are often not only exclusive and parochial, but also dominated and controlled by powerful elites. Within much restorative justice literature, there is little acknowledgement of intra-community diversity and conflict.

> The image of the community is purified of all that might convey a feeling of difference, let alone conflict, in who 'we' are. In this way the myth of community solidarity is a purification ritual (Sennett 1996: 36).

Moverover, much restorative justice over-exaggerates the role that communities can play in responses to, and preventing, crime (Crawford 1999). The central lessons from research into community crime prevention are: first, that it is difficult to mobilize and sustain community interest and participation in matters of crime, alone, over long periods of time; and secondly, that there tends to be an inverse relationship between activity and need (see Rosenbaum 1988). In other words, given that participation (and volunteering in particular) is more likely to prosper in low crime, well organized and affluent communities what are the implications of community-based restorative justice for equity?

Appeals to 'community' within restorative justice often fail to address the relations that connect local institutions to the wider civil society and political economy of which the community is a part or the manner in which local justice may impact upon neighbouring areas. The inequitable distribution of security imposes upon the state obligations in harnessing public safety to avoid disadvantaging the less affluent members of society. In this regard, the role of community as a force for social cohesion is limited by the current reality of geographic inequality, the spatial con-centration of wealth and poverty and increased social polarization. Some communities are better able to provide for their members than are others. As such, restorative justice may not always be an appropriate site of redistributive justice, more generally (Crawford and Clear 2001). Local restorative justice initiatives are unlikely to be capable of reversing structural inequalities that both divide societies and foster crime.

Butterfly collecting

Like butterfly collecting there is a tendency within much restorative justice literature to extract examples (often drawn from around the world or across time) which are abstracted and removed from the cultural and social environment which sustains them.[7] Again, like the butterfly collector, the examples sought are 'pretty' or 'exotic' ones that seek to illustrate the case for restorative justice, rather than engage with the less attractive aspects of social arrangement and human relations. This butterfly collecting operates at two levels. First, it is reflected in the way in which restorative justice proponents select the benign aspects of community self-regulation and the spectacular examples of forgiving and reintegration, be it from the jungles of Papua New Guinea or the corporate boardroom, without having to recognize or engage with the less attractive forms of that often co-exist alongside each other. The anecdote and 'one off' case study as methodologies have an all too prominent place in restorative justice literature. This is not to suggest that case studies and anecdotes are not powerful (and at times appropriate) means of story-telling which have an important emotive and subjective appeal. Nor is this to suggest that such examples are not useful means of making legitimate points or conveying meaning. As methodologies they have their place. The point here is that they lack any rigorous understanding of their connectedness to the environment from which they are drawn. Moreover, we are beginning to see the emergence of rigorous and extensive evaluation studies of restorative justice programmes which should provide data to supplement (although not completely displace) the small-scale case study or anecdote.[8]

At a second level, butterfly collecting is to be found in the inter-nationalization of restorative justice. Family group conferencing, community conferencing, mediation and sentencing circles, we are told, transcend cultural differences, as they accommodate such diversity. Implicitly, therefore, models of family group conferences etc. can be moved between cultural settings with little implications for our understandings of those processes. Hence, participants in international meetings or collections of essays often speak and write about restorative justice initiatives as if they, like the butterflies in the glass-cased collection, were easily understood abstracted from the habitat which nourishes them. And yet, the relationships between cultures, crime and responses to it are both crucial and complex (Nelken 1994). As Blagg (2001: 230) notes, restorative justice proponents have 'tended to selectively appropriate certain elements of traditional practice without acknowledging the wider universe of obligation, reciprocity and meaning that gave these elements their purpose and significance to the actors involved'. We need to understand more, rather than less, about the differences and similarities in connections between responses to crime and cultures, as well as the manner in which such strategies derive their sense and meaning from their cultural ties; the limits to the transferability of crime control mechanisms or policies, which advocates may claim to be universal, often derive from precisely such cultural connections.

This tendency to abstract examples of restorative justice extends beyond questions of culture, to the legal and political institutions and social practices which influence the manner in which forms of family group conferencing or other restorative justice practices are received and implemented. For me, what is fascinating is the nature of differences in the implementation of restorative justice practices in divergent social and cultural contexts (Crawford 2000c). For example, the origin, development and practice of conferencing has been very different in New Zealand and Australia (and even within Australian states) despite the apparent similarity of the two countries to the outsider (Daly 2001). We need to know more about the prevailing political and social forces that shape the resultant restorative justice practices. It is only on the basis of this knowledge that we can begin to understand the applicability of given practices beyond the confines from which they emerge. The problem for the observer of the butterfly collection is not knowing the contexts that give life to and sustain each exhibit nor how transferable any example is from one environment to another.

Whither the state?

The legacy of the assumptions drawn from the 'theft of conflict' thesis is that it suggests a dichotomous account whereby the state is seen as malign whereas civil society – and community in particular – is benign. What is perceived to be needed is less state, greater de-professionalization and a returning of conflicts to their 'owners'. Many restorative justice proponents appear to have been carried away with 'a giddy sense at the moment among many intellectuals that the state is *passé*' (Bayley 2001: 212). Like Bayley, I question both whether it is and whether it should be considered *passé* in relation to criminal justice. This is not to suggest that critiques of the monopolistic and paternalistic tendencies of modern states are not appropriate nor that there is not scope for a greater role for public participation within criminal justice (to which I return later). Rather, I am suggesting the notion of the 'theft of conflict' over-emphasizes this point. More problematically, it blinds us to the ambiguous position that restorative justice occupies within contemporary criminal justice policy and its relation to ongoing social and political change, which simultaneously generate the appeal of restorative justice (at this particular historic juncture) but also may undermine or challenge its realization. This includes the following.

- The anti-state appeal within restorative justice coincides with a neo-liberal assault upon the welfare state. To this end, Bazemore and Schiff (2001: 36) note: 'Restorative justice advocates will ultimately stand with libertarians on many issues because they question the value of much government intervention'.[9] The concern here is that restorative justice may be the benign cloak under which the management of conflicts are thrown back onto communities and individuals, representing a 'privatization of disputes' and a responsibilization of communities with little acknowledgement of the differential capacity of groups and communities to regulate conflict, support victims and offenders and resource their reintegration. Whilst the responsibilization of families, groups and communities may be a desirable aim, the shedding of responsibilities by the state, particularly in the field of justice, I suggest is not.

- There are continuities between the growth of private security – and the modes of governance that it heralds – and restorative justice, not only in that they challenge state-based criminal justice but also in that they share an emphasis upon particularistic crime prevention rather than deterrence (Bayley 2001). Like the privatization of security, the privatization of justice raises fundamental questions about the nature of social solidarity and the institutions through which this may be delivered.

- The anti-professional appeal within restorative justice coincides with the increased institutionalization of distrust and the managerialist-inspired encircling of professional discretion with logics of accounting and audit (Crawford 2000a). This institutionalization of distrust runs counter to claims about the centrality and virtue of strong fabrics of trust as the mainspring of social capital (Putnam 1995), upon which restorative justice draws strength.

- This same managerialist ideology may serve to undermine the practical realization of restorative justice ideas (Crawford 2000b). The managerialist obsession with speed, cost reductions, performance measurement and efficiency gains, has often led to a move away from 'local justice' – understood as local people contributing to the handling of cases in their own local area – and encouraged both pro-fessionalization (in which lay members of the public have less involvement) and centralization (in which government departments and related agencies closely govern local practices).

- The growing recognition, acknowledgement and accommodation of the subjective and emotive (biographical) accounts and testimonies of victims which restorative justice enables, coincides with a growing emphasis upon more actuarial and risk-based management of offenders which treats them as a biographical aggregates, rather than individuals. Perversely, the 'individualization of the victim' as a subject of criminal justice has occurred at precisely the moment when this has been abandoned in relation to offenders (Sebba 2000).

- The 'return of the victim' as central to criminal justice policy and its associated discourse of 'public protection' paradoxically may allow for a 'getting tough through restorative justice', whereby victims are drawn into 'the service of severity' (Ashworth 2000). The diminished emphasis on offender's rights within restorative justice, in the current punitive climate, may see 'the corruption of benevolence', a recurring theme within criminal justice (Levrant et al. 1999).[10]

- The appeal of community – mutuality, interdependencies and connectedness – within restorative justice coincides with its observed absence. Hobsbawm, the historian, puts it succinctly: 'Never was the word "community" used more indiscriminately and emptily than in the decades when communities in the sociological sense became hard to find in real life' (1994: 428). Here lies a tension for restorative justice. Contemporary weak communities simultaneously are seen as the cause of endemic social ills and held out in defence of the way in which communities can allow sufficient space for individual autonomy, minority dissent, innovation and difference.

- In an increasingly globalizing world – simultaneously uncertain and uncontrollable – we are witnessing an increasing individualization, whereby how one lives becomes the 'biographical solution of systemic contradictions' (Beck 1992: 137). Likewise restorative justice has the capacity to become the individualized quest for biographical solutions to systemic contradictions, as it offers a 'therapeutic' response to structural problems. As such, it may be a conservative rather than radical force (Abel 1981).

Restorative justice is not merely 'a good idea whose time has come' – which is not to suggest that it is not a good idea in the first place. Rather it needs to be seen in terms of the way in which it connects with, is facilitated or undermined by, wider social, political and cultural transformations.

The owners of disputes

Christie's idea of 'giving back conflicts to its owners' highlights the question: who are the legitimate owners of a given dispute? At one level, the offender and victim are the obvious 'owners'. However, this provokes two issues. First, in specific cases these concepts often prove problematic. There is a thin and frayed line between victim and offender: offenders are often victims and victims are often offenders (Miers 2000). The ascription to an individual of the status 'victim' (or offender) involves complex processes of self-perception and social reaction. Second, returning disputes merely to individuals would herald an unacceptable 'privatization of disputes' – a Hobbesian nightmare of competition and dominance. Instead, restorative justice relies upon some notion of the communal by reconfiguring the idea of the 'public interest' through appeals to a different set of 'stakeholders'. These stakeholders are believed to be more directly affected – or 'victimized' even – by given acts of harm than the state.

At one level, all restorative interventions require a minimum conception of 'community', in that the victim and offender must share a 'minimum common interest in settling together the aftermath of the crime constructively' (Walgrave 2002a: 6). At another level, restorative justice departs from victim–offender mediation in that it seeks to incorporate wider relations of care and to work through networks of inter-dependencies, less prevalent (but not absent) from traditional criminal justice. These levers of social control beyond the immediate family are usually referred to as communal forms of regulation. Without getting into semantic debates about the nature of 'community', we can note that it is an essential element of, and occupies a central position within, restorative rhetoric and ideals (Kurki 2000: 267; Bazemore and Shiff 2001). Some commentators go as far as to suggest that 'community strength is the ultimate outcome measure for [restorative] interventions' (Pranis 1998: 3). Reference to communities in restorative justice generally alludes to some form of regulatory authority or moral value system with persuasive power to induce conformity beyond the family and below the state (the political community). These communities are often differently conceived in different restorative justice contexts. Nevertheless, most restorative justice practices hold a particular place for some community involvement.

This may take the form of the direct involvement of community representatives in some capacity: as facilitator, panel member, surrogate victim or merely contributor to proceedings. Family group conferencing, for example, in its reference to 'groups' explicitly seeks to draw upon kinship networks beyond the immediate family. Other examples include local representatives at community conferences in Australia, community members in peacemaking and sentencing circles in North America (La Prairie 1995; Stuart 2001) and Community Board members in the Vermont Reparative Probation Programme in the US (Karp and Walther 2001), as well as other forms of community representation in victim–offender mediation and conferencing programmes.

However, it is rarely clear exactly what the purpose of community involvement is or what the lines of legitimacy, accountability or representation, particular community members have. What precise stake does the community or specific community members hold with regard to a given offence? Whose business is it to be involved? On whose behalf do they speak? What value does community input or participation contribute to the process? If someone is not involved as a state representative or as a representative of one of the immediate parties, then what is their mandate?

For me, these questions were given particular poignancy as I was part of a research team tasked with evaluating the introduction of referral order pilots and youth offender panels in England and Wales by the Youth Justice Board and Home Office. The introduction of referral orders, as part of the Youth Justice and Criminal Evidence Act 1999, constitutes arguably the most significant attempt by the British government to integrate restorative justice into the heart of the youth justice system. The referral order is a mandatory sentence for all young offenders before the court for the first time unless they are given an absolute discharge or a custodial sentence is being considered (see Crawford 2002b). Referral orders may be made for a minimum of three and a maximum of twelve months depending on the seriousness of the crime (as determined by the court). During this period the case is referred to a 'youth offender panel', managed by local youth offending teams (YOTs). Panels seek to agree a 'contract' with the young offender, involving activities for the duration of the referral order. Contracts should always include reparation to the victim or wider community, as well as a programme of activity designed primarily to prevent further offending.

Importantly, panels consist of at least two, trained community volunteers (recruited by the YOT), one of whom will lead the panel meeting, together with a YOT member. The intention is that panel meetings will be held in locations as close as possible to where the young person lives and from which the community panel members will be drawn. Panels are designed to provide a less formal context than court for the offender, the victim, their supporters and members of the community to discuss the crime and its consequences. Panels are to be guided by the principles underlying the concept of restorative justice, defined as the '3Rs' of 'restoration, reintegration and responsibility'. According to Dignan and Marsh, as decision-making forums youth offender panels are 'potentially one of the most radical aspects of the entire youth justice reform agenda' (2001: 99).

Panels seek to adopt a conference-type approach to decision-making that is intended to be both inclusive and party-centred. Not only does the panel have the symbolic power to 'sign off' the referral order once it has been discharged successfully but also this has the effect of purging the offender of the offence (as it is considered spent). In addition, the reintegrative element of referral orders is strengthened by the fact that panel meetings are not merely 'one off' events, but entail structured meetings over the lifetime of the referral order. Consequently, panels meet to review developments as well as support, discuss and where appropriate congratulate the offender on progress made. The panel, therefore, is not only a forum for deliberation about the harm and its consequences, but also acts as a means of monitoring contract compliance and championing reintegration.

Findings from the pilots have been published elsewhere (Newburn *et al.* 2001, 2002) and I do not intend to rehearse them. What interests me here are the broader issues provoked by the involvement of community representatives as panel members. Interestingly, these issues are intensified in the English context for two reasons, first by the fact that it was not the government's original intention to include community representatives. Initially, the intention had been that panels 'would contain a mix of youth justice practitioners – a magistrate (if possible, one of the magistrates responsible for the referral), a YOT member, and perhaps a police officer' (Home Office 1997: 33, para. 9.35). The idea of community volunteers making up the majority on youth offender panels did not appear as part of the original philosophy of referral orders. The government appears to have opted for this approach rather late in the day and more by accident than design, largely in response to concerns over potential conflicts of interests on behalf of criminal justice professionals who may have had contact with and knowledge about the young people appearing before them (had they been panel members). The second factor amplifying these debates is that in the English context, community panel members sit alongside a professional YOT member, albeit that they are in the majority and tasked with leading the panel meeting. This introduces a dynamic, if potentially tense, relationship in which different organizational and cultural understandings, conflicting aims and ways of workings as well as power differences can clash (Crawford and Newburn 2002). Both of these elements beg the question: what is it that lay volunteers as community representatives can and/or do bring to the workings of panels which may be of intrinsic social value?

Reasons for community involvement in restorative justice

Let us consider some of the rationales offered for community involvement in restorative justice generally in order to shed some light on this and related questions raised earlier.

Community has a right to be involved as victim

For many restorative justice commentators the community is a secondary victim of crime (Pranis 1998). As the community has been adversely affected, it has a right to be involved in how to deal with the crime. This understanding gives the community a 'direct stake' in the resolution of the dispute due to its need for redress and its responsibility for the resolution and prevention of crime (McCold 1996: 90–2). Thus, 'community input' may come through the voice of the extended victim, as representative of community as victim. This connects with discussions about the community as stakeholder. However, it is rarely clear what the nature of this 'stake' is and, consequently, where this conception of community ends. For some commentators this includes 'everyone affected'. Indirectly, however this could be extended to include all members of the broader political community, namely the nation state. This merely returns us to the conventional understanding of the role of the public within the traditional criminal justice process. This malleable essence of victimhood – or 'victimalization' as Boutellier (this volume) suggests – has become a dominant narrative for contemporary criminal justice. As Garland notes: 'In the high crime society, tiny crimes are viewed cumulatively and "the community" is the collective, all-purpose victim' (2001: 181). The problem with the 'community as victim' is that it does not take us very far in clarifying the nature of community input or public participation and merely reinforces the notion of 'victim' as an elastic and all-pervasive cultural symbol.

Can act as a bulwark against greater punitiveness

There is a strong argument for greater public involvement in criminal justice as a cultural and political impediment against more punitive responses and the growing use of imprisonment. It may challenge the presupposition in policy discourse that public opinion, at every turn, demands more punishment. Despite the powerful association between 'punitiveness' and 'populism', 'punitive populism' does not equate with public involvement or participation in criminal justice. Whilst broad opinion surveys do often reveal a more punitive public, such opinion is not the same as the public interest. Here, we need to distinguish between 'public opinion' and 'public judgement'. The former is impromptu, not informed by serious discussion or weighing the facts and the arguments of others. Neither is it followed by taking responsibility for the argued-for position. Whereas public judgement incorporates all these characteristics. Research suggests that when provided with more information about offenders and the circumstances under which they offend, the public is more tolerant and less punitive than politicians would have us believe (Hough 1996).

Not only does failure to involve the public exacerbate legitimacy deficits and crises of confidence. But also, informed public debate and dialogue as a central aspect of criminal justice allows for regulated ways in which people can deliberate upon, and search for ways of resolving, conflict. As Girling *et al.* (2000: 177) notes:

> if the punitive passions (and actions) of citizens are the impotent cries of spectators watching dramas in which they play little part, and for whose outcomes they exercise no responsibility, then keeping such sentiments 'in the shadows' also has its costs. It leaves the impassioned demands of citizens undiscussed and unchallenged and does nothing to make good the legitimation deficits suffered by institutions from whose actions attentive, concerned citizens have been excluded.

Justice should be about citizens deliberating over the consequences of crimes and how to deal with them, as well as how to prevent their recurrence. Such a vision of justice seeks to restore the deliberative control of justice to citizens. Moreover, criminal justice as deliberative justice has important historical and philosophical roots.

Encourages civic responsibility

Conflict processing and responses to crime are social events that reflect, and are reflected in, our cultural sensibilities. Participation in the processing of disputes, as Christie suggested, allows the parties and others opportunities for 'norm-clarification', civic engagement and the promotion of active citizenry beyond the confines of criminal justice processes. It is understood as an element in the construction of shared values and commitment. The involvement of community participation in deliberative forums affords the potential to encourage a stronger and more participatory civil society. It allows an approach to restorative justice that engages communities in owning and resolving problems, rather than outsourcing them to state bureaucracies and professional expertise. As such, participation may facilitate community empowerment and communal self-governance. As it affords processes of restorative justice to operate through informal relations of interdependencies and mutual knowledge, community participation may help to cement relations and encourage greater synergy between formal and informal systems of control.

Assures a human and relational dynamic and professional accountability

The participation of ordinary citizens in the deliberative processes of criminal justice can help to ensure that proceedings which may otherwise be dominated by technical, bureaucratic or managerial demands also accord to the emotional and expressive needs of responses to crime and in a similar vein ensures fairness. It can facilitate the 'opening up' of otherwise introspective professional cultures, which militate against greater public participation. Significant community participation can act to open up processes which may otherwise see professionals guided by detached and disinterested performance standards often of a kind which are more concerned with internal organizational legitimacy than responsiveness to public interests. It can help break down inward-looking cultures and paternalistic attitudes held by professionals and in their place encourage responsiveness to the concerns articulated by citizens, as the guidance of professionals. Community involvement can counter scepticism on the part of participants (notably offenders) that decision-makers are removed from their concerns and understandings, precisely because of their professional attachments. As such, community involvement may act as a safeguard against the excesses of managerialism within criminal justice.

Community as a resource – it reduces the cost

It is often argued, primarily by governments, that community involvement in criminal justice reduces the cost to the public purse by drawing upon the untapped resource of 'voluntary collective action'. Some restorative justice proponents also see 'community as a resource' for reconciliation of victims and offenders and as a resource for monitoring and enforcing community standards of behaviour (Pranis 1998). Some research has sought to show that restorative justice interventions cost less (Miers *et al.* 2001).

However, there is also a growing recognition that lay volunteers tend to work at a slower pace than do professional counterparts. It is this relative inefficiency of lay volunteers which has resulted in the recent increase in the number of professional stipendiary magistrates and the increasing perception in government circles that the lay magistracy 'as a symbol of the unmodernized court' is 'now under pressure as never before' (Raine 2001). Even though a system may be based on unpaid volunteers (such as the lay magistracy and youth offender panels), this, of itself, does not mean that it is necessarily cheap. There are significant costs associated with training, advice and information providing for volunteers as well as with other supporting infrastructures which are required simply because volunteers are involved.

The danger is that governments see public participation as a way of devolving certain 'auxiliary duties' to lay people as a cheap alternative to professional service delivery or as a cost-efficient way of reducing the burden upon professionals. This is a concern for at least two reasons. First, as suggested above, it is not clear that public participation is in all instances a cheaper alternative. Secondly, such an approach reduces public participation to a limited and secondary supplemental role and maintains a paternalistic relationship between public and criminal justice institutions and professionals.

The limits of public participation in restorative justice

However, public participation is limited by both normative and practical difficulties. At a practical level, to what extent is it possible to accommodate, bring together and assemble extended community input?

- It is becoming harder to attract lay volunteers, given the time demands of training, the travel demands (which may require lay people travelling across a county – particularly with the closure of local police stations, courthouses etc) and the difficulties for those in employment of matching voluntary work with their careers, whilst those unemployed may jeopardize their chances of obtaining a job. There is not always an unambiguous correspondence between volunteering and representativeness. Representatives may poorly represent the diverse publics from which they are drawn, and may be perceived by others to be unrepresentative and less legitimate. The experience of recruiting community panel members for youth offender panels in

England and Wales shows that members were seen as being predominantly female, middle class and middle aged. There is a danger that community panel members – like other community representatives – may come to constitute something of a 'new magistracy', whose normative appeal may be undermined by their empirical lack of representativeness (Crawford and Newburn 2002: 483).

- Lay people drawn into criminal justice may become 'professionalized' – co-opted into the values and culture of the institutions into which they are drawn. Hence, they may lose their attachments to the wider civil society or the qualities of 'layness', which inspired their initial participation.

- There is an ambivalent relationship between participation and concern about crime. Participation in local crime prevention activities is highest among people who are moderately concerned about crime but where crime levels are low. High levels of fear of crime can become incapacitating, whilst low levels of fear are often de-motivating. As well as implications for equity, this has practical consequences for levels of participation in high crime areas.

- There are limits to what citizens can accomplish through institutions of civil society alone. Particularistic, local and parochial interests may conflict with promoting social justice. Moreover, the increasing frag-mentation of civil society, and the growing concentration of poverty and wealth, mean that different social groups are better placed to exploit their own social capital and access to resources. As noted above, with regard to crime prevention there tends to be an inverse relationship between activity and need, as well as knock-on con-sequences (through crime displacement) of private or collective activity for others. One person's (or community's) security may adversely impact upon that of others. We need to be as aware of dangers of 'unsocial capital' as the advantages of 'social capital'.

- The involvement of lay people within the processes of justice necessitates that due concern is given to any conflict of interests that lay people may bring to their participation, particularly where they are cast in a decision-making role. Private and parochial interests should not be allowed to affect public decisions. This creates a tension between, on the one hand, the notion that lay members should be from, and of, the community (share a social and geographical proximity) and, on the other hand, the reality that the more attached to the community (from which the cases come and their greater proximate relationship to the participants) they are, the less likely they may hold the required 'detached stance' which constitutes a central value in establishing neutrality and legitimacy. Such conflicts may also place community representatives at risk of retaliation. This fear may put people off getting involved in the first place.

- People may legitimately prefer not to get involved in criminal justice because of its association with punishment and the infliction of pain, coercion and intrusions into the freedoms of individuals, regardless of whether this is cloaked in a restorative justice discourse.

- Enhancing public participation in criminal justice is not merely a matter of making opportunities for participation available.

The deliberative potential of restorative justice

Responses to crime are fundamentally social and cultural events which seek to reaffirm a collective consciousness. Criminal justice as a public good, therefore is rooted in its participatory and norm clarifying roles. Here, processes of deliberation within criminal justice are fundamental. Yet in the quest to professionalize and bureaucratize justice we have tended to lose sight of the important deliberative framework of justice and the involvement of the public in that deliberative process. Braithwaite has advanced the case for restorative justice to accord to a notion of 'deliberative justice' (1998: 329). Like Christie, he is correct to emphasize the social importance of civic engagement with, and participation in, dispute processing. I suggest that the deliberative potential of restorative justice should be its primary *raison d'être* and over-arching principle.

One of the deficits of traditional criminal justice is that when the public are asked to participate as defendants, witnesses or victims, they are usually involved in passive, rather than active responsibility, which is both after-the-event and backward-looking (Braithwaite and Roche 2001). With a greater emphasis upon deliberation justice can seek to shift the emphasis of dialogue from questions of individual incidents to systemic patterns, from individual conscience to social values, from passive responsibility to active responsibility, from punishment to prevention, and from individual interests to common goods. As such, justice should require that outcomes are grounded in a dialogue that recognizes and takes account of under-lying inequities and injustices. Ultimately, however, it is social and economic policies (including employment, education, health and housing) rather than criminal justice policy that should remain the primary vehicle for the construction of a just and equal social order.

Criminal justice involves conflict and difference. As such it is a fertile –

albeit complex – terrain for deliberation. But rather than settle conflict by asserting one version of events and rejecting another in the context of blame allocation, it should be the source of dialogue that extends beyond the allocation of blame and guilt and which is focused upon problem solving. Justice as a deliberative process encourages public discussion emphasizing reasoning, debate, communication and normative appeals – a form of 'practical reason' offering proposals for how best to solve problems or meet legitimate needs. In this, deliberative justice should also allow space for the expression of emotions without this supplanting reason. Deliberation can also challenge professional cultures and assumptions and require those who defend impersonal bureaucratic processes to account for them.[11] As such, forms of deliberative participation open up opportunities for changing conditions of injustice and promoting justice. For, as Pavlich (this volume) notes, justice itself is not a state of being but an elusive end-point: a journey never completed.

In line with Walgrave (2002) and Braithwaite (1999a), restorative justice needs to outline ethical values and principles which enable researchers and practitioners to navigate between the malign and benign elements and attributes of community self-regulation and which simultaneously impose limitations upon the state itself. Deliberation in justice, as in democracy itself, should be structured around the ideals of inclusion, political equality, reasonableness and publicity which Iris Marion Young elaborates as follows (2000: 21–25).

- 'Inclusion' refers to the ideal that all those affected by a decision should be included in the process of discussion and decision-making.

- 'Political equality' refers to the equal right and effective opportunity to express interests and concerns.

- 'Reasonableness' refers to a framework for discussion or a 'set of dispositions that discussion participants have' (Young 2000: 24), including a willingness to listen, a tolerance of dissent and difference, a responsiveness, an openness to challenge and a quest to solve collective problems (even if this is not the outcome).

- 'Publicity' refers to recognition that participants to a deliberative process are accountable to others, which means explaining views held and claims made, as well as openness and transparency.

This overlaps and connects with Jones and colleagues' seven criteria for testing how far the arrangements for making policing policy follow democratic principles, namely: equity, delivery of service, responsiveness, distribution of power, information, redress and participation (Jones *et al.*

1994: 42–8). Whilst they relegate participation to last place in their list – in part given a wariness of the less savoury forms that participation can take – they importantly note that participation is itself a vital democratic ideal.

Like Iris Marion Young, they have helped steer debate towards the need to connect notions of democracy in crime control with conceptions of social justice. What their complex criteria embody are both elements of procedural and substantive justice. This suggests the need to maximize the opportunities for participation while constructing minimal, yet critical, limitations on the nature and form of participation. To this end, we should seek to encourage processes that serve as a means of discovering and validating the most just policies available in individual cases and with respect to broader social issues. As a consequence, mutual tolerance must be a prerequisite of participation.

As an element of democratic renewal, public participation in criminal justice implies representation. All of the public cannot (nor will they necessarily want to) participate all of the time. Certain members of the public – through their participation in criminal justice – will need to act as representatives of public interests. As such, they need to be authorized and held to account. This suggests further anticipatory and retrospective discussion as to public participation and representation. Participation should not stand as an opposite to representation but one should require and imply the other. Without citizen participation, the connection between representative and constituents is most liable to break down – potentially turning the 'representative' into a detached élite.

Certainly, there is a need for professionals and procedures to contain and regulate aspects of public participation by mitigating power differentials between the parties, challenging arbitrary outcomes, rendering procedures open, accountable and contestable under the rule of law. However, it is not clear that this cannot occur in interest-based and party-centred negotiations as distinct from rights-based and lawyer-centred proceedings. An emphasis upon forms of negotiation of the parties' common interests, rather than their legal entitlements as the basis for settlement, requires legal oversight. What is important is that these two polarities are kept in a tense relationship, in which one serves to correct the excesses of the other. Formal legal rights and due process act as bounding mechanisms that empower and constitutionalize informal processes. The principle of proportionality – with regard to the relationship between the harm done and the agreed outcome – has a role to play as a principle in deliberative justice. This does not suggest that all outcomes will be the same for the same offence, but that there are accepted boundaries as to both minimum and excessive outcomes.

In implementing participatory deliberation, what is not being argued for is the replacement of criminal justice by an untamed form of community justice – as some commentators advocate (McCold and Watchel 1998) – but that the two be held in a complementary, dynamic tension such as to enhance a form of deliberative justice: reducing but not eradicating the specialist professional management of crime. This is in accordance with Braithwaite and Parker's call for a 'rule of law' that 'percolates down into restorative justice' and 'restorative justice' that 'percolates up into the rule of law' (1999: 115–21 cited in Walgrave 2002: 9).

In this, the state and law are necessary to tame the excesses of community self-regulation, promote the equitable provision of security and justice, develop the capacity of communities to be more involved in conflict resolution and enhance the conditions for deliberative justice. In addition, the state is necessary as a means of striving against the powers that would seek to undermine public participation and deliberation. Advancing restorative justice necessitates working through, in and against the state.

> the paradox may be that the path to relational organisational governance may be state imposition on bureaucracies of participatory decision-making and accountability to local communities. Restorative justice needs state authority to prevent powerful fractions of the state from destroying restorative justice... (Braithwaite and Strang 2001: 9)

Nevertheless, even a deliberative form of justice has its limitations along the lines already outlined. Deliberative justice is facilitated where there are existing relations of care and trust and where a commitment to collective problem-solving is apparent. However, there will be circumstances in which individuals refuse to engage in deliberative processes for a variety of reasons and where deliberation cannot even begin. In these instances, a greater emphasis upon the professional management of cases and problem-solving will be required. Moreover, the role of criminal justice in solving problems remains severely limited. Synergy with other policy arenas – education, health, employment, housing and so on – more able to deliver solutions is paramount. The challenge, here, for criminal justice agencies, local authorities and other relevant organizations, is to dissolve the internal compartmentalization of social problems, to connect and collaborate with other – private, public and voluntary sector – organizations and to 'join-up' services around harm reduction (Crawford 1997).

Conclusions

In a prophetic insight Bauman has recently commented that:

> The century likely to go down in history as one of violence perpetrated by nation-states on their subjects has come to its close. Another violent century, this time a century of violence prodded by the disablement of nation-states as agencies of collective solutions and the progressive individualisation of human condition and fate, is likely to succeed it. (2002: 57)

The great challenge of future governance is how to regulate, co-ordinate and mitigate the forces of fragmentation and pluralization which affect both security and justice in ways which include citizens such that they can deliberate upon, and search for ways of resolving, conflict. In this, the enduring importance of the state as 'power-container' remains as pre-eminent as ever. The contemporary state needs to re-articulate a relationship with its populations encouraging and facilitating a more participatory civil society.

There is a need to maximize the opportunities for participation while constructing minimal, yet critical, limitations on the nature and form of participation. To protect against majoritarian rule and safeguard vulnerable minorities from the coercive and oppressive power of communal morality or private interests, there is a need for a socially inclusive process. This requires procedural mechanisms governing conflict negotiation and communication that seek to mitigate power differentials and structure the normative boundaries of the process. In addition, it is essential to ensure a minimum respect for diversity in both process and outcomes. Thus envisaged, public participation should be located within a human rights agenda as a check upon state power, but also in order to maximize its democratic and civic potential. McEvoy and Mika (2002: 18) rightly note that restorative justice's engagement in human rights discourses 'provides a mutually acceptable language within which both state and community can engage'. As Braithwaite and Strang (2001: 13) note: 'We come to see the restorative justice agenda not as a choice between civil society and state justice, but as requiring us to seek the most productive synergies between the two'. In this, the state has a crucial task in mitigating inequalities and the abuse of private power as well as fostering and enhancing the conditions for public participation in deliberative justice. However, there is ultimately the question as to the willingness of states to pursue and implement such radical projects. It is likely that in the interplay between state, law and culture lie the seeds of the form that restorative justice will take in different societies. We need to understand more, not less, about these wider forces and the manner in which they influence, affect and promote the potential for greater restoration and deliberation in justice.

Notes

1. Recent exceptions to this include a useful edited collection by Strang and Braithwaite (2001) and a special edition of the *British Journal of Criminology* 42(3) published in 2002.
2. Christie, of course, does not refer to, or use, the term 'restorative justice', in large part because it has come to popularity since the publication of his essay. Nevertheless, his focus is clearly upon forms of community dispute resolution, mediation and forms of restitution, which clearly fall within the restorative justice umbrella.
3. This is an insight that I have developed elsewhere with regard to deficiencies in much of the practice of community safety partnerships (Crawford 1997: Ch. 3). At a very different level, Stanley Cohen (2001) has elaborated with great eloquence upon the way in which individuals and states deny knowing about atrocities and suffering.
4. In an important essay McEvoy and Mika (2002) revisit the critique of informalism in the context of restorative justice in Northern Ireland.
5. This is not to suggest that all such 'informal' ways of dealing with conflict are appropriate, nor that people may prefer not to have recourse to the criminal justice system, precisely because of the arguments put forward by restorative justice proponents: that it denies the victim a significant voice, is destructive of relationships, denies the parties responsibility, is backward-looking, punitive etc. (although victimization surveys do not suggest that these are the primary reasons for non-reporting of crimes). Moreover, this raises more fundamental issues. If restorative justice initiatives are 'more attractive' to victims or offenders and thus encourage higher levels of reporting what will be the 'net-widening' consequences? Will restorative justice initiatives result in the formalization of previously informal conflict processing?
6. By contrast, Christie prefers the idea that; 'Ours is a society of task-monopolists' (1977: 7)
7. Christie's anecdotal conversations with a friendly lawyer and his selective (rhetorical) juxtaposition of dispute processing in a small village in Tanzania against a Scandinavian court case are examples of this 'butterfly collecting'.
8. Such as the RISE evaluation in Canberra (Strang 1999; Sherman *et al.* 2000), the South Australian Juvenile Justice (SAJJ) research (Daly 2001; 2002a); the evaluation of referral order pilots and other restorative justice initiatives in England and Wales (Newburn *et al.* 2001; 2002; Miers *et al.* 2001); to go with the earlier evaluation of the New Zealand family group conferencing for juveniles (Morris and Maxwell 2000).

9. Interestingly, they go on to reference Christie's article in support of such a proposition.
10. Levrant *et al.* (1999: 7) note that the recent history of criminal justice reminds us: 'Progressive sentiments are no guarantee that reforms will not be corrupted and serve punitive ends'.
11. One of the key findings from the experience of implementing the youth offender panel pilots in England and Wales has been the manner in which lay involvement has challenged, often in very positive ways, many of the cultural and organizational assumptions of those working in the delivery of youth justice (Newburn *et al.* 2002).

Chapter 7

Creating restorative systems

Daniel W. Van Ness

Restorative justice gatherings in North America fifteen years ago featured much more limited discussion than conferences today. There was only one restorative programme at that time, called Victim–Offender Reconciliation Program (VORP). In virtually every instance the groups running VORP were community based, meaning that they were run and funded by volunteers or small NGOs, and not by any part of the justice system. Most presentations at those conferences focused on the mechanics of VORP: the role of the mediator, the kinds of cases best suited for VORP, how to get funding, how to get cases referred, how to recruit and train volunteer facilitators, and (such was the extent of optimism) how to avoid being co-opted by a system that hardly even took notice at the time.

Things certainly have changed. In the past decade or so there has been an explosion of interest and activity in restorative justice. New pro-grammes and new philosophical and political explanations have emerged and mingled. There has been a growing awareness that these 'new' ideas are in fact the rediscovery of old approaches to crime and conflict, and those have helped shape the conversation. Governments have tested restorative programmes and in some instances have embraced them. But what does all this activity amount to?

A few years ago, Michael Tonry prepared a report for the US National Institute of Justice. He began as follows: 'After a quarter century of changes, there is no longer anything that can be called "the American system" of sentencing and corrections. As recently as 1975, there was a distinctively American approach, usually referred to as indeterminate sentencing, and it had changed little in the preceding 50 years' (Tonry 1999: 1). He then described how in the past quarter century that consensus had fragmented into four competing conceptions of sentencing – indeterminate, structured sentencing (e.g. guidelines), risk-based sentencing and restorative/community justice.

Why did he include restorative/community justice in that list? 'A fully elaborated system exists nowhere,' he acknowledged, 'but there is considerable activity in many States, and programs based on community/ restorative principles are beginning to deal with more serious crimes and criminals and to operate at every stage of the justice system, including within prisons'. It is, he continued, 'spreading rapidly and into applications that a decade ago would have seemed visionary. These include various forms of community involvement and emphasise offender accountability, victim participation, reconciliation, restoration and healing as goals (though which goals are emphasised and with what respective weights vary widely)' (Tonry 1999: 3, 4).

Tonry's comment that there is no fully elaborated system of restorative/community justice is correct, not only in the sense that no jurisdiction has fully embraced restorative/community values and practices but also in the sense that no one has clearly articulated how such a system might work. It is time to begin that work, for reasons I will go into in some detail later. To do so, we must consider several issues.

First, are there degrees of restorativeness, or is a system either restorative or not? Karen Strong and I have assumed the former (Van Ness and Strong 2002), as have others,[1] although we have approached the problem differently. This assumption seems merited for several reasons. First, change is usually incremental, which means that restorative approaches that work as designed will begin to have some effect even before all the restorative reforms are implemented. Second, restorative justice reflects values, and is not limited to particular programme elements, which means that it is possible to reflect those values fully or partially. When they are partially expressed, there will be some restorative impact, but not a fully restorative outcome.

What I would like to do in this chapter is further develop how we might assess whether a system is minimally, moderately or fully restorative. Second, I would like to similarly suggest a way that we might think about the relative roles of the state and community in overseeing a restorative response. Finally, I would like to propose the broad outlines of a restorative system.

Plotting the 'restorativeness' of a system

A variety of values or attributes have been used from time to time to describe restorative processes and outcomes. Sometimes these are treated as though they were discrete elements that are either completely present or else completely absent. Experience shows, however, that these may be partially present and absent. For example, amends – making things right – is certainly a value of restorative justice. But one offender might make amends by paying restitution, offering an apology and agreeing to acts of rehabilitation and generosity that the offender and victim have agreed to. Another offender may only pay restitution. Both have taken steps to make amends, but one has done more than the other has.

Similarly, processes may reflect restorative values in degree or fully. Non-coercion or voluntariness is affirmed as a restorative value, but in fact many – perhaps most – offenders participate in restorative programmes not because that is what they desire, but because it is the least onerous of the options given them. Surely we would acknowledge that programmes that use such limited options have a less stringent definition of 'non-coercive' than do others that would use no coercion at all.

For these reasons, it is best to think of restorative values or attributes as lying on the end of a continuum on the other end of which is a value or attribute that characterizes contemporary criminal justice. Furthermore, it would be helpful for us to include values or attributes regardless of whether they seem to concern restorative processes or restorative out-comes. During the recent exchanges between Paul McCold, Lode Walgrave, Gordon Bazemore and others on the Purist and Maximalist models of restorative justice,[2] several observers and the participants themselves noted that this discussion hinged in part on whether restorative values relate to process or outcome. It may be my own inclination to look for harmony when two notes are struck, but it seems apparent to me that both process and outcome are important in a restorative perspective.[3]

Let me propose four values or attributes that might be described as restorative processes and four that are more in the nature of restorative outcomes. I suggest that we think of each of these as lying on a continuum, the other end of which represents its antithesis. The four values related to restorative processes are inclusion, balance of interests, voluntary practice, and problem-solving orientation. [4] They and their antitheses are sum-marized in Figure 7.1.

Inclusion means that all stakeholders are invited to participate. Traditional stakeholders are the government and the offender. Restorative justice adds the victim and community to those two (more on community

Attributes of Restorative Processes

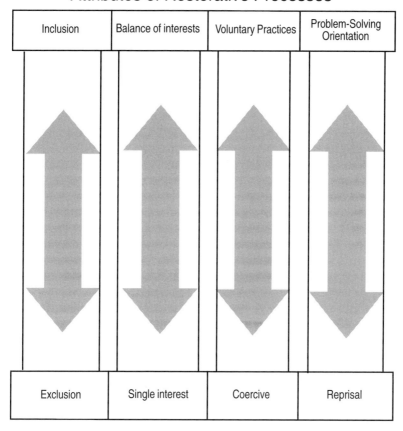

Inclusion	Balance of interests	Voluntary Practices	Problem-Solving Orientation
Exclusion	Single interest	Coercive	Reprisal

Figure 7.1. Continuum of attributes of the restorative process.

later). It is understood that the victim and community have their own interests to pursue; they are not involved only to help the government or defence with their cases. This means that the process will need to be adapted when necessary to allow the parties to participate and to look after their interests. At the other end of the continuum is the exclusion of all parties except to the extent required to determine whether the offender broke the law (see Van Ness and Strong 2002).

Balance of interests means that restorative programmes avoid focusing on one task alone, and instead attempt to accommodate the interests of all the parties. For example, while restorative programmes respect the importance of the public interest in resolving crimes, they do not address that to the exclusion of the interests of others. The objective is to maintain an appropriate balance between of all the interests at stake. At the other end of the continuum is the situation in which the only interest pursued is that of determining guilt.

Voluntary practice means that parties participate and assume responsibilities because they have chosen to, and not because they were required to. In practice, the choice to participate is made in the context of other alternatives, so the 'voluntariness' of a party's decision may be limited to the lesser of available evils. For example, an offender may summon the courage to meet with the victim in order to avoid going to prison. At the other end lies a process that routinely relies on coercion to gain the participation of the accused and of witnesses.

The *problem-solving* orientation of restorative justice causes it to look to the future even as it addresses the past. Among other things, this means that it is more likely to view crime in its social context than as an isolated event. Contemporary criminal justice focuses instead on whether and how to impose some sort of reprisal on the guilty offender (Dignan and Lowey 2000: 6).

Figure 7.2 depicts the values or attributes of restorative outcomes. The first continuum addresses the extent to which the parties have come together in arriving at the restorative resolution. At one end is the situation in which all interested parties were able to encounter each other. This will have given them an opportunity to work together to achieve the other restorative outcomes. At the other end is the situation in which the parties have been separated by the criminal justice process.

The second continuum represents differing understandings of how to respond to the offender's criminal behaviour. At one end is amends, in which the offender has made restitution, offered an apology, undertaken specific behaviours that will lead to change and acts of generosity. At the other end is the situation in which the offender has been required to 'pay' for committing the crime by suffering harm.

The third continuum depicts the relationship between the parties and their communities at the end of the process. At one end is the full integration of both into their communities as productive and contributing members. At the other end is ostracism either through enforced separation of the offender (perhaps through a sentence to prison) or through continuing stigmatization of both in their roles as victim and offender. In contemporary criminal justice, the separation of the offender is a desired outcome, and stigmatization of victims and offenders is a consequential outcome.

The final continuum concerns the nature and extent of the truth that is discovered in the course of the process. At one end, the parties discover the

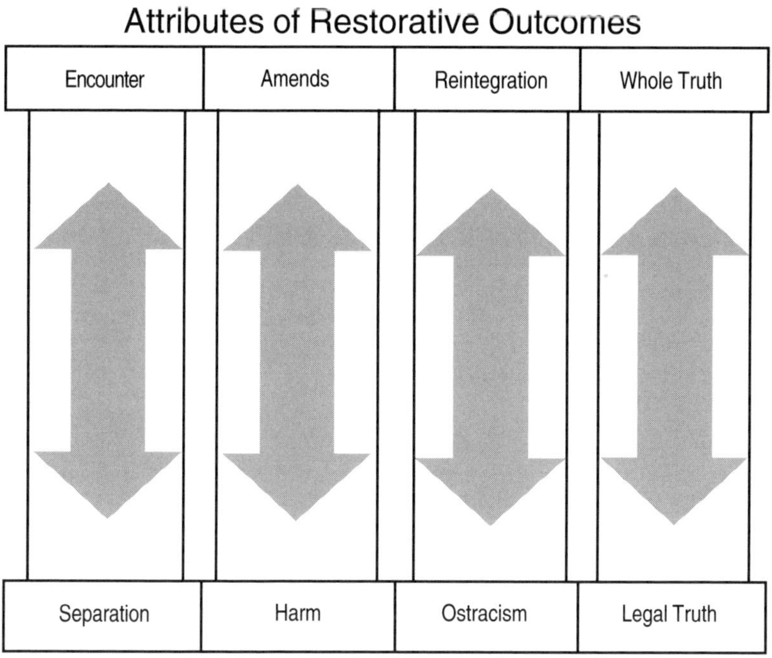

Attributes of Restorative Outcomes

Encounter	Amends	Reintegration	Whole Truth
Separation	Harm	Ostracism	Legal Truth

Figure 7.2. Continuum of attributes of restorative outcomes.

whole truth about the offence, including matters of culpability, harm, the perspectives of the parties, community impact and the shared values of the parties. They are able to explore any matter that concerns them. At the other end lies the more limited legal truth around which contemporary criminal justice focuses its efforts. It is concerned with what law was broken and whether the defendant is the one who broke it. Other matters are considered irrelevant and perhaps prejudicial.

Assume for a moment that these eight continuums capture the key values of restorative processes and outcomes. Assume as well that we are able to calibrate where a programme or system lies along each of these eight continuums. Under those circumstances, we could identify degrees of 'restorativeness' for both processes and outcomes.

I will give examples to illustrate why we might think in terms of degrees of restorativeness, although I do not want to suggest that particular restorative programmes are necessarily more or less restorative than others. What makes any process restorative is the extent to which it reflects restorative values and attributes, not the name it goes by. An example of a fully restorative process might be the circles of Hollow Water,

Attributes of Restorative Processes

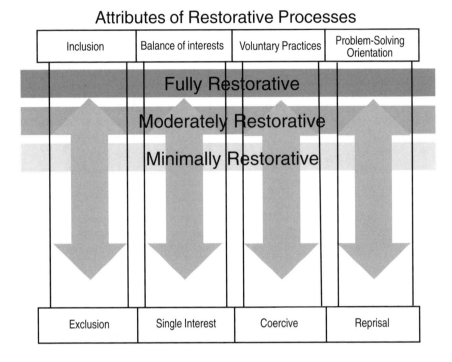

Inclusion	Balance of interests	Voluntary Practices	Problem-Solving Orientation

Fully Restorative

Moderately Restorative

Minimally Restorative

Exclusion	Single Interest	Coercive	Reprisal

Figure 7.3. Attributes of restorative processes.

a First Nations community in Canada. In instances of sexual violence, for example, there will be separate healing circles for the victim and the offender, together with their families, supporters and members of their community. After a time, these give way to new circles in which all parties may participate, with the objective being to develop a plan for the future. An example of a moderately restorative process could be a conference in which the victim, offender and their supporters meet to discuss the crime and work toward a resolution. The offender chooses to participate rather than go to court. Because of the relative brevity of the meeting, there is little time to probe underlying issues. An example of a minimally restorative process might be a conference that involves only the offender and his supporters. The victim has chosen not to participate, and a police officer or community volunteer attempts to provide the kind of perspective that the victim would have offered.

In the same way we might construct a range of restorative outcomes. An example of a fully restorative outcome might be one in which the

Attributes of Restorative Outcomes

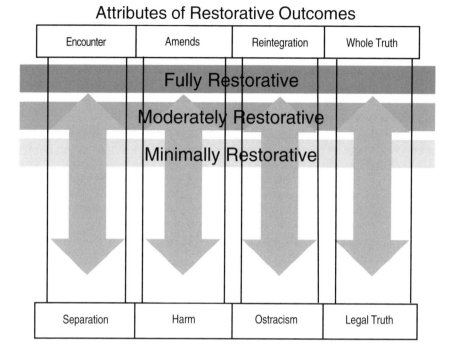

Figure 7.4. Attributes of restorative outcomes.

victim, offender and community members were able to meet and talk, all came to a more complete understanding of what took place and of the harm that resulted, the offender offered an apology as well as restitution, and the community members helped organize necessary support for each of them. An example of a moderately restorative outcome might be one in which the victim and offender met and talked about what took place and the fear the victim experienced, the offender answered all questions the victim had and then apologized, and the offender agreed to return to school and participate in a substance abuse treatment programme. An example of a minimally restorative outcome might be one in which the offender met with community members and the victim of a similar crime (the actual victim chose not to participate), the offender agreed to pay restitution and perform community service rather than face a potential prison sentence, and the offender agreed to return to school.

When we design our restorative system, we want one that includes restorative processes and outcomes. This forces us to consider a constellation of options more complex than two sets of four continuums, because we will need to explore how the two interrelate. A moderately restorative process will not necessarily yield a moderately restorative outcome. Figure 7.5 shows a grid with one axis representing processes and another representing outcomes. Many processes and outcomes are not restorative at all (these portions are represented in white). Others are minimally, moderately or fully restorative (dark grey, medium grey and light grey, respectively). If we require a restorative programme or system to exhibit both restorative processes and outcomes, we narrow the possibilities significantly. Further, if we assume that a lower degree of restorativeness on one axis is only marginally improved by a higher degree on the other, we see that there are a number of ways that systems can be at least minimally restorative but only one way to make them fully restorative.

This may inform the Purist and Maximalist discussion in several ways. It illustrates graphically that the Maximalist approach increases (maximizes) the number of people and programmes falling within its scope by aiming to be at least minimally restorative. By the same token, it shows that there are indeed differences between it and the Purist model (which is similar to the fully restorative category in this discussion). Finally, it allows us to begin categorizing restorative programmes based on their values and attributes related to process and outcome.

Considering the community–government relationship

Restorative justice proponents have had an ongoing discussion about community: What is it? How do we define it? Why do some feel that community involvement is valuable or essential? Is the community necessarily benevolent? In part this is because the term is sometimes used in an almost sentimental way ('longing for a sense of community that never existed') when, as Lode Walgrave has argued, other terms such as solidarity and responsibility might be more precise (Walgrave 2002b). Further, the term is used in significantly different ways: to describe localities ('the community I grew up in') affinity groups ('the restorative justice community'), or supporters ('the community of care').

However, when we speak of the roles of the government and of the community, I suggest that the meaning of community becomes clear: community refers to the non-governmental actors who respond to crime, to victims and to offenders. A volunteer who listens to a crime victim is doing so as a member of the community, not part of a governmental response. A privately funded NGO that helps ex-prisoners return from prison is part of the community. In this sense, community has a similar meaning to civil society.[5]

System of Processes and Outcomes

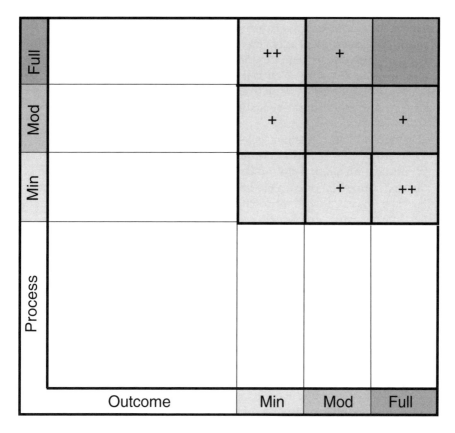

Figure 7.5. System of processes and outcomes.

Lode Walgrave has suggested that the experiences of Americans and Europeans with their governments and communities might have coloured the attitudes of restorative justice proponents in those continents (Walgrave 2000b). He suggests that Americans think of government as bureaucratic, impersonal and formal, whereas Europeans tend to view their state as a tool of the community, and when needed as a protection against intolerance within communities. There are undoubtedly other influences as well. Many of the early articulators of restorative justice were Mennonites, a religious community with a distrust of even the most benevolent governments. As they developed victim–offender encounter programmes, they worked outside of government and argued that this was an important strategy for restorative justice. Historians have noticed the parallels between the rise of the current paradigm of justice and the rise of both centralized governments and the professionalization of justice, typically by government agencies. Probation, for example, started out as a volunteer movement and then was incorporated into the formal governmental response. Political perspectives certainly influence the debate. Carolyn Boyes-Watson draws this distinction between the current justice system and restorative justice:

> The current justice system seeks to use rationalized and impersonal procedures to respond to crime. This paradigm of justice views individuals in isolation from others, and expects their behavior to be judged, punished or corrected by disinterested parties. Punishment is expected to be proportionate to the crime and procedures for evaluating truth are, ideally, uniform, adversarial, and objective. Even those persons deemed less responsible for their actions are handled by professionals equipped with expert knowledge to sort and channel them into appropriate arenas of state management and control.
>
> Proponents of restorative justice use starkly different criteria to determine what constitutes a just response to crime. Since crime is defined primarily as a violation of human relationships, rather than an abstract violation of the law, a restorative response seeks to heal those relationships above all else. While state forms of justice discourage participation of individuals personally known to the parties because they are supposed to lack neutrality, restorative justice processes seek out participation of all who have a stake in the incident and its resolution (Boyes-Watson 1999: 261).

Whether we are suspicious of governments or of communities, it seems clear that we agree that both exist. Furthermore, we understand that they have a dynamic and complicated relationship. In democracies, the leaders of governments are persons who have been elected by members of the community. Sometimes governments side with majority or minority groups within the community in asserting those groups' values or interests. Governments are overthrown when they lose support of the community.

At different times in history, governments and communities have carried out similar functions in responding to crime. Not long ago victims were expected to investigate their own crimes, and arrest and prosecute their offenders. Their reward, in addition to the satisfaction of seeing justice done, was the possibility of receiving judicial orders providing for multiple restitution. Policing was carried out by volunteers who raised the 'hue and cry' when they noticed a criminal running away. Passers-by had a duty to help apprehend the suspect. However, experience showed that victims, volunteers and passers-by were not reliable performers of their responsibilities. They were amateurs who often did not know what they were doing. They were distracted by other responsibilities and failed to complete the tasks they were expected to carry out.

Government officers, on the other hand, could be trained and hired to do this work full time. Policies could be set that gave consistency and uniformity to the discretionary decisions that necessarily are part of the investigation and prosecution of crime. Support structures and staff could be established to respond efficiently to demand. Increasing professionalization helped ameliorate the provincial interests and biases that the community volunteers might bring. In other words, government assumed community responsibilities in responding to crime because it could do it faster, more efficiently, more fairly and more uniformly than community members operating individually or even in groups.

My point is that the relationship and relative roles of the government and the community in responding to crime are dynamic and flexible. While some North American conversation about community may reflect distrust of government, much of it – perhaps most of it – is directed toward communities as a challenge to assume neglected responsibilities. The sense is that people have found it easier to let the police or other government agencies handle problems rather than to become personally involved.

Why not let the state handle these matters? Are there principles that might help identify the unique contributions that government and communities can make in the mutual effort to create safe societies? Karen Strong and I have suggested that government's role is to establish and preserve a just order and that the community's role is to build and preserve a just peace. We defined the two terms as follows:

> Peace requires a community's commitment to respect the rights of its members and to help resolve conflicts among them. It requires that those members respect community interests even when they conflict with their individual interests. It is in this context that communities and their members assume responsibility for addressing the underlying social, economic, and moral factors that contribute to conflict within the community. Order, on the other hand, is imposed on the community. It establishes and enforces external limits on individual behavior to minimize overt conflict and to control the resolution of

conflict. Like peace, a just order is important in preserving safety, and government has both the power and mandate to establish such an order (Van Ness and Strong 2002: 42).

Where there is sufficient community peace, there will be relatively little need for order. Where there is little peace, more order will be needed. This has two implications. The first is that communities concerned about safety may, rather than building peace through respectful dialogue and problem solving, resort to police and the courts. They have this right, of course, but a regular abdication of the responsibility to build peace on the part of community can contribute to a reliance on governmental order.[6]

Second, governments typically recognize that community involvement increases their capabilities and credibility. Consequently, police departments may form citizen advisory boards and jails and prisons will appoint volunteer prison visitors. These groups may in some instances have an adversarial posture toward the government agency, but often they help the agency avoid problems or find alternative approaches that work more effectively. Furthermore, recent initiatives in some jurisdictions have attempted to establish closer ties with communities. Examples include community policing, with police officers who walk their beats or ride bicycles, and community courts with smaller geographic scope.

I suggest that when we think of government and community co-operation in bringing about safe societies, we will do better if we contemplate a range of cooperative relationships rather than a binary choice of one or the other being responsible. Figure 7.6 illustrates this point. While there are some situations that may be handled solely by the government or community, most involve some combination of the two.

For example, a trial that does not involve a jury could be considered solely a governmental process (although community members will probably be asked to testify). A jury, on the other hand, introduces community members into the process, although they are now expected to be unfamiliar with the parties and circumstances. On the other side of the continuum, a circle might be solely a community process, since even though criminal justice system personnel may participate, the process ensures that this is done as a private individual and not as a representative of the justice system (Boyes-Watson 1999).

Conferencing and mediation programmes might be placed in different positions along the continuum depending on who administers and facilitates the programme. An NGO-run programme is more community-based than one that is run by social services departments of governments. Those run by probation are more governmentally-based (at least in jurisdictions where probation performs a 'control' function. Police-run

Community/Government Cooperation

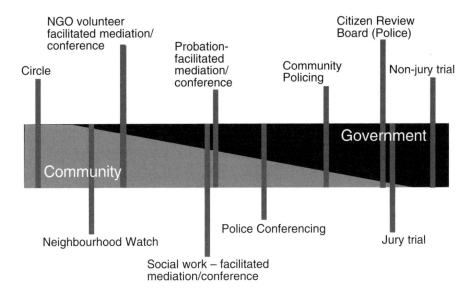

Figure 7.6. Cooperative relationships in the exercise of justice.

conferences are certainly more governmentally-based than the other conferencing options.

Finally, we can also plot examples of community–government co-operation related to various policing models. Neighbourhood Watch is principally a community programme, but it is formally linked to the police and is predicated on the volunteers contacting the police department if they see evidence of criminal activity. Community policing is largely a governmental activity, but the emphasis on building stronger community ties and actively seeking cooperation of people in the community makes it more community-based than traditional models. Establishing a citizen advisory or review board adds a modest degree of community involvement.

Certainly other examples could be offered, and there may be dis-agreement about the relative placement of the examples given. However, two observations seem to be worth making at this point. First, the question debated in restorative justice should not be whether the community should take responsibility for parts of a restorative response. Instead we should ask what the optimal role for the community and government may be in particular contexts and for particular purposes. Second, while political and philosophical perspectives will certainly inform that discussion, this is also an area in which research could be very useful. What are the outcomes of various programmes, and do those improve or decline (from a restorative perspective) when the extent and nature of community involvement changes?[7]

Constructing a unified restorative model

Now we come to the third area of discussion: how we might go about constructing a model of a restorative system. For a number of reasons, it is important to begin designing such a system now, even as restorative applications continue to spread rapidly and as we consider issues such as relative restorativeness and community–government cooperation.

First, if changes continue to be made incrementally, restorative justice runs the risk of becoming marginalized. Rather than letting the values and principles of restorative justice transform our entire approach to crime, particular restorative programmes will be annexed to existing structures in such a way that their influence is contained.

Second, many proponents have made the claim that restorative justice represents a paradigm shift, a change in patterns of thinking, a new lens through which we look at crime. If so, one would expect a wholesale change in how we approach crime and justice. A shift of the magnitude we claim would surely produce an entirely new system with very different programmes, institutions, processes and outcomes.

Third, some policymakers are asking for a system model. The not unreasonable expectation is that after a decade of experimentation, development, evaluation and experience, restorative justice practitioners and advocates would have reasonably clear ideas about what a restorative system might look like. We run two risks in responding to that expectation. The first is to offer incomplete and ill-considered proposals that if implemented would short-change the transformational potential of restorative justice. The second is to lose credibility when it becomes clear that we have done only a limited amount of thinking about what such a system might look like.

Finally, there are hard questions about the feasibility and comprehensiveness of restorative justice that may never be answered until serious attempts are made to construct a restorative system. Comprehensiveness is an issue because some conditions have traditionally been viewed as prerequisites for a restorative response (admission of guilt, willingness to participate, ability to make reparation, etc.). What happens when those conditions are not present? How could a system respond restoratively with all serious crimes as well as all minor ones? With offenders and victims who are unwilling or unable to participate, as well as to those who are willing and able? With cases in which the accused denies guilt? A fully restorative justice system of the sort anticipated by this project must be capable of effectively and restoratively addressing the myriad conditions and issues that are normal and routine in the administration of justice.

The second issue has to do with the feasibility of such a system. The 'criminal justice system' is not a system at all, but a collection of responses by public and private agencies, often in the context of conflicting goals and interests. Is it reasonable to suggest that a system with restorative values and norms could be implemented when so many different players must be involved? Furthermore, political concerns are (and should be) of great importance to policymakers. How might a policymaker consider alternative strategies for introducing and implementing a restorative system? Finally, can a restorative system handle high volumes of cases efficiently yet restoratively? Not simply the current high volume of criminal cases (which represent only a fraction of all crimes because they are only those in which accused offenders have been identified and caught) but also all those other crimes in which there are victims, but no identified offenders.

I have previously suggested that a restorative system might take one of four forms in the way it would relate to conventional criminal justice systems (see Figure 7.7) (Van Ness 2000). The first is a unitary model in which the restorative system is the only one available. The second is a dual-track model in which both systems stand side by side, with designated passages between them for parties to move back and forth. The third is a safety-net model in which the restorative system is the basic response to crime, but conventional processes are available when needed (for example, for determining guilt when that issue is contested). The final model is a hybrid, in which both approaches are linked into a single system. The example showed in Figure 7.7 is one that uses conventional processes until guilt is ascertained, at which point it shifts to restorative processes.

Models one and two assume that restorative justice is capable of dealing with all kinds of crimes and at all stages of the justice system. Models three and four assume that for either conceptual or practical reasons, it will not do so. Consequently, the more challenging models to examine are the first two, since they must be able to address the issues of comprehensiveness and feasibility. Perhaps a way to begin is to construct the second model, the dual track system, and then explore how that could be transformed into a unitary model.

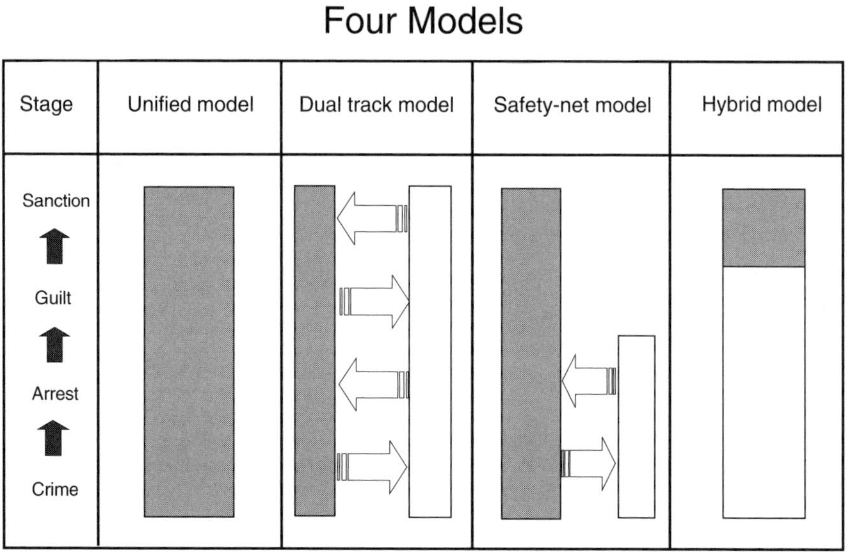

Four Models

Stage	Unified model	Dual track model	Safety-net model	Hybrid model
Sanction ↑ Guilt ↑ Arrest ↑ Crime				

Figure 7.7. Four models of the relationship between conventional and restorative justice systems.

I think that there are several likely elements to either of the two models. The first is a significant governmental role in organizing the restorative system and making it available to all. This is how the New Zealand Family Group Conferencing programme is organized. The government arm responsible for this (we might call it the Office of Restorative Interventions) will require sufficient staff to provide a stable programme, but built into its operations would be a large number of volunteer participants recruited from communities. These volunteers would play critical, not cosmetic or supportive roles, which means that both they and the Office of Restorative Interventions would understand their critical nature.

The Office would need to organize responses from the moment that a crime occurs until the final restorative elements have been completed. This means that victim services and support would need to be made available regardless of whether the accused offender is apprehended. These services and support would continue to be available at the request of the victim regardless of the pace of the processes determining offender accountability and response. The Office would also need to organize an investigatory service that would seek to minimize harm even as it explored what happened, who participated and what steps are needed to insure that this person is available for determining accountability.

I anticipate the development of a restorative method of dealing with situations in which the defendant denies having caused harm or violated laws to prevent harm.[8] The defendant and the victim should have the opportunity to get a full and complete explanation of the available processes so that they could make informed decisions. This briefing would probably be given by carefully trained volunteer supporters who would be available to both parties. Furthermore, to the extent that the community had been adversely affected by the crime, a representative of the community might be invited to participate in all future proceedings as a representative of the community. This would ensure that a general invitation to the community is neither ignored or unheard.

A full range of restorative processes should be available during the adjudication and sentencing or responsibility phases.[9] It may be that these processes will be used multiple times in the same matter. For example, there may be a need to proceed with an encounter programme without the victim because the victim is unable or unwilling to participate within the time in which it is reasonable to seek to determine the defendant's responsibility. Conferences may take place without the direct victim, and instead community members or surrogate victims may participate. At a later date, if the victim decides that it would be useful to meet with the defendant, then a conference, circle or mediation/dialogue might be conducted for those purposes.

The restorative processes used to facilitate the adjudication and responsibility phases would be modified to ensure that the agreement is carried out. If some sort of incapacitation were needed, a form of prison would be available, characterized by two features. First, the goal would be to work with the prisoner so that the need for prison was eliminated. Second, the prison should have meaningful work opportunities within it so that the prisoner could work, earn money and pay restitution.

Conclusion

Much has changed in fifteen years in the restorative justice movement. The question we must ask is whether in another fifteen years restorative justice will play a marginal role in a criminal justice system dominated by other values, or whether it will become the principle response to crime in at least some jurisdictions. The answer to that question will depend on our abilities to measure the restorativeness of systems and programmes, to understand and take full advantage of the community–government relationship, and to construct conceptual models.

Notes

1. Paul McCold, for example, in describing his Purist model of restorative justice has proposed that programmes could be classified based on the extent to which they meet the needs of victims, offenders and their communities. He assigns the name holistic to programmes that meet the needs of all three parties. Mostly restorative programmes are those that address the interests of only two. Partly restorative programmes meet the needs of only one. Pseudo-restorative programmes are those that call themselves restorative but in fact fail to address the interests of any of the parties (McCold 2000). In other words, the degree of restorativeness of programmes (and presumably of systems) is based on the extent to which they meet the needs of all, as opposed to some, of the parties.

2. A thorough discussion of the Purist and Maximalist models, featuring articles by McCold, Walgrave, Bazemore and others, may be found in *Contemporary Justice Review*, Dec. 2000, 3(4).

3. Part of the difficulty here may be that the distinction between processes and outcomes, while seeming clear, becomes cloudier on close inspection. Can a process really be examined independently of the outcome that results? Can an outcome be considered restorative regardless of how it was achieved? The answers to both questions seems to be 'no', which is why I suggest that we address both processes and outcomes as each relates to the other.

4. These are adapted from Dignan and Lowey 2000.

5. Of course, not all examples of community involvement are positive. In my country, lynch mobs circumvented the justice process by delivering informal vigilante justice. Furthermore, many communities maintained 'peace' by relegating some of its members to second-class status through limitations on education, voting, employment and housing (among other examples) based on race. The community's participation may be constructive or negative, as can that of the other three stakeholders. This is one reason it is important for government's balancing influence to be present in restorative justice.

6. According to the National Crime Prevention Council, 'Successful Neighborhood Watches move beyond the basics of home security, watching out for suspicious activities, and reporting them to law enforcement. They sponsor community cleanups, find solutions to local traffic problems, collect clothing and toys for homeless families, organize after-school activities for young people, help victims of crime, tutor teens at risk of dropping out of school, reclaim playgrounds from drug dealers, and form task forces that influence policymakers.' (www.ncpc.org/2success.htm (April 8, 2002)). This means that active community involvement is more than a communitarian ideal; it is also (at least in the United States) an effective means of reducing the amount and the harm of crime.

7. For example, one study found improved results when volunteer counselors were added to traditional probation with high-risk young male offenders. Compared to other high-risk offenders, those with volunteer counselors committed fewer and less serious criminal offences, were employed more regularly, made better educational progress, and appeared to be somewhat less

rebellious, less impulsive, and more responsible as measured on the California Psychological Inventory at the end of probation (Moore 1987).
8. I use the name given to the accused under contemporary criminal justice processes only so that it is clear to whom I am referring. Presumably different names would be assigned that better reflect the person's true position in what should be a less adversarial process.
9. See the disclaimer concerning names in the previous note.

Chapter 8

In search of restorative jurisprudence

John Braithwaite

The restorative consensus on limits

It is of course far too early to articulate a jurisprudence of restorative justice. Innovation in restorative practices continues apace. The best pro-grammes today are very different from best practice a decade ago. As usual, practice is ahead of theory. The newer the ideas, the less research and development (R&D) there has been around them.

Within the social movement for restorative justice, there is and always has been absolute consensus on one jurisprudential issue. This is that restorative justice processes should never exceed the upper limits on punishment enforced by the courts for the criminal offence under con-sideration. Retributive theorists often pretend in their writing that this is not the case, but when they do, they are unable to cite any scholarly writings, any restorative justice legislation or any training manuals of restorative justice practitioners to substantiate loose rhetoric about restorative justice being against upper limits or uncommitted to them. Moreover, the empirical experience of the courts intervening to overturn the decisions of restorative justice processes, which has now been con-siderable, particularly in New Zealand and Canada, has been over-whelmingly in the direction of the courts increasing the punitiveness of agreements reached between victims, offenders and other stakeholders. In New Zealand, for example, Maxwell and Morris (1993) report that while courts ratified conference decisions 81 per cent of the time, when they did change them, for every case where they reduced the punitiveness of the order there were eight where they increased it. Similar results have been obtained in the Restorative Resolutions project for adult offenders in Manitoba (83 per cent judicial ratification of plans, with five times as much modification by addition of requirements as modification by deletion) (Bonta *et al.* 1998: 16). While there were no cases where the restorative process recommended imprisonment and the court overruled this, there were many of the court overruling the process by adding prison time to the sentence.

Retributivist voices have been absent in condemnation of excesses of courts in overturning non-punitive restorative justice outcomes while persisting with rhetoric on the disrespect of restorative justice for upper limits. I suspect this is not a matter of bad faith on their part, but simply a result of their acceptance of a false assumption that the problem will turn out to be one of punitive populism as the driver of punitive excess.

Secondly, there is near universal consensus among restorative justice advocates that fundamental human rights ought to be respected in restorative justice processes. The argument is about what that list of rights ought to be. I have suggested that there could be consensus on respect for the fundamental human rights specified in the Universal Declaration of Human Rights, the International Covenant on Economic, Social and Cultural Rights, the International Covenant on Civil and Political Rights and its Second Optional Protocol, the United Nations Declaration on the Elimination of Violence Against Women and the Declaration of Basic Principles of Justice for Victims of Crime and Abuse of Power (Braithwaite 2002b). While restorative justice advocates would agree that it can never be right to send an offender to a prison where his fundamental human rights are not protected, in Australia there is never likely to be consensus on whether it can be right to allow traditional Aboriginal spearing as an indigenous response to the problem of Aboriginal deaths in custody. The dilemma here is that for some traditional Aboriginal people in outback Australia, imprisonment is a fundamental assault on their human rights because it deprives them of spiritual contact with their land, which is everything to their humanity. When they feel strongly that ritualized spearing is less cruel and more reintegrative than imprisonment, little wonder that here it is difficult for westerners to be sure about what is right.

Basically, however, the restorative justice consensus on limits and rights is very similar to the retributive consensus: there ought to be upper limits on punishment, while there is disagreement on what should be the quantum of those upper limits, and fundamental human rights should constrain what is permissible in justice processes, with disagreements about what some of those rights should be and how they should be framed.

Ferment on proportionality

Where there is both strong disagreement between restorativists and retributivists, and among restorativists themselves, is on proportionality. Some restorativists are attracted to calibrating the proportionality of restorative agreements in terms of whether the repair is proportional to the harm done. This cuts no ice with retributivists who see this as a tort-based form of proportionality. For retributivists, punishment must be proportional to culpability. The harm in need of repair is only one component of culpability. An attempted murder where no one is hit by the bullet is more culpable than injuring someone seriously as a result of unintentionally or slightly exceeding the speed limit. Such restorative proportionality is also unattractive to cultures who seek healing by allowing victims to give a gift to the offender (for examples, see Braithwaite 2002a: Box 3.3). The grace that comes from such gift-giving by victims can be helpful for their own healing and trigger remorse in offenders. It might be nurtured as a practice attractive to a number of cultural groups present in Western societies, not condemned as negative proportionality when what is required is positive proportionality.

For my part, I am not attracted to any conception of proportionality in restorative justice programmes. Limits are essential, but an upper constraint is quite a different matter from believing that the amount of punishment or repair ought in some way to be proportional to the seriousness of the crime. It may be that an underlying difference between retributivists and people like myself is that while retributivists tend to be deeply pessimistic that whatever the justice system does will make little difference to the safety of people. In contrast, my theoretical position is that poorly designed criminal justice interventions can make the community considerably less safe and well designed ones can help make it much safer. While it seems true that most attempts to reduce crime through restorative justice, rehabilitation, deterrence and incapacitation fail in the majority of cases where each is attempted, it is also true that all of these things succeed often enough for it to be true that there are cost-effective ways of reducing crime through best-practice restorative, rehabilitative, deterrence and incapacitative programmes. More importantly, I am an optimist that through programmes of rigorous research we can learn how to design a criminal justice system that has places for restorative justice, rehabilitation, deterrence and incapacitation that cover the weaknesses of one paradigm with the strengths of another. Through openness to innovation and evaluation, it should be quite possible for us to craft a criminal justice system that is both more decent in respecting rights and limits and more effective in creating community safety.

There is no evidence that upper limits inhibit this R&D aspiration. If they did, from my republican perspective we would have to scale back our aspirations (see Braithwaite and Pettit 1990). But there is no dilemma here. It is not true that if only we could execute murderers, or boil them in oil, we could reduce the homicide rate. There is no reason for thinking that we could reduce crime by locking up first-time juvenile shoplifters for five years. If it reduced shoplifting without generating subcultural defiance, it would only do so by shifting resources away from combating much more serious crimes.

Unlike upper limits, proportionality is an obstacle to crime prevention. In my corporate crime work, I believe I have shown persuasively that mercy for corporate criminals (disproportionate leniency) is often important for making the community safer (see Braithwaite 1984, 1985; Braithwaite and Pettit 1990). That is why corporate regulators have policies that they inelegantly call leniency policies. Regulators routinely face a choice between the out and out warfare of a criminal prosecution aimed at incarcerating the CEO and cutting a deal where the company agrees to increasing its investment in safety, internal discipline, staff retraining, in internal compliance systems and industry-wide compliance systems, and to compensation to victims in return for dropping criminal charges against top management. Or the individual penalties are reduced in a plea agreement that keeps top management out of prison. The reason this mercy works is that the power of major corporate criminals for ill is matched by their power for good. The consequentialist impulse is to harness that power for good. Once we have done that, we must be troubled by the fact that while power is the reason we let the white corporate criminal free, it is also the reason we lock up the black street criminal. The social movement for restorative justice here might set as its aspiration showing the path to progressively reduce the incarceration of the poor in a way that increases community safety. This is no less plausible a policy idea than largely dispensing with the incarceration of corporate criminals in a way that increases community safety.

Obviously, we can never hope to do either if we are morally constrained in both domains to inflict punishment proportional to the wrongdoing. Many retributivists are attracted to Hart's (1968) move of seeing consequentialist considerations as general justifying aims of having a criminal justice system, but proportionality as a principle that should guide the distribution of punishments. A justifying principle that is consequentialist;

a distributive one that is retributive. This is the formulation that appeals to von Hirsch (1993), for example. But what if I am right that proportionality destroys our capacity to experiment with crime prevention programmes that sometimes grant mercy, sometimes not, depending on the responsiveness of offenders to reform and repair, or depending on the agreement of victims and other stakeholders in restorative processes that this responsiveness justifies mercy? If I am right that often it will prove to be in the interests of community safety to give offenders other than a proportionate punishment, the Hartian principle of distributing punishment will defeat the general justifying aim of having an institution of punishment. That is, if we honour the distributive principle of proportionality, we will increase crime. The effect of the distribution will be to defeat the aim of establishing the punitive institution. The Hartian move of separating justifying and distributive principles is incoherent. It is only rendered coherent by the empirical assumptions that punishment reduces crime, and that while excessive punishment might reduce crime even more, we must place proportionality constraints on the pursuit of that good.[1] That is, the general justifying aim is to reduce crime through punishment. While we might achieve that aim even more through disproportionately heavy punishment, we still achieve it by proportionate punishment. If, on the other hand, these empirical assumptions fall apart in the way I suggest, then the distributive principle actually defeats the justifying aim of reducing crime (instead of simply limiting it).

Proportionality is a hot issue with surveillance and policing, just as it is with 'sentencing'. Just as there is a liberal impulse for equal punishment for equal wrongs, there is also the compelling intuition that black people should not be subject to more police surveillance than white people. This is the dilemma in US cities where Compstat computer targeting of crime hotspots for special police surveillance both seems able to reduce serious crimes like gun homicides and disproportionately targets black people (Sherman 1998).

Here I think there are lessons for restorative justice jurisprudence in the contrast between the Boston and New York police targeting of recent years, both of which make some plausible claims for reducing crime through improved targeting (Berrien and Winship 2000). In early 1999, both law enforcement officials and community members became greatly concerned at the shocking number of violent incidents in Boston's Cape Verdean community. The police believed they knew who were the gangs behind the violence. They believed they 'had the right guys' each of whom they could take out with several charges for offences not necessarily having anything to do with the violence (Berrien and Winship 2000: 30). They also wanted to do an Immigration and Naturalization Service sweep, with the threat of deportation for certain youths, unless the gang violence threatening the community stopped. Such an aggressive targeted swoop on a non-white community was obviously controversial and open to the interpretation of being racist. But what the lead police officer did was consult with both city-wide leaders of colour who had been critical of the police in the past for racist enforcement and consulted with the local Cape Verdean community. The police would not go ahead with this aggressive targeting unless it would be well received by the affected community. In the event, locals did seem so fed up with the violence that they wanted decisive policing. The targeting was of course still controversial, but it occurred with considerable local buy-in and it did not come as a shock to the local community when these young people were targeted. As far as I understand the case, limits and fundamental human rights were not breached. People were charged with offences they had actually committed. What is controversial is that many in white communities might have been targeted for the same kinds of offences. There are two relevant differences: the race difference and the fact that such a swoop in some other community that did not have the level of violence of the Cape Verdean community would not have picked up guns, would not have given a signal that might end gang violence. Police paralysis in the face of the moral dilemma seems a bad option. But a New York style police pounce aimed at reducing gun violence is also an inferior option to the Boston path of targeting combined with community consultation. While 'New York has gained national attention for dramatic reductions in violence ... Boston has found a way to achieve dramatic reductions in violent crime while making equally strong efforts to build partnerships with the community' (Berrien and Winship 2000: 32). A better option still than the Boston approach might involve consultation with the community followed by offering the targeted youths an option of a restorative community justice process as an alternative to incarceration (see Braithwaite 2002a: Chapter 2).

While I doubt there will ever be a settled restorative justice view on proportionality, my submission would be to abandon proportionality in favour of a commitment to limits and to honouring rights. Then under those constraints we might rely heavily on richly deliberated consent when the interventions that seem necessary to secure public safety involve selective enforcement against some but not others.

The jurisprudence of responsibility

Declan Roche and I have argued that restorative justice involves a shift towards an active conception of responsibility, while still finding a more limited place for passive responsibility than is standard in criminal jurisprudence (Braithwaite and Roche 2000). While passive responsibility means an offender being held responsible for a wrong he has committed in the past, active responsibility is a virtue, the virtue of taking responsibility for repairing the harm that has been done, the relationships that have been damaged. Restorative justice is about creating spaces where not only offenders, but other concerned citizens as well, will find it safe to take active responsibility for righting the wrong.

With respect to offenders, Roche and I found appeal in Fisse's (1983) concept of reactive fault. This means that even though an individual can reasonably be held passively responsible for a crime, if she takes active responsibility for righting the wrong, she can acquit that responsibility. She does not need to be punished for it; indeed in many contexts it would be wrong to do so.

In recent years, I have noticed on visits to women's prisons, not only in my own country, a new feminist consciousness that sees posters in public areas of the prison that point to the injustice of the revelation in research studies that a majority of the inmates of womens' prisons have been victims of sexual abuse in their past. When I read those posters their feminist polemic is always persuasive to me: 'Yes', I think, 'that is the most profound injustice about most of these women being in this place.' I particularly thought that recently when I met Yvonne Johnson (see Wiebe and Johnson 1998), a Cree woman raped as a child by a number of men, in prison for the brutal murder of a man she believed had sexually molested her children. Then I would quickly move to the thought that it would nevertheless be dangerous to excuse terrible crimes on these grounds.

Shadd Maruna's (2001) wonderful book, *Making Good: How Ex-Convicts Reform and Rebuild their Lives* is relevant here. It showed that serious Liverpool offenders who went straight had to find a new way of making sense of their lives. They had to restory their life histories. They defined a new ethical identity for themselves that meant that they were able to say, looking back at their former criminal selves, that they were 'not like that any more' (Maruna 2001: 7). His persistent reoffender sample, in contrast, were locked into 'condemnation scripts' whereby they saw themselves as irrevocably condemned to their criminal self-story.

This suggests a restorative justice that is about 'rebiographing', restorative storytelling that redefines an ethical conception of the self. Garfinkel (1956: 421–2) saw what was at issue in 'making good': 'the former identity stands as accidental; the new identity is the basic reality. What he is now is what, after all, he was all along.' So, Maruna found systematically that desisters from crime reverted to an unspoiled identity.

Desisters had restoried themselves to believe that their formerly criminal self 'wasn't me'. The self that did it was in William James' terms, not the I (the self-as-subject, who acts) nor the Me (the self-as-object, that is acted upon), but what Petrunik and Shearing (1988) called the It, an alien source of action (Maruna 2001: 93). Restorative justice might learn from this research how to help wrongdoers write their It out of the story of their true ethical identity. Maruna (2001: 13) also concluded that 'redemption rituals' as communal processes were important in this sense-making because desisting offenders often narrated the way their deviance had been decertified by important others such as family members or judges – the parent or policeman who said Johnny was now his old self. Howard Zehr (2002: 10) makes the point that whether we have victimized or been victimized, we need social support in the journey 'to re-narrate our stories so that they are no longer just about shame and humiliation but ultimately about dignity and triumph.'

Maruna (2001: 148) commends to us the Jesse Jackson slogan: 'You are not responsible for being down, but you are responsible for getting up.' In the all-too-common cases of children in poverty who have been physically or sexually abused, they do frequently feel that they are not responsible, that their life circumstances have condemned them to regular encounters with the criminal justice system. While there is moral peril in allowing the law to accept poverty as an excuse, an attraction of restorative justice is that it creates a space where it can be accepted as just for such victimized offenders to believe: 'I am one of the victims in this room. While I am not responsible for the abused life that led me into a life of crime on the streets, I am responsible for getting out of it and I am also responsible for helping this victim who has been hurt by my act.' Maruna (2001) found empirically that desisters from crime moved from 'contamination scripts' to 'redemption scripts' through just this kind of refusal to take responsibility for being down while accepting responsibility for getting up. In short, by accepting a jurisprudence of active responsibility, it may be that we can respond more compassionately to the injustices offenders have suffered while increasing community safety, instead of threatening community safety in the way implied by our moral hazard intuitions against allowing poverty as an excuse. Hence, when a woman like Yvonne Johnson has good reason for thinking that she has been the most profound victim of injustice in the events swirling around her, yet has remorse for her crimes, wants to do the best she can to right the wrongs of her past, help others to avoid that path themselves, why not let her keep the interpretation that she was not really responsible for her terrible circumstances, so long as she takes responsibility for getting out of them and for doing what she can to heal those she has hurt? Why not say, 'because you have acquitted your fault reactively, because you are not a danger but a blessing to others, go in peace.' Because you have taken active responsibility for making good, you will no longer be held responsible for any debt to the community. This links to the core restorative intuition that because crime hurts, justice should heal. And punishments that obstruct healing by insisting on adding more hurt to the world are not justice.

Contextual justice, not consistent justice

Restorative processes put the problem in the centre of the circle, not the person (Melton 1995). The right punishment of the person according to some retributive theory will almost always be the wrong solution to the problem. By wrong I mean less just. Both restorative justice and responsive regulation (Ayres and Braithwaite 1992) opt for contextual rather than consistent justice. With restorative justice, it is the collective wisdom of the stakeholders in the circle that decides what is the agreement that is just in all the circumstances, not perhaps the ideal agreement in the view of any one person in the circle, but one that all in the circle can sign off on as contextually just. That agreement that seems contextually just to all of them may or may not include punishment, compensation, apology, community work, rehabilitation or other measures to prevent recurrence. Because punishment, apology and measures to dissuade others from taking the same path are not commensurable in the terms of retributive theory, asking if the outcomes are consistent across a large number of cases makes little sense.

Similarly, responsive regulation is contextual justice. With responsive regulation, the regulator moves up a regulatory pyramid in the direction of progressively more onerous state interventions until there is a response to improve compliance with the law, compensate victims of wrongdoing, put better compliance systems in place, and so on (see the example of a responsive regulatory pyramid that integrates restorative justice with deterrence and incapacitation in Figure 8.1).[2] So restorative justice and responsive regulation share the notion that state response can become contextually more punitive if offenders are not responsive to appeals to take their obligations more seriously. Reactive fault again.

Retributive intuitions are that such contextual justice on both fronts is inferior to the consistent justice of equal punishment for equal wrongs. Rather restorative justice, as I have conceived it here, involves unequal punishment in response to unequal reactions (to unequal active responsibility). With restorative justice, a particular concern from the consistent punishment perspective is that whether you get a lighter or a

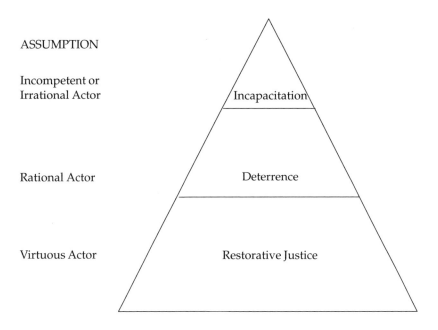

ASSUMPTION

Incompetent or
Irrational Actor

Incapacitation

Rational Actor

Deterrence

Virtuous Actor

Restorative Justice

Figure 8.1. Toward an integration of restorative, deterrent and incapacitative justice.

harsher punishment will depend on how punitive or forgiving victims and others in the circle are. A rich victim might not need full compensation as desperately as a poor one. But that is part of the point for the restorativist. If the poor victim is in more desperate trouble then she has a greater need and it would be a greater injustice to fail to fully respond to it.[3] For most of the great philosophers of the past, and for contemporarily influential ones such as Dworkin (1986) as well, fundamental to genuine justice is equal concern and equal respect for the needs of all of those hurt by an injustice. It follows that privileging equal punishment for offenders narrows us to concern for only one type of justice affecting one type of actor. Philosophers who take the equal application of rules very seriously in a wide range of contexts – from Cass Sunstein to Fred Schauer – are also clear that if we could perfect equal concern for all affected by an injustice we would not do it by enforcement of simple rules like equal punishment for equal wrongs. As Sunstein puts it; 'If human frailties and institutional needs are put to one side, particularized judgments, based on the relevant features of the single case, represent the highest form of justice' (Sunstein 1996: 135). And indeed the presumptive positivist Schauer argues even more emphatically:

When we entrench a generalization, therefore, we do not further the aim of treating like cases alike and unalike cases differently. On the contrary, it is particularism that recognizes relevant unlikeness, drawing all the distinctions some substantive justification indicates ought to be drawn. And it is particularistic rather than rule-based decision-making that recognizes all relevant similarities, thereby ensuring that substantively similar cases will in fact be treated similarly (Schauer 1991: 136–137).

Schauer's case for rules is arguments from reliance, efficiency, from stability and about enabling a proper allocation of power. The restorativist can argue that reliance that punishment will be prevented from exceeding upper limits that track the seriousness of an offence is quite enough reliance. Who wants the reliance of knowing that you are prevented from getting less than this, or much less? Reliance makes a good case for the existence of criminal law with upper limits, as opposed to open-textured evaluation of wrongdoing unconstrained by rules. But it does not make much of a case for lower limits or proportionality all the way down. I could work through a restorativist spin on all of Schauer's reasons for rules and why in criminal law they do not make a case for equal punishment for equal wrongs. But this would distract me from my core point, which is that equal punishment for equal wrongs is a travesty of equal justice.

Restorative justice has no easy escape from the horns of the dilemma that equal justice for victims is incompatible with equal justice for offenders. First, because it is a trilemma; restorativists are enjoined also to be concerned with justice for the community. So of course restorativists must reject a radical vision of victim empowerment that says that any result the victim wants she should get so long as it does not breach upper constraints on punishment. Restorativists must abandon both equal punishment for offenders and equal justice (compensation, empowerment, etc.) for victims as goals and seek to craft a superior fidelity to the goal of equal concern and respect for all those affected by the crime. The restorative justice circle is an imperfect vehicle for institutionalizing that aspiration. We can improve it without ever perfecting it. But I would argue that the aspiration is right.

The restorative circle heads down the path of the holistic consideration of all the injustices that matter in the particular case (Zehr 1995; Van Ness and Strong 1997; Luna 2002), as suggested in the quotation from Schauer (1991), but in a way constrained by limits on punishments, rights and rules that define what is a crime and what is not. We might be stumbling as we feel our way, but it does seem a better path than the narrow road of proportional punishment.

While we should not seek to guarantee offenders equal punishment for equal wrongs, the law can and should assure citizens that they will never be punished beyond upper limits. While victims cannot be guaranteed their wishes, the law should assure them of a right to put their views in their own voice. It should also guarantee a minimum level of victim support when they are physically or emotionally traumatized by a crime. This falls far short of an equal right of victims for full empowerment and full compensation. But the minimum guarantees I propose on the offender side and the victim side put some limits on how much inequality we can produce as we stumble down the path that pursues holistic justice. We are constrained that however we try to implement the ideal of equal concern and respect for all affected, we must assure that certain minimum guarantees are always delivered to certain key players. This puts limits on the inequality of the justice any one person can suffer, just as it enjoins us to eschew the error of single-minded pursuit of equality for the one that produces inequality for others.

The difficult choices were well illustrated by the Clotworthy case in New Zealand (see the Box below). Clotworthy is a paradigm case, albeit an extreme one, because, as we saw earlier, the evidence is that when courts overrule restorative justice conferences it is overwhelmingly to increase punishment, to trump the mercy victims have agreed to, and is rarely to reduce punitive excess demanded by victims. In my view, it was Justice Thorburn who decided the case correctly. But the more important point to emphasize is that the retributive presumption here tends to be empirically wrong. That presumption is that the problem is that victims will demand more punishment than the courts deem proportionate, whereas in fact the 'problem' is that they more often demand less than the courts deem proportionate. This is another instance of where the retributive philosophers have been led to unbalanced, decontextualized analyses by adopting a perspective which grows out of the less likely rather than the more likely empirically arising ethical dilemma.

CLOTWORTHY

Mr. Clotworthy inflicted six stab wounds, which collapsed a lung and diaphragm, upon an attempted robbery victim. Justice Thorburn of the Auckland District Court imposed a 2 year prison sentence, which was suspended, a compensation order of $15,000 to fund cosmetic surgery for an 'embarrassing scar' and 200 hours of community work. These had been agreed at a restorative conference organized by Justice Alternatives. The Judge found a basis for restorative justice in New Zealand law and placed weight on the wish of the victim for financial support for the cosmetic surgery and emotional support to end through forgiveness 'a festering agenda of vengeance or retribution in his heart against the prisoner'. The Court of Appeal allowed the victim to address it, whereupon the victim 'reiterated his previous stance, emphasising his wish to obtain funds for the necessary cosmetic surgery and his view that imprisonment would achieve nothing either for Mr. Clotworthy or for himself' (p.12). The victory for restorative justice was that 'substantial weight' was given by the court to the victim's belief that expiation had been agreed; their honours accepted that restorative justice had an important place in New Zealand sentencing law. The defeat was that greater weight was given to the empirical supposition that a custodial sentence would help 'deter others from such serious offending' (p.12). The suspending of the two year custodial sentence was quashed in favour of a sentence of four years and a $5,000 compensation order (which had already been lodged with the court); the community service and payment of the remaining compensation were also quashed. The victim got neither his act of grace nor the money for the cosmetic surgery. Subsequently, for reasons unknown, the victim committed suicide,

The Queen v Patrick Dale Clotworthy, Auckland District Court T. 971545, Court of Appeal of New Zealand, CA

Principles of restorative justice

How do we evaluate the adequacy of this elusive contextual justice? How do we assess how satisfactorily active the active responsibility has been? Are there ever circumstances where we should dishonour rights and limits on punishment? I have written on these questions elsewhere, so I will not traverse them here except to say that Philip Pettit and I have argued that freedom as non-domination or dominion, republican freedom, is an attractive ultimate yardstick of the justice of any criminal justice practice (Braithwaite and Pettit 1990). More recently, Walgrave (2002) has worked through, in a manner I find congenial, the way dominion can guide the day to day practice of restorative justice.

What comes with civic republicanism is an approach to insti-tutionalizing plurally deliberative justice under a rule of law and a separation of powers that accepts that citizens will often, indeed mostly, argue from a non-republican perspective. This is a great strength compared to retributivism or utilitarianism, which are stuck with the problem that if some judges are retributivists and some are utilitarians, the theory of the second best outcome is of a disastrous outcome. The republican argues for republican institutions and procedures without expecting that most people will manifest republican values within them. Sadly, sometimes they will be retributivists. But republicans must support giving voice to retributivists, indeed influence to them in deciding matters in which they are stakeholders. They can join hands with retributivists in defending upper limits, respectful communication and fundamental human rights as the only limits restorativists would want to place on the sway of retributive arguments. So when a restorativist is deeply disturbed by the threat to dominion in the agreement proposed in a restorative justice conference, what she should do, and all she should do, after failing to persuade others that the agreement is unjust, is argue that there is no consensus on the agreement and, this being so, the matter should be sent to court.

For most restorative justice advocates, freedom as non-domination is rather too abstract a philosophical concept to offer detailed practical guidance. I am grateful to Lode Walgrave for saying in his comments on this chapter that restoring freedom as non-domination is not for him too abstract, 'but a very clarifying principle'. While it is my hope people will come to this conclusion, I hope the following discussion will help them to do so, and even if they come to reject it, they might find the longer derived list of values useful for guiding evaluation research. At this early stage of the debate around restorative jurisprudence we must be wary against being prematurely prescriptive about the precise values we wish to maximize. Elsewhere, I have combined a set of still rather abstract restorative justice values into three groups. I will not defend the values again here (Braithwaite 2002b). Yes, they are vague, but if we are to pursue contextual justice wisely, both considerable openness and revisability of our values would be well advised, especially when the values debate is still so immature. The first group of values I submit for consideration by restorative jurisprudence are the values that take priority when there is any serious sanction or other infringement of freedom at risk. These are the fundamental procedural safeguards. In the context of liberty being threatened in any significant way, if no other values are realized, these must be.

Priority list of values 1

- Non-domination.
- Empowerment.

- Honouring legally specific upper limits on sanctions.
- Respectful listening.
- Equal concern for all stakeholders.
- Accountability, appealability.
- Respect for the fundamental human rights specified in the Universal Declaration of Human Rights, the International Covenant on Economic, Social and Cultural Rights, the International Covenant on Civil and Political Rights and its Second Optional Protocol, the United Nations Declaration on the Elimination of Violence Against Women and the Declaration of Basic Principles of Justice for Victims of Crime and Abuse of Power.

The second group of restorative justice values are values participants are empowered to ignore. Their being ignored is not reason for abandoning a restorative justice process. It might, however, be reason for asking the participants to agree to an adjournment so new participants might be brought in to give these values more chance of realization. While the second group are values that can be trumped by empowerment, they are values against which the success of restorative processes must be evaluated. Moreover they are values around which the restorativist is democratically active, seeking to persuade the community that these are decent values.

Priority list of values 2

- Restoration of human dignity.
- Restoration of property loss.
- Restoration of safety/injury.
- Restoration of damaged human relationships.
- Restoration of communities.
- Restoration of the environment.
- Emotional restoration.
- Restoration of freedom.
- Restoration of compassion or caring.
- Restoration of peace.
- Restoration of a sense of duty as a citizen.
- Provision of social support to develop human capabilities to the full.
- Prevention of future injustice.

The third list are values that restorativists do not actively encourage participants to manifest in restorative justice processes. To urge people to apologize or forgive is wrong and cruel. These are gifts that have no power as gifts when they are demanded. Being on the third list does not mean they are less important values. It means they are values we promote simply by creating spaces where it is easy for people to manifest them.

Priority list of values 3

- Remorse over injustice.
- Apology.
- Censure of the act.
- Forgiveness of the person.
- Mercy.

List 3 are emergent values, list 2 maximizing values, list 1 constraining values. What follows from the above is that the evaluation of restorative justice should occur along many dimensions. Narrowly evaluating restorative justice in terms of whether it reduces crime (the preeminent utilitarian concern) or honours limits (the preeminent retributive concern), important as they are, are only two of 25 dimensions of evaluation considered important here. If 25 is too many, we can think of restorativists as concerned about securing freedom as non-domination through repair, transformation, empowerment with others, and limits on the exercise of power over others. From a civic republican perspective, the 25-value version, the four-value version and the one-value version (freedom as non-domination) are mutually compatible.

Conclusion

The point of jurisprudence is to guide us in how we ought to evaluate the justice of disputing practices. That also implies an obligation to be empirically serious in measuring performance against these evaluation criteria. The restorative justice research community has a long way to go before it can marshall empirical evidence on all the outcomes discussed in this essay. Yet in a short time, a considerable portfolio of studies of variable quality has been assembled. The critics of restorative justice have not been as empirically serious. A contribution of this chapter has been to illustrate how this has rendered their analyses myopic. One illustration is that retributive critics launch their attacks from an assumption that the disturbing problem will be victims insisting on excessive punishment. Yet the empirical reality is of courts insisting on overruling restorative processes that include victims for not being excessive enough in their punishment. Hartian critics assume that punishment is justified because it reduces crime, and that this is still true of punishing proportionately. Yet empirically punishment often increases crime in a way that makes it plausible that we can reduce crime by abandoning proportionality (while maintaining upper limits). The possibility of this empirical conjuncture is a blank page of the leading jurisprudential texts.

I have conceived the fundamental principles of restorative jurisprudence here as the republican dominion of citizens secured through repair, transformation, empowerment with others, and limits on the exercise of power over others. Repair is a very different value to punishment as hard treatment; repair does not have to hurt, though of course it often does. While restorativists share with retributivists a concern to limit abuse of power over others, restorative justice is distinguished from retributive justice by its obverse commitment to empowerment with others. Finally, our discussion of responsibility has illustrated how restorative justice aspires to transform citizens through deliberation into being democratically active. The active responsibility ideal is a republican transformative ideal or a positive liberty ideal. Retributive passive responsibility is an ideal of negative liberalism, of non-interference beyond holding citizens to legal obligations. In action, of course, retributivism is not liberal at all, but is the stuff of law and order conservatism at best, totalitarianism at worst. In action, restorative justice is a bit better than this, though it too will forever suffer a wide gap between normative ideal and political practice.

Notes

1. A restorative theory of deterrence (see Braithwaite 2002a: Chapter 4) suggests that the Hartian assumptions are wrong. Empirically, there is now a lot of evidence that increasing punishment produces both increasing deterrence and increasing defiance (or reactance) effects (Sherman 1993; Brehm and Brehm 1981). Where the defiance effect is stronger than the deterrance effect, higher penalties increase crime. In their meta-analysis of correctional studies, Cullen and Gendreau (2000) found that the punitive severity of sentences actually had a small positive coefficient – more punishment, more reoffending.
2. The pyramid implies a willingness to abandon restorative justice in favour of more determinedly punitive justice primarily oriented to either deterrence or incapacitation when restorative justice fails (Braithwaite, 2002a: Ch. 2). It assumes that restorative justice will often fail and fail again and in such cases the safety of the community requires escalation to more punitive approaches. Even when this means imprisonment, however, restorative justice values should be given as much space as possible within the punitive justice institution. More importantly, however, responsive regulation means con-

textually responsive de-escalation back down the pyramid to restorative justice whenever punishment has succeeded in getting the safety concerns under control.

3. On the idea of a restorative justice philosophy based on responding to needs see Sullivan and Tifft (2001). See also the discussion in Braithwaite (2002a) of the compatibility between a concern with freedom as non-domination and the approach of Nussbaum (1995) of nurturing human capabilities.

Chapter 9

Restorative justice and the law: the case for an integrated, systemic approach[1]

Jim Dignan

Introduction

The growth in the range, diversity and geographical spread of restorative justice initiatives in recent years has been remarkable. Even more remarkable is the extent to which restorative justice thinking appears to be increasingly influencing the direction of criminal justice policy-making at almost every level: international, governmental, and also sub-governmental within a wide range of criminal justice agencies, including the police, probation service and prison service. As its influence develops, however, one inevitable consequence will be to expose ever more starkly a number of significant 'fault-lines' within the restorative justice 'movement', necessitating some fundamental reappraisals of hitherto taken-for-granted assumptions, and some difficult policy choices regarding the future direction of restorative justice endeavours. In this chapter I will address three of the most important fault-lines that delineate different strands of restorative justice thinking, and will attempt to 'map out' the policy implications that are associated with each tendency. In doing so I will argue the case for restorative justice to be conceptualized and developed as a fully integrated part of the 'regular' criminal justice system, with the important proviso that the system itself needs to be radically and systematically reformed in accordance with restorative justice precepts.

Restorative justice fault-lines and their policy implications

In the early days of the restorative justice movement, there was a tendency to portray the relationship between the emerging restorative justice approach and the regular criminal justice system in highly dichotomous terms, as being 'polar opposites' in almost every respect. The best-known and most influential example involves Howard Zehr's (1985, 1990) powerful use of photographic metaphors involving the imagery of 'changing lenses' to reveal radically different perspectives on a given subject. His writings probably did most to popularize the portrayal of restorative justice as a completely new paradigm that has little or nothing in common with the regular criminal justice system. Although he was by no means the first to advocate the need for an alternative paradigm, others had done so on grounds that only loosely anticipated the restorative justice movement. Some (for example Cantor 1976), had advocated a wholesale substitution of civil law for criminal law processes with a view to 'civilizing' the treatment of offenders, while others (for example Christie 1977), had argued in favour of informal methods of offence resolution that would return criminal conflicts to the parties directly involved with a view to empowering them.

Although the tendency to dichotomize may be understandable when advocating new concepts to people who may be unfamiliar with them – since it may enhance their appeal when contrasted with existing institutions that are widely, and often justifiably, felt to be failing – it may also be misleading. It may mislead firstly by exaggerating the differences between the two systems, and playing down their similarities; and secondly by implying that the two systems are more homogeneous than they really are, thereby overlooking important differences (or shades of opinion) within each system.

The tendency to 'play up' differences between the two systems is illustrated by the long-running debate over whether restorative justice measures are 'punitive'. Some restorative justice advocates (see e.g. Wright 1991: 15 and 1996: 27; Walgrave 1999: 146) deny that they are punitive – regardless of the way they are actually perceived by their recipients – on the ground that their primary purpose is intended to be 'constructive'. This denial that restorative justice is engaged in the business of punishment is then contrasted with the conventional criminal justice system. The latter *is* characterized as punitive – even though the deprivations that it imposes may be identical to those entailed in restorative justice measures – because they are said to be inflicted 'for their own sake' rather than for any 'higher' purpose.

I have argued elsewhere (Dignan 2002) that this purported distinction is misleading because it relies for its effect on the confusion of two distinct elements in the concept of intention. One element relates to the motive for doing something (its intended purpose); the other (which we may think of as the element of volition) refers to the fact that the act in question is being performed deliberately or wilfully. However, the reason for taking issue with those who insist on distinguishing between punishment and restorative justice interventions is not just that the purported distinction is misleading; nor is the debate a mere semantic quibble. It arises from a concern that it is likely to be harmful to the cause of restorative justice to deny that it is also engaged in the business of punishment. For if we were to accept such a distinction, then there would be no obligation to provide any moral justification for imposing restorative justice interventions on offenders in the way that there is for punitive interventions; nor would there be any need to specify any limits on the extent or intensity of those interventions.

However, those restorative justice advocates who insist on such a distinction would do well to recall that similar 'motivational' arguments were used by previous generations of penal reformers in support of rehabilitative measures that were also claimed not to be subject to the same normative restrictions as punitive measures, because they, too, were said to be inflicted with purely benevolent intentions. They would do well to remember also that such arguments were justifiably challenged,[2] and ultimately rejected, on the ground that they failed to provide adequate safeguards to protect offenders from being treated unjustly.

A far more principled, defensible, and strategically advisable line[3] for restorative justice advocates to adopt in my view is to accept that whenever pain or unpleasantness of any kind is deliberately imposed on a person this calls for a moral justification and needs to be subject to normative restrictions. This applies regardless of the motive for inflicting the pain or unpleasantness and irrespective of the name that is given to it, whether this be punishment, treatment or a restorative justice 'sanction'. So, instead of engaging in such fine semantic distinctions, there is a far more urgent need for restorative justice advocates to articulate and refine a clear set of normative principles that are capable of providing a coherent and defensible normative framework for the practice of restorative justice, whatever form it takes. Although this is not the aim of the present chapter, it is an issue that I have tentatively addressed elsewhere (Dignan 2002, see also Cavadino and Dignan 1997).

Conversely, the tendency to 'play down' similarities between restorative justice approaches and the conventional criminal justice system is exemplified by a reluctance to acknowledge that the latter may also comprise certain restorative elements (in the form of 'compensation orders', 'reparation orders', or even certain forms of 'community service', for example), however attenuated they may appear in the eyes of some restorative justice advocates. Instead of depicting the relationship between restorative justice approaches and the conventional criminal justice system in terms of a dichotomy of opposites, therefore, it may be more helpful to think in terms of a continuum of restorative approaches (see Dignan and Marsh 2001). These might range from fairly narrowly focused court-ordered reparative measures on the one hand, to potentially much more wide-ranging restorative measures that may have resulted from some form of inclusionary decision-making process at the other end of the spectrum.

A third weakness that is associated with this 'dichotomizing tendency' is its implicit assumption that the two contrasting models are themselves relatively homogeneous, thereby glossing over important distinctions (including major differences of opinion) within each model. With regard to the restorative justice model, there are at least three major sets of 'fault-lines'[4] that delineate significantly different strands of restorative justice thinking.

The first fault-line relates to the concept of 'restorative justice' itself, and the way this has been defined by restorative justice advocates. It encompasses an important split between those who conceptualize restorative justice exclusively or primarily in terms of a particular kind of process, and those for whom the concept also extends to outcomes of a particular kind, irrespective of the decision-making process that is involved. The second fault-line relates to the focus of different restorative justice practices, and the primacy or 'standing' that is accorded to each of the main 'stake-holders' – victim, offender, community and state – with regard to specific offences. And the third fault-line relates to the kind of relationship that is envisaged between restorative justice initiatives – whatever form they take – and the 'regular' criminal justice system. To some extent, as we shall see, there may be a tendency for attitudes to 'polarize' in a consistent direction, or in the same 'plane', across all three sets of fault-lines and, to that extent, the fault-lines themselves may help to delineate a number of quite distinct lines of potential development for restorative justice to take in the future. Or so I shall be arguing. But first it is important to expose the three principal fault-lines themselves and the differences of opinion with which they are associated.

First restorative justice fault-line: process vs. outcome definitions

Despite numerous attempts, it has not been possible for restorative justice advocates to formulate a definition of the concept that all are able to subscribe to. On one side of this 'definitional fault-line' are those who conceive of restorative justice as a distinctive type of decision-making process.[5] Marshall's formulation (1999: 5) of this process – as one that enables those who have a stake in a specific offence to 'do justice' by collectively resolving how to deal with its aftermath and also its implications for the future – epitomizes this perspective. Most restorative justice advocates and practitioners who conceive of restorative justice as a distinctive process for dealing with crime and its aftermath also subscribe to certain core ethical values that underpin the process itself. They include the need for consensual participation on the part of the principal stake-holders; for dialogue based on the principle of mutual respect for all parties; for a balance to be sought between the various sets of interests that are in play; and for non-coercive practices and agreements. Another significant attribute of the process is its forward-looking, 'problem-solving' orientation (Dignan and Lowey 2000: 14). Such values provide an important and welcome acknowledgement of the potential abuses to which informal restorative justice processes might otherwise be subject. Where they are respected and enforced – and particularly when they are incorporated into more detailed sets of ethical standards for regulating restorative justice practices[6] – they may provide valuable safeguards to minimize the risk of abuse.

Although the formulation proposed by Tony Marshall is reasonably flexible, since it incorporates a variety of possible processes (including victim–offender mediation, various forms of conferencing and sentencing circles), in another sense it is also highly restrictive. For the adoption of a process-based definition of restorative justice also appears to limit its scope – possibly drastically – firstly to those cases that are deemed appropriate for this kind of intervention, and secondly – within this category – to those in which both parties are willing to participate and abide by the ground rules.

Different jurisdictions have adopted different policies with regard to the first of these issues, though all of them are inherently problematic. In New Zealand, for example, family group conferencing is currently restricted in the main to young offenders whose offences are considered too serious to be dealt with by means of a police caution. In other words conferencing is reserved as a routine alternative to prosecution in the youth court. There may be strong arguments in favour of this approach, since conferencing is undoubtedly a resource-intensive process, and it may make sense to limit its use to cases where the victim's need is felt to be greatest. But the effect is to restrict the scope for this kind of restorative justice process (together with its potential benefits) to a minority of those

New Zealand young offenders whose cases are formally dealt with by the criminal justice system, and to withhold it from the majority of young offenders – and also their victims – who are cautioned by the police.[7]

In other common law jurisdictions the tendency has been to restrict the use of restorative justice processes to the less serious offences that are committed by young offenders, either by linking them to police cautioning initiatives[8] or to relatively minor court-based disposals. For example, younger offenders in England and Wales may be given reparation orders,[9] that could include mediation meetings with their victims, though this is just one of a number of possible forms that reparation might take, and will only happen where the victim is willing to take part. In addition, young offenders who are prosecuted for the first time, and who plead guilty, are in most cases now automatically made subject to a referral order,[10] which requires them to participate in a meeting, the purpose of which is to conclude a contractual agreement binding the young offender to an agreed 'programme of behaviour' for the duration of the order. Victims are among those who might be invited to take part in such meetings, but again only if they wish to attend.

The effect of this approach is to withhold the availability of restorative justice processes from cases that are deemed to be too serious, which are therefore prosecuted and sentenced in the normal way. And even though the pool of less serious cases is potentially far greater – as in New Zealand – the fact that truly restorative justice processes can only be resorted to where the victim's consent is forthcoming has so far restricted their use in practice to a tiny minority of cases only. Indeed the rate of victim participation that has been reported in connection with a variety of recently introduced restorative justice style processes aimed at young offenders has been little better than the rates that were achieved by two experimental schemes catering for more serious adult offenders in the period preceding these recent reforms.

Thus, Umbreit and Roberts (1996: 27), for example, reported that only 7 per cent of all referrals to two well-established and highly respected English Victim Offender Mediation Projects (Coventry and Leeds) during 1993 participated in direct (face-to-face) mediation.[11] Similarly, following the introduction of reparation orders in the Crime and Disorder Act 1998 only 9 per cent of these involved mediation between victims and young offenders during the time of the pilot evaluation (Holdaway et al. 2001: 89). Reports on the evaluation of the referral order pilots also suggested a low rate of victim participation in the new youth offender panels (Newburn et al. 2001a and b, 2002). The final report of the evaluation indicated that victims attended panel meetings in only 13 per cent of cases in which an initial panel was held, and in respect of which there was an identifiable victim. Finally, the level of victim participation in the police-led Thames Valley restorative cautioning initiative is much closer to those encountered in other restorative justice processes in England and Wales than to those achieved by its Australian or North American counterparts, where victim participate rates have been very much higher.[12]

To some extent the disappointingly low rates of victim participation that have been reported recently in England and Wales may reflect shortcomings in the way some of the newer restorative justice-type initiatives have been implemented.[13] A lack of adequately trained and suitably experienced practitioners may also have been a contributory factor (though the low level of victim participation predates these latest initiatives). Nevertheless, if those who advocate an exclusively process-based definition of restorative justice insist that it must involve those with a stake in the offence, and that the 'eligibility' for the process is restricted to those cases that can satisfy the exacting ethical standards outlined above, then it follows that the scope for restorative justice processes may be quite narrow. Moreover, the prospects for future development and expansion would also appear to be correspondingly limited, at least in the short term.

One response to these problems has been to relax the 'eligibility' criteria, in effect, for example by developing forms of restorative justice practice that do not depend on direct participation by victims. The use of 'indirect mediation', involving the mediator as a 'go-between' is one of the earliest and best-known adaptations of this kind.[14] Analogous techniques have also been developed in connection with the Thames Valley style restorative cautioning scheme, whereby police facilitators may seek to convey the absent victim's perspective during the 'conference'.[15] Attempts have also been made to relax the criteria for participation by offenders, notably in New Zealand, where a formal admission of guilt is not insisted upon provided an offender 'does not actively deny' responsibility for the behaviour that gave rise to the charge.

On the other side of the 'definitional fault-line' are those (e.g. Bazemore and Walgrave 1999: 48, see also Dignan 2002) who take the view that the process-based definition of restorative justice is at best incomplete, because it has little to say on the subject of 'restorative outcomes', or how these might be defined and evaluated. The neglect of any reference to restorative outcomes in the definition of restorative justice is problematic on a number of counts. First, with regard to restorative justice processes of the 'standard' type, that do involve participation by the appropriate parties, it is important for others – not just the parties themselves – to be able to say what counts, or does not count, as a 'restorative' outcome. In principle it seems desirable to be able to do this with reference to criteria that may be derived either from the definition itself, or from objective normative standards that are accepted as underpinning the definition. This may be particularly important where juvenile offenders are concerned, even when their own families are involved in the process for, as Braithwaite's (1999a: 66–7) example of the authoritarian 'Uncle Harry' reminds us, families are not necessarily the most effective guarantors of 'fair outcomes' that also reflect the best interests of the children for whom they may be responsible.

Second, the need to be able to determine what counts as a 'restorative outcome' is arguably all the more important in cases that are dealt with by means of 'non-standard' restorative processes, as when the victim is absent. This is partly because it may be more difficult to determine what might count as an appropriate form of 'direct reparation' when the victim is not present; and partly because it may increase the likelihood of a power imbalance. The risk of this happening may be even more acute when the offender is confronted by one or more 'authority figures' – especially if the police are involved in the process, as in some forms of police-led conferencing – rather than the victim. Cases such as these raise serious doubts regarding the extent to which the process can be fully restorative in such circumstances, whether from an offender's or a victim's perspective, and make it all the more important to consider what should count as a restorative outcome.

The third and most important problem that is posed by a failure to address the issue of restorative outcomes is that it leaves restorative justice advocates with nothing to say regarding the way cases should be dealt with that – for whatever reason – do not lend themselves to some form of informal offence resolution process. More specifically, it represents a missed opportunity to consider whether, and if so how, restorative justice thinking might contribute to a broader and much more far-reaching programme of reform encompassing the entire penal system. Instead, by tying the definition of restorative justice to a particular kind of informal dispute-resolution processing it increases the likelihood that restorative justice theory and practice will largely be confined to a set of diversionary practices operating on the margins of the regular criminal justice system.

Second restorative justice fault-line: 'civilian' vs. 'communitarian' tendencies

Restorative justice advocates are united in their belief that the conventional criminal justice system is seriously flawed on two principal counts: first in the way it defines crimes as offences 'against the state'; and second in concluding from this that the appropriate response should be based on official assessments of what the 'public interest' demands (Dignan and Cavadino 1996: 155). This has the effect of relegating all other interests (including those of the victim, the offender and 'the community') to a subordinate status at best, and relevant chiefly as a means of determining what the 'public interest' might entail. Beyond this 'unity in opposition', however, there are important differences of opinion within the restorative justice movement, even among those who subscribe to a 'process definition'. These differences relate to three main sets of issues: first the precise range of interests that need to be accommodated when dealing with an offence; second the extent to which it is felt important for these interests to be represented in the appropriate decision-making process; and third the extent to which it is considered that such interests need to be reflected in the outcomes that emerge from that process. As with the definitional issue, these differences represent a second significant 'fault-line' within the restorative justice movement: one that relates to the identity of the key 'stakeholders'; the most appropriate 'forum' or decision-making process in which they should be represented; and also the role they are expected to play in determining the outcome of this process.

One side of the fault-line is represented by a 'civilian' tendency, for whom the key stakeholders are thought to be the parties who are most directly affected by an offence. When taken to its logical conclusion (as in the writings of Gilbert Cantor 1976), the appropriate decision-making forum for resolving disputes of this kind is one that is analogous to a civil court system. However, many restorative justice advocates (e.g. Wright 1991) would prefer to substitute informal methods of offence resolution such as face-to-face mediation, which allow far greater involvement by the parties themselves both in the process itself, and also in determining the outcome. The arguments in favour of such an approach (assuming the parties agree, and subject to the safeguards considered above) are highly persuasive in the case of less serious offences, since here the most important interests in play are those relating to the personal harm that is experienced by the victim. And even in more serious cases it may be argued that the victim should be entitled to receive reparation from the offender for the personal harm that has been sustained, including the opportunity to take part in a process of mediation if desired.

In its most uncompromising form, the 'civilian' approach would favour mediation as the *sole* response to an offence, even in cases such as this, but this argument is much more difficult to sustain. The problem with this extreme variant of the civilian tendency is that it collapses the distinction between crimes and civil wrongs and, in so doing, fails to acknowledge that offences – particularly where they are serious – may have broader social implications which go beyond the personal harm or loss that is experienced by the direct victim (Duff 1988; Dignan and Cavadino 1996). By redefining the concept of crime as a purely interpersonal matter, other relevant interests are neglected. The most important of these is the anxiety that may be caused to potential victims since their presumption of security may be undermined, especially in the case of a particularly serious offence (Watson *et al*. 1989). Consequently, in cases such as these, the use of informal dispute resolution processes such as victim–offender mediation is unlikely to be acceptable as the sole response, even though there may be scope for it to feature as part of the overall response to an offence.

On the other side of this particular fault-line is the 'communitarian' tendency, which accepts that the victim's personal losses are not the only key interests in play. It favours some form of 'conferencing' process rather than a conventional court hearing as the most appropriate forum within which the key stake-holders, including the wider community, can be represented. There are a number of important differences in the way 'the community' is defined by different conferencing advocates, however, and once again it may be helpful to think in terms of a continuum within the communitarian approach rather than a single model. Some advocates of a conferencing approach identify the key stake-holders as encompassing all those who are 'concerned' in some way about the offence. They include those who are concerned for the well-being of either the victim or the offender, those who have concerns about the offence and its consequences, and those who may be able to contribute towards a solution to the problem presented by the offence. Collectively, this group of potential stake-holders is sometimes referred to as the 'community of interest' (Young and Morris 1998: 10), though 'offence community' might be an even more apposite term.

For other conferencing advocates the concept of 'community' means more than simply an extension of the 'bilateral' approach that is associated with the civilian tendency and also encompasses the 'community at large', whose interests may be 'represented' by those acting in an 'official' capacity such as the conference facilitator. Braithwaite and Mugford (1994: 147) and Moore (1993: 30), for example, have suggested that, in cases where the breach of social norms that is involved in an offence is inadequately addressed by the outcome that may have been negotiated between the conference participants, the facilitator has a duty to stress the wider public interest, and to seek to ensure that this is also reflected in the resulting plan of action.

This may be acceptable when the social norms in question are those that are associated with the liberal and tolerant 'republican' political tradition that Braithwaite himself espouses (Braithwaite and Pettit 1990). But what when this is not the case, as when 'restorative justice' processes are advocated within the context of local sectarian communities? Many of these are authoritarian, intolerant and unrestrainedly punitive in their attitudes towards 'wrongdoers', and possibly also towards those who are perceived to be deviant, or simply those who reject the prevailing social norms. And what when those informal community justice processes are intended to operate without recourse to the regular criminal justice system which, for all its failings, does at least afford some degree of protection against abuse of power and denials of due process? This is not a mere hypothetical example, and concerns have been raised (e.g. Cavadino *et al.* 1999: 48-50; Pavlich 2000; Crawford and Clear 2001; Walgrave 2002a) regarding the risks that restorative justice processes and rhetoric might be invoked to provide a façade not only for illiberal populism, but also for vigilantism and community despotism. These risks are not confined to divided and polarized communities such as might be found in parts of Northern Ireland (see Dignan and Lowey 2000) but are just as real and immediate in many 'ordinary' non-sectarian communities throughout England and Wales, as the recent controversy over the treatment of paedophiles all too graphically demonstrates.

In this section I have identified a split within the restorative justice movement between those who advocate a 'civilian approach' and those who advocate a 'communitarian approach' as alternatives to the regular criminal justice system. In both cases, I have suggested that these divergent tendencies are best seen as a continuum and that both may result in undesirable consequences, if taken to extremes. Although I believe that both mediation and conferencing have an important and valuable part to play as part of the overall response to crime they seem incapable of displacing altogether the 'regular' criminal justice system; nor does it seem desirable that they should. This conclusion throws into even sharper relief the third and, in many respects the most fundamental fault-line of all, concerning the relationship between 'restorative justice' on the one hand and 'criminal justice' on the other.

Third restorative justice fault-line: 'separatist' vs. 'integrationist' tendencies

Particularly in the early days of the restorative justice movement, there was a tendency for some of its most enthusiastic supporters (see e.g. Fattah 1995, 1998) not only to contrast it with the regular criminal justice system in the highly dichotomous terms to which I referred earlier, but also to present it as an alternative paradigm, that might, one day, come to displace the latter. However accurate or inaccurate such predictions may turn out to be in the fullness of time, they were barely plausible in the absence of a reasonably coherent and realistic 'transitional strategy', which was missing from most early accounts of restorative justice. Other restorative justice proponents have shown a surer appreciation of the 'realpolitikal' context within which the fledgling movement was struggling to assert itself.

Once again, however, two distinct schools of thought can be identified. On one side of this third restorative justice fault-line are those who argue for restorative justice programmes to operate completely outside the existing criminal justice system, in a supplementary capacity, rather than as a fully-fledged alternative to it.[16] Although this completely 'separatist' approach afforded a number of advantages during the early 'developmental' phase of the movement, these benefits were greatly outweighed by the considerable limitations that came to be experienced once the emphasis shifted from 'innovation' to 'implementation' (Dignan and Lowey 2000: 47). One of the biggest drawbacks with stand-alone programmes is the difficulty they almost invariably experience in recruiting and retaining sufficient numbers of referrals to remain viable. Another problem is the risk of 'double punishment' for offenders, if they take part in restorative justice programmes that operate entirely outwith the regular criminal justice system. But the biggest drawback of all with the 'separatist' approach is that 'it virtually ensures that a restorative justice approach will in practice be doomed to a precarious and marginal existence at the periphery of the criminal justice system. Consequently, whatever potential such an approach might have to offer as a means of contributing to the long-overdue reform of the existing criminal justice system is likely to remain unfulfilled' (Dignan and Lowey 2000: 48). If restorative justice is not to be 'doomed to irrelevance and marginality' in this way, then some form of accommodation with the regular criminal justice system will need to be devised, though it would be foolish to pretend that this approach is free from dangers of its own. One of the most obvious of these is the risk of co-optation, which could result in a distortion of its principal aims and a compromize of its own distinctive ethos.[17]

On the other side of the 'implementational fault-line', John Braithwaite has recently proposed a model showing how such an accommodation might be reached (see Chapter 8, Figure 8.1).

Although Braithwaite refers to the model as an integration of restorative, deterrent and incapacitative strategies, it may be more apposite to think of it as incorporating a hybrid or twin-track approach, in which restorative justice processes operate alongside deterrent and incapacitative measures rather than one that is systemically reorganized according to restorative justice principles. Thus, at the base of the enforcement pyramid, a restorative justice approach to criminal law enforcement is reserved exclusively for virtuous or well-intended actors (including repeat offenders up to a point) who are willing to enter into informal restorative justice negotiations in good faith. To guard against the risk of rational actors who might be tempted to pursue a 'free-loading' strategy by making a deceitful pretence at participating in a restorative justice negotiation, however, Braithwaite envisages an enforcement strategy based on the principle of 'active deterrence'. The latter involves the strategic use of escalating threats in response to recalcitrance on the part of the offender, and could result in custodial incapacitation. This aspect of Braithwaite's approach has provoked understandable concerns on the part of deserts-based theorists, who are alarmed at the absence of proportionality constraints. The danger with this kind of twin-track approach is that it could readily lend itself to an escalation in the level of punitive responses towards repeat and recalcitrant offenders.[18] Moreover, it does nothing to address the manifest defects of the existing system of punishments, about which restorative justice enthusiasts and just-deserts proponents alike are justifiably critical.

If restorative justice is to play a part in addressing these defects, then it will need to be founded on a very different type of enforcement strategy to the one proposed by Braithwaite. This in turn will necessitate a reconceptualization of restorative justice itself so that it is no longer tied to an informal consensual decision-making process requiring active participation by all the relevant stakeholders. For provision will also need to be made for all those cases that are deemed ineligible or inappropriate for referral to a diversionary informal restorative justice process (the 'recusants, the rejected and the recalcitrant', to use Ashworth's (2000: 9) alliterative terminology).[19]

Figure 9.1 shows an alternative enforcement model[20] that I have previously proposed in a slightly different context (Dignan 1994),[21] in which restorative justice is intended to operate as a systemic and fully integrated part of the 'regular' criminal justice system. One of the most important features of the model, however, is that the latter is itself radically reformed according to restorative justice precepts. This is essential in order to avoid the risks of co-optation that were referred to above. A second feature of the model is that it is intended to apply to both juvenile *and* adult offenders.

First, with regard to those offences that are currently diverted from prosecution by means of a caution or warning, a system that is formulated along restorative justice lines would need to incorporate procedures for ensuring that, where appropriate, the needs of victims could be

ASSUMPTION

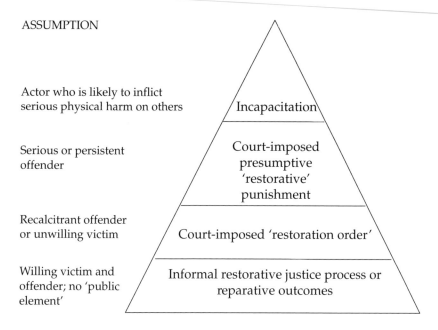

Actor who is likely to inflict
serious physical harm on others

Serious or persistent
offender

Recalcitrant offender
or unwilling victim

Willing victim and
offender; no 'public
element'

Figure 9.1. Toward a form of replacement discourse based on a 'systemic' model
of restorative justice

satisfactorily addressed. This could either take the form of a police-led
conferencing approach, of the kind described above, or alternatively the
police or other appropriate agencies (prosecution authorities for instance)
could be given the power to promote or impose suitable reparative
undertakings. For example, an offender might agree to apologize to a
victim, or to provide direct reparation if appropriate and desired by the
victim, or alternatively might be required to undertake a limited amount
of indirect reparation for the benefit of the community. Before the
introduction of the recent youth justice reforms in England and Wales,
limited attempts had been made in some areas to develop such an
approach, which was known as 'caution plus'. Likewise, the police in New
Zealand also have similar powers when dealing with the 70 per cent or so
of offenders who are cautioned each year, though this mechanism for
securing 'restorative outcomes' is usually overshadowed by the attention
that is devoted to the much better known family group conferencing
system.

For cases that are too serious to be diverted in this way, the standard
response for the vast majority of criminal offences, as in Braithwaite's

model, would again be for the matter to be dealt with, where possible, by means of the most appropriate restorative justice process (victim–offender mediation, restorative conference etc.). Provided that reparation is agreed and performed to the satisfaction of both parties, and at least where there is no evidence of a lengthy history of similar offences, the fact that the offender has been willing to make suitable amends should normally be taken as evidence of a renewed respect for the rights of others. In the absence of any other 'public element', the case for any additional punishment in such cases would appear very weak. However, it would still be desirable to incorporate some form of 'judicial oversight' in such cases.[22] This is partly to ensure that whatever is agreed by the parties does not exceed a reasonable level of reparation, and partly in order to safeguard the public interest (i.e. the human rights of people other than the individual victim and offender), for example in cases where the victim does not seek any reparation from the offender despite suffering serious personal harm.

Recourse to the courts would not normally be allowed unless either the accused denied guilt, the victim was unwilling to participate in any way, the parties were unable to reach agreement on the subject of reparation or the offender refused to make reparation as agreed. In cases such as these (which include not only Braithwaite's rational free-loading actor but also other cases in which informal restorative justice processes might not be considered suitable), the court would necessarily become the 'default option' (see also Wundersitz 1994: 94). However, the sentencing powers of the courts would be restricted in such cases to the imposition of a 'restoration order', which would either entail compensation or reparation for the victim, or else some form of restorative justice-based community service. There would thus be no need for a strategy of 'active deterrence', of the kind advocated by Braithwaite, since the court would in principle be able to enforce compliance on the part of offenders making a deceitful pretence at co-operation.

In more serious cases, (including cases in which the offender has unreasonably refused to make adequate amends, or there is a prolonged history of repeat offending followed by a refusal to make adequate reparation), greater weight would need to be placed on the 'public' aspect of the offence. In cases such as these, the offender could be said to represent a potential threat to the rights of other law-abiding citizens, whose interests therefore need also to be taken into account in determining the final outcome. However, this 'rights-based' approach also requires the 'private element' to be addressed. Consequently, an opportunity should still be afforded for suitable reparation to be informally negotiated in such cases. And due weight would need to be given by the court to the outcome of such negotiations when determining the kind and amount of additional punishment that might be appropriate, since a willingness to undertake reparation does represent an acknowledgement that an offender has done wrong. It could also indicate a commitment to respect other people's rights in future. Where no adequate reparation is forthcoming, however, or reparation alone is not an adequate response to the 'public' element that needs to be addressed, what principles should apply regarding the type and amount of punishment to which an offender should be liable?

Rethinking the role of non-custodial penalties within a systemic model of restorative justice

If restorative justice *is* to furnish a more constructive alternative to the current repressive approach, it will be necessary to reformulate the existing range of punishments so that, as far as possible, every kind of penalty applies restorative justice principles in the pursuit of restorative outcomes. Some existing forms of punishment are already geared (in principle at least) towards the pursuit of broadly restorative outcomes – notably compensation orders and reparation orders. At present, however, the way in which compensation works is far from ideal from a restorative perspective (Cavadino *et al*. 1999: 175). Compensation orders are not always considered despite a statutory duty on courts to do so. And even when compensation is imposed, the duty to take the offender's financial circumstances into account means that it may not represent the full amount that the victim has lost as a result of the crime, particularly where the offender has committed a number of offences with multiple victims. Moreover, the victim often has to wait a considerable time for any compensation to be paid, frequently in small sums according to the means of the offender; and often having to go back to the court when instalments are missed.

Furthermore, the kind of reparation that such penalties are capable of providing is inferior in many respects to the kind of reparation that might be expected to emanate from an appropriate restorative justice process. For example, it is far less flexible, is less likely to address the particular needs and sensitivities of the parties, and lacks the empowering potential that may ensue when victims and offenders are given the opportunity to participate actively in the offence resolution process. But in less serious cases that do not lend themselves to restorative justice processes for one reason or another, the use of a compensation (or reparation) order is nevertheless likely to result in a more constructive and restorative outcome than is likely to emanate from most other conventional forms of punishment, particularly if it is modified to take account of some of the operational shortcomings identified above.

Another conventional form of punishment that could in principle be modified in pursuit of restorative outcomes is the fine. This is not the case at present, since the revenue that is generated by fines is paid to the Treasury. But in principle it would be possible to strengthen the reparative potential of the fine. One way of achieving this would be to develop closer links between the fine and the compensation order, which might also attend to some of the deficiencies that have already been noted. For example, the income from fines (and also from proceeds that are con-fiscated from convicted offenders) could be used to create a 'Reparation Fund' that would enable victims to be compensated immediately.[23] The fund could then be reimbursed by the offender at whatever rate the court feels is appropriate after taking account of the offender's financial circumstances. There is still an important distinction between the fine, a financial compensation order that is imposed on an offender by the court, and a voluntary agreement on the part of an offender to make reparation (whether financial or non-financial) to a victim. Although the latter is preferable, it is not always achievable and, in such cases, it would be consistent with the idea of restorative justice as a form of 'replacement discourse' to develop a much more explicit and transparent link between crimes which infringes the right and well-being of others, including the community at large, and the principle of reparation for such wrongs.

It may also be possible to adapt other penalties, such as the community service order, to ensure that they are capable of producing more reparative outcomes (Cavadino *et al.* 1999: ch. 4; Walgrave 1999), though it will almost certainly be necessary to divest them of their more overtly repressive and denunciatory elements in order to do so. Thus, as Bottoms (2000) has recently pointed out, the community service order can be, and often is, conceptualized in an unambiguously punitive manner as a 'fine on the offender's time', as where an offender is required to undertake meaning-less and sometimes demeaning tasks that are unrelated to the crime.[24] However, it can also be conceptualized in a straightforwardly reparative manner as a more constructive and meaningful undertaking that is more closely related to the original offence, particularly where the victim is keen to receive direct reparation. Alternatively, it could be conceptualized as a more broadly restorative or reintegrative intervention. This might be attempted, for example, where the task is related to the offender's skills or interests, or is intended to reinforce the offender's sense of self-esteem by providing a meaningful and worthwhile service to others. It is important to note at this point that, although these 'reparative' or 'restorative' variants of the community service concept may be preferable to the more denunciatory and repressive versions, they are nevertheless still punitive. For, however benevolent the motive for resorting to them, they are nevertheless imposed deliberately on offenders, and require them to act in ways that they would not otherwise have wanted to. So their imposition still requires a defensible moral justification, and needs to be subjected to appropriate normative restrictions regarding length or severity, just as with any other punitive intervention.

With regard to other forms of non-custodial punishment, the restorative potential may not be so clearly discernible, but is rarely completely absent. In the case of probation, for example, attempts to promote compliance with the law by engaging in normative dialogue with an offender have some affinity with the kind of discourse that is encouraged during restorative justice processes such as conferencing. In principle it would be possible to move probation practice much closer to a model involving the 'dialogic regulation of social life' of the kind that is posited by Braithwaite (1999: 60) as part of the conferencing process. This might be done, for example, by encouraging probation officers to involve other people – including those that the offender cares about and also victims where appropriate – during discussions about the offence and the offending behaviour that gave rise to it.

Even the imposition of more restrictive measures such as curfew orders (with or without electronic monitoring) could in principle help to promote restorative outcomes; for example if they are adopted to enable an offender to maintain a job and so undertake financial reparation for a victim instead of being given a custodial sentence.[25] However, there is also a danger of 'up-tariffing' where such measures are used as substitutes for other forms of non-custodial punishment, or the conditions that are imposed are so restrictive that the offender faces an increased likelihood of imprisonment in the event of a breach (see also Roberts and Roach 2002). The risk of up-tariffing is likely to be lower where such measures are introduced within the context of a 'systemic' model that prioritizes restorative outcomes, but it would be naïve to imagine that it could be eliminated altogether; hence once again the need for effective constraints on the amount of punishment that can be imposed (see Dignan 2002), and for effective procedural safeguards to ensure that those constraints are observed.

It is also worth noting that even within a punishment system in which the primary aim is to repair the harm caused by an offence and promote the restoration of victims, offenders and communities, this does not necessarily preclude the pursuit of other sentencing aims such as rehabilitation or even public protection in appropriate cases (see below). Indeed, many victims would like to feel that any response to 'their' offence would reduce the likelihood of others being victimized in the way they have been, irrespective of their views on the subject of personal reparation for themselves.

Rethinking the role of imprisonment within a systemic model of restorative justice

So far I have been arguing that, even in cases for which informal restorative justices processes may be inappropriate, inapplicable or inadequate by themselves, it is possible to envisage a range of non-custodial court-imposed punishments that could be adapted to promote restorative outcomes. To this extent, at least, restorative justice could form the basis of a 'replacement discourse' in which the emphasis would be on more constructive and less repressive forms of intervention.[26] The use of custody would not normally be permitted within this kind of approach because it is rarely consistent with the pursuit of restorative outcomes. For that reason, it would not be routinely available as either a purely punitive or a deterrent measure, whether in an active or passive sense.

The use of custody would not be prohibited altogether, however, since some offenders do threaten the freedom and well-being of others to such an extent that protective measures are called for. But it would need to be strictly reserved instead for offenders who pose a serious and continuing threat to the personal safety of others.[27] Even where custodial sentences are warranted, however, much more could and should be done to promote restorative outcomes, for example by enabling offenders to undertake adequately paid work in prison in order to provide financial compensation for or on behalf of their victims. Moreover, experience in a wide range of penal jurisdictions has shown that there is also scope for facilitating victim–offender mediation in appropriate cases within a prison context. In England and Wales, for example, some victim–offender mediation services (notably those serving the West Yorkshire[28] and West Midland areas) have regularly mediated in serious cases where the offender is either still serving, or has recently been released from, a custodial sentence. In Belgium each of the 30 prisons now has its own restorative justice counsellor, whose responsibilities include the facilitation of a wide range of restorative activities (including but not restricted to mediation between victim and offender where requested) during the detention period (Verstraete *et al.* 2000).

Equally important, however, is the need to apply wherever possible relevant insights that are derived from experience with informal restorative justice processes to the regulation of social life within the prison setting. Thus, much more could and should be done to foster constructive and mutually respectful relationships between staff and prison inmates, since such interactions normally afford the only context within which any kind of constructive dialogue, emotional engagement and behavioural or attitudinal change is likely to be possible (Cavadino and Dignan 2002: 214ff). Within this setting, there is also a strong argument for adopting normative or 'moralistic' forms of reasoning with offenders. This kind of 'relational' approach is not only more humane and respectful of the rights of offenders, but offers a potentially much more constructive and effective response than the cruder forms of instrumental reasoning based on sanctions and incentives that have typically been favoured – all too often with predictably damaging consequences – in the past (Liebling 2001).

Conclusions

In this chapter I have identified a number of potentially seismic 'fault-lines' running through the restorative justice movement. In the early days of the movement, the existence of these fault-lines was of relatively little consequence and, indeed, was almost entirely overlooked. But as the influence of restorative justice grows stronger, and particularly as it increasingly attracts the interest of criminal justice and penal policy-makers, the existence of such fault-lines can no longer be overlooked; nor can their significance be denied. For it is important, not only to be aware of the different tendencies within the movement, and the policy options with which they are associated, but also to be prepared to make some hard choices about the directions in which, and terms on which, restorative justice policies should be developed in the future. In this chapter I have argued against the tendency to equate restorative justice exclusively with a particular kind of informal dispute resolution process; against the tendency to adopt extreme and potentially damaging 'civilian' or 'communitarian' positions; and against a policy of 'separatism' *vis-à-vis* the regular criminal justice system. Instead, I have advocated the need to be at least as much concerned about the promotion of restorative outcomes as the promotion of restorative justice processes; and the need for restorative justice to operate within, and as a fully integrated part of, the regular criminal justice system. But above all else I have argued for restorative justice precepts to be used as a catalyst for reform of the entire criminal justice and penal systems. My hope is that the promotion of 'restorative outcomes' may become the primary goal of the entire system instead of an incidental product of an admirable process that functions intermittently and inconsistently on the margins of that system.

Notes

1. An earlier and much less developed version of this chapter was presented at the fifth international conference of the International Network for Research on Restorative Justice for Juveniles, entitled 'Positioning Restorative Justice', which was held in Leuven on 16–19 September 2001. The current version has benefitted from comments made by Michael Cavadino, David Miers, Gwen Robinson and Lode Walgrave, though none of these colleagues should be held responsible for the final product.
2. See for example the American Friends Service Committee (1971); and also the Canadian Ouimet Report (Canada, 1969) as cited by Roach (2000: 265).
3. To insist on distinguishing between punitive measures and restorative justice measures is strategically inadvisable because it is likely to alienate other campaigners for penal reform, notably those associated with the just deserts movement, who might otherwise be supportive of a more principled approach.
4. There is arguably a fourth fault-line, separating those restorative justice advocates whose approach is principally 'offender-focused', and those whose approach is principally 'victim-focused', but this is not an issue that I am proposing to address in this chapter.
5. This process, involving as it does some form of dialogue between the principal 'stake-holders', may itself produce a variety of 'outcomes'. One such outcome is a subjective sense of 'having been restored' as a result of the process. But other, more tangible, outcomes in the form of material reparation are also possible. However, for many restorative justice advocates it is the dialogical process itself that constitutes the essential meaning of restorative justice, rather than any consequential outcomes to which it may give rise.
6. As in the 'Standards for Restorative Justice' (SINRJ) that have been formulated by the Restorative Justice Consortium (1999 and 2002).
7. Approximately 70 per cent of young offenders in New Zealand are cautioned, leaving a maximum of 30 per cent whose cases may be dealt with by means of a family group conference.
8. As in the 'Wagga Wagga' model that operated, for a time, in New South Wales (see Moore and O'Connell, 1994), from which a number of other police-led conferencing initiatives have been derived, including one operating in the Thames Valley in England (see Hoyle et al. 2002). The latter has been endorsed by the Home Office (2000) as a model for other police forces to emulate.
9. These were introduced by the Crime and Disorder Act in 1998 and were implemented nationally in June 2000, after a period in which they were piloted in a small number of areas. Reparation orders were envisaged as an 'entry level' penalty for offenders who might in the past have been dealt with by means of a conditional discharge.

10. Introduced by the Youth Justice and Criminal Evidence Act 1999. Like the reparation order, these were also piloted at first, and were 'rolled out' nationally in April 2002. N.B. Referral orders need not be imposed where the offence is considered sufficiently serious to warrant a custodial penalty.

11. See also, Miers *et al.* (2001: 25). This government-funded study of seven pioneering English restorative justice schemes (five of which dealt principally with juveniles and two with adults) reported even lower rates of direct mediation for all but two of the schemes (both of which dealt with juvenile offenders) in which the rates were 13 per cent and 19 per cent.

12. Notably the Canberra RISE experiment, and also the Wagga Wagga conferencing evaluation. Here, recorded rates of victim participation are as high as 85 per cent (Braithwaite 1999a: 22) and over 90 per cent (Moore and O'Connell 1994) respectively. In marked contrast, the rate of victim participation in the Thames Valley Cautioning project was 16 per cent overall, diminishing slightly over the three years of the project (Hoyle *et al.* 2002).

13. Various problems have been identified. They include tensions between conflicting objectives such as a desire to 'speed up' the system of trial and the need to allow adequate time for victim consultation; and also difficulties arising from the restrictive way in which recently introduced data protection legislation has been interpreted; see Dignan 2000, Holdaway *et al.* 2001 for further details.

14. Another approach involves the use of 'surrogate' victims, though care is needed in the selection and preparation of such victims to ensure both that they are suitably motivated and that they are not themselves further victimized as a result of their experience (Dignan, 2000: 25).

15. Likewise, the referral order evaluation reported that a range of creative and innovative approaches was being developed in some of the pilot areas, to promote other forms of victim input into the panels (Newburn *et al.* 2002: 44).

16. Those who have advocated a 'separatist' or 'stand-alone' approach as the basis for developing restorative justice programmes include Wright 1991; Marshall and Merry 1990, and Davis *et al.* 1992.

17. Such problems were associated with some of the earliest attempts to develop restorative justice initiatives alongside the regular criminal justice system (Davis *et al.* 1988; 1989).

18. Such concerns are by no means fanciful. In England and Wales Halliday's report (2001: 15) recommends the introduction of an explicit presumption that the severity of a sentence should no longer be determined primarily by the seriousness of a given offence, but also by the degree of persistence shown by an offender.

19. Similar considerations may also apply even in those jurisdictions (for example New Zealand), where restorative justice processes such as conferencing have been mainstreamed, in cases where victims decline to participate or offenders prove recalcitrant.

20. This model was itself adapted from one that had originally been proposed by Braithwaite (1991) in the context of business or agency regulation.

21. As part of an initial attempt to set out a 'transitional strategy' showing how restorative justice might be integrated into the regular criminal justice system. See also Walgrave (2000), whose proposals for the reform of the Belgian juvenile justice system have independently adopted a similar course.
22. As in the New Zealand family group conferencing model.
23. Similar forms of hypothecation already operate within the criminal justice system; for example the channelling of the confiscated financial gains of drug offenders into programmes working to combat drug abuse and proposals to channel income from speeding fines to cover the cost of installing and operating road-side cameras. Moreover, the government has recently indicated (Home Office 2001: para. 3.118) that it is contemplating the creation of a Victims Fund to ensure that every victim receives immediate payment of any compensation that is ordered.
24. For example one of the areas piloting reparation orders under the Crime and Disorder Act 1998 routinely required offenders to redecorate 'derelict' houses that no one lived in (Holdaway *et al.* 2001: 91).
25. The use of conditional sentences of imprisonment in Canada provides an interesting example of an attempt to pursue restorative outcomes in sentencing as an explicit alternative to imprisonment (see Roberts and Roach 2002) even though the Canadian sentencing system as a whole falls a long way short of the 'systemic' approach that is advocated here.
26. At the risk of being overly repetitive, this argument is not based on a dichotomous approach, in which restorative justice interventions are heralded as an alternative to punishment; rather, they are advocated as a less destructive form of punishment, albeit one that still stands in need of moral justification and has to be subject to the standard normative safeguards that have been referred to above.
27. There may also be a case for using imprisonment as a default sanction in order to secure compliance with a non-custodial order, but this would only be justifiable in fairly limited circumstances where the offence itself was serious and all other non-custodial options had been tried and failed.
28. See, for example, Wynne 1996.

Chapter 10

Restorative justice and the law: socio-ethical and juridical foundations for a systemic approach

Lode Walgrave

Introduction

Restorative justice basically is a bottom-up approach to the settlement of the aftermath of a crime. Its re-emergence is based on deep dissatisfaction with traditional criminal justice, which is reproached for being guided by top-down rules, leading to alienation from real life. Instead, informal deliberation – as a means of repairing harm caused by crime – is advanced as a more effective and appropriate response than formal interventions in law enforcement. Restorative justice has been a succes so far. In two or three decades, it has become all over the world a busy field of experimentation, an important domain of empirical and theoretical research and of socio-ethical reflection, and a crucial theme in the debates on juvenile justice and criminal justice reform. Its success has helped promote restorative justice as the mainstream response to crime, raising high on the agenda the question of how to incorporate it into the principles of a democratic constitutional state. In other words, how to find an appropriate relationship between restorative justice and its support for informal deliberative processes, and the law in a democratic state, with its need for formalization and external control?

The search for this relationship requires several steps. First, the essentials of the restorative option on doing justice must be unravelled. Second, specific 'particularities' of this option must explain why the relationship between restorative justice and the law cannot just replicate the way traditional criminal justice is legalized. Finally, these particularities will make it possible to conceive a system which would guarantee to all parties democratic rights and freedoms, while leaving maximum space for informal deliberation in constructively settling the aftermath of an offence.

This chapter is not conceived as a synthesis of the positions taken earlier in this volume. The authors of the preceding chapters have been invited to contribute because of their original, often controversial standpoints on themes which are important in the discussion on the relation between restorative justice and the law, not because they present complementary views which together could provide a coherent model. Different approaches have been sought deliberately because they provoke additional reflection and debate. The positions and arguments set out in this final chapter have often been supported by the earlier chapters, but often also deviate from them. Agreements deliver additional arguments. Disagreements offer opportunities for clarification and challenges for justification.

Restorative justice

While no generally accepted definition of restorative justice exists, I refer to an earlier definition (Bazemore and Walgrave 1999: 48), and consider restorative justice as 'an option on doing justice which is primarily oriented towards restoring the harm that has been caused by a crime'. From this definition, three important comments are derived. (1) Restorative justice is characterized by its aim of restoration, and not by the process which typically favours restorative outcomes. This definition thus also includes interventions as a means of restoration which are not based on voluntary deliberative processes. (2) Restorative justice considers all kinds of harm caused by a crime, including the harm to social life. As a consequence, there is a need to define the public interests and harm to be restored, and to find out how they may be included in the processes and procedures towards restoration. (3) The focus on the reparation of the harm caused by the offence constitutes a paradigm shift. It is the key difference from both the punishment and the treatment approaches to crime, which focus on the kind of treatment which the offender is to undergo. Basically, restorative justice is neither punishment nor treatment oriented. It follows that procedures to achieve reparation cannot be just copies of the existing procedural rules.

Including coercion in restorative justice

Defining restorative justice by its aim of restoration is not commonly accepted. Many restorative justice proponents consider voluntary deliberative processes in an informal context as the key to restorative justice (Marshall 1996; McCold 2000; Boyes-Watson 2000). In this volume, Adam Crawford considers the 'deliberative potential of restorative justice' as 'its primary *raison d'être* and over-arching principle' (Ch. 6: 123). George Pavlich (Ch. 1) typifies restorative justice as basically an exercise of 'being with others' in a context of 'hospitality'. They all rightly promote informal voluntary settlements as being crucial for achieving the fullest degree of restoration. The communicative potential of mediation and family group conferences indeed favours the authentic assessment of the harm suffered and may more easily lead to a true agreement on how it can be reasonably repaired or compensated. The offender's acceptance of the need to compensate the victim expresses his understanding of the wrongs committed and harms caused, and his compliance with social norms; the recognition of harm confirms the value and recognizes the rights of the victim. This is all much more restorative for the victim, community and for the offender as well, than if a sanction on the offender is simply imposed.

Nevertheless, restorative justice cannot be reduced to such a process, for two reasons. First, as Daniel Van Ness also argues in Chapter 7, a process cannot be defined and valued without referring to the purpose for which it is undertaken. Defining a process without referring to the goal it aims at is like pedalling in the air. The process is valued not because of the deliberation on its own, but because of the outcomes it helps to achieve. Why would a deliberative process be more 'restorative'? Because the expressions of remorse, compassion, apology and forgiveness which it facilitates lead more easily to feelings of being respected, of peace and satisfaction. These feelings are outcomes, even if they are not explicitly written in the agreement.

Secondly, restricting restorative justice to voluntary deliberations would 'limit its scope – possibly drastically' (Dignan, Ch. 9), and condemn it to the margins of the system. One can imagine two models here. In the currently predominant model, the mainstream response to crime is coercive and punitive, but the criminal justice system can refer a number of cases to deliberative restorative processes. As the system is the gate-keeper to the opportunites for restoration, it will probably refer less serious cases only, excluding from the restorative benefits the many victims who most need restoration. John Braithwaite proposes another model which functions the other way round (Ch. 8). Restorative processes are given priority, but they are complemented by punishment when they cannot be achieved. This option will be discussed at greater length later in the chapter, but the problem I see here is that it would lead to two separate systems, one restorative for offenders and victims of goodwill, one punitive and exclusionary for the others. Giving up priority for restoration at a certain point seems to hand over a category of citizens to the punitive a priorism, its unethical and inefficient aspects included.

Therefore, the recognition of deliberative processes as crucial tools to enhance the quality of restorative practice must not lead us to consider them to be the key characteristics of restorative justice. Restoration is the key objective. In many cases, agreement cannot be reached or may be insufficient, for a variety of possible reasons. Coercion may then be considered, but so far as possible it must still primarily serve restoration. In Chapter 9, Jim Dignan lists a number of possible restorative sanctions. We can think of imposing formal restitution or compensation, paying a fine or doing work for the benefit of a victims' fund, or community service. Other forms of deprivation of liberty, such as an enforced stay in a closed facility, are used to enforce compliance with the restorative sanctions, or to incapacitate offenders who are considered to represent a high risk to public safety. Granted, such sanctions do not fulfill the potential of the restorative paradigm completely, because they are enforced and do not result from voluntary agreements. This is, however, no reason to give up the principle of priority for restoration and to leave the floor to punitiveness. As Daniel Van Ness (Ch. 7) and others (McCold 2000) point out, restorative justice is not just a black and white option; restoration can be achieved in different degrees.

This position provokes a challenge for legalizing restorative justice. Possible coercive sanctions with the objective of achieving restoration can indeed only be imposed by the judicial system. However, as is evident in earlier chapters, especially chapter 9, judicial procedures and sanctions also can be considered from a restorative perspective (see also Bazemore and Walgrave 1999; Walgrave 2000).

Defining public harm in restorative justice

The harm considered for reparation by restorative justice includes all kinds of damage and suffering, as far as it has been caused by a particular crime. Restorative justice thus addresses material damage, psychological and other forms of suffering in the victim and his[1] proximate environment, but also the harm to social and public life, and the social damage which the offender has caused to himself by his offence.

This subsection focuses on the harm to social and public life. Its inclusion in the restorative scope makes clear that restorative justice is not limited to settling a tort according to civil law, but deals with crimes, which are also public events traditionally subject to criminal law. A major problem is to define this public harm. What makes a crime a crime and not a tort should also be asked from a restorative perspective. In traditional retributive justice, legal order is seen as the value to be preserved, but this is too abstract and too top-down a value for restorative justice. For this justice option the need is to come closer to what is experienced in community life, and to define the problem in terms of harm. The notion of 'collectivity' undeniably suffers harm by the occurrence of crime. That becomes obvious through considering what would happen if the community and/or society were not to intervene after the occurrence of an offence; besides the possible material damage, the community would probably suffer from a loss of peace. The victim and his supporters (family, peers) would not accept what had been done, and they would try to 'make things even'; acts of revenge might escalate into a kind of vendetta, dragging down the community as a whole. The community would lose its peace and be dominated by the fear of crime. It would affect the general quality of life through the loss of solidarity and mutual respect. Common values might fade away. What is at stake here is more than just the individual victim's losses; an offence is a threat to peace and quality of life in the community, which it will lose if nothing is done about it.

But the state has much to lose also. If institutionalized society does not intervene adequately against crime, the public's belief in public rules and in the authorities' power to preserve order and justice in social life will diminish. People would not feel secure, and see each other as rivals and the government as a threat. Society would collapse or would deteriorate into tyranny.

As Daniel Van Ness writes: '... government's role is to establish and preserve a just order and ... community's role is to build and preserve a just peace' (Ch. 7: 41–2, see also Van Ness and Strong 2002). McCold considers macro-communities and society/government as secondary stakeholders, and lists a number of injuries, needs and responsibilities (McCold 2000). But still the question remains of how to define them in a way which allows the link to legal formalization and inclusion into the constitutional democratic state. This is a major challenge for restorative justice. How to define and measure the public or collective interests? How to organize representation? How to achieve possible reparation of public harms? Later on in this chapter, we shall base our proposal on the dominion concept advanced by Braithwaite and Pettit (1990).

Restorative justice as an original paradigm

Contrary to both punitive and rehabilitative justice, restorative justice is not primarily concerned with the kind of action to which the offender must submit. Restorative justice therefore represents an original paradigm. Restoration can in fact proceed a considerable distance without the involvement of the offender. If the offender is not caught, while the harm inflicted is assessed, (partial) justice should be done by trying to repair or compensate the victim, which also is crucial to restoring the public's assurance that the crime is rejected.

The authorities' action in involving the offender in the aftermath of the offence is a means of enhancing the restoration of both the victim and public confidence. It expresses disapproval of the norm transgression, and it contributes to the reassurance of the norm and norm enforcement, in the public, the victim and the offender as well. A consistent restorative justice approach implicates the offender not primarily because something must be done to him, but because it will promote restoration. The nature and extent of obligation is determined by the needs of reasonable restoration, not by the needs of adequate treatment, nor of proportionate punishment.

This position raises questions on the relation between restorative justice and both rehabilitative and punitive justice. Chapter 3 by Gordon Bazemore and Sandra O'Brien and Chapter 4 by Ido Weijers deal with the question of rehabilitation, but from different positions. Ido Weijers examines family group conferencing, but only in so far as it may contribute to offender rehabilitation. 'An FGC [Family Group Conference] aims, first of all, to make an emotional and moral appeal to the young offender…' (Ch. 4: 74). He states, for example, that the conference must rely on basic trust between the adolescent and his parents, and that in cases of absence of such trust, 'a FGC approach must be excluded' (Ch. 4: 79). How family group conferences contribute to restoring harm to victims and community is no part of this view. It is difficult therefore to hold to this approach to the restorative justice perspective, because it does not correspond to the definition we have advanced. It uses the family group conference as a technique for rehabilitation, not for restoration.[2] It does not fully recognise the needs of the victims, and chooses the path of rehabilitation, including the risks of neglecting legal rights (Feld 1999).

In Chapter 3, Gordon Bazemore and Sandra O'Brien repeatedly make clear that they adhere to the core idea 'that doing justice requires repairing the harm of crime', and that 'presenting restorative justice as primarily aimed at reducing recidivism is inappropriate' (Ch. 3: 32). Within that framework, however, they argue that 'there is great untapped potential in the application of core restorative values and principles to treatment and rehabilitation' (Ch. 3: 32). Priority for restoration sets the scene, but the broader picture can (and must) include rehabilitative concerns. As we have seen, the advantages of this position are, first, that it seems socio-ethically more constructive, and, second, that it provides a better foundation for constructing a decent legal framework than do the 'preventionist' (Braithwaite and Pettit 1990: 133–136) rehabilitative justice systems.

Whereas restoration and rehabilitation appear not to be intrinsically contradictory, this is different for restoration and punishment. We shall devote an entire section to this crucial distinction, which will at the same time make clear the peculiarities of restorative justice with respect to its legalization.

The awareness that restorative responses are not limited to voluntary deliberative processes, and that they also need to include repair of collective harms, makes it essential to provide a proper legal context for this. Retributivists, for example, express deep scepticism toward restorative justice, because of what they observe as shortcomings in procedural and sentencing safeguards (Ashworth 1993; von Hirsch 1998; Feld 1999). However, there is no reason to believe that retributivism would have the monopoly of safeguarding rights.[3] John Braithwaite advances strong arguments for saying that 'the right punishment ... according to some retributive theory will almost always be the wrong solution to the problem. By wrong I mean less just' (Ch. 8: 158). The remainder of this chapter will develop arguments for the position that restoration must remain clearly distinguished from punishment, in order to ensure that responses to crime are more ethically just, and that restoration has the potential to provide answers which are also legally just.

Crucial distinctions between restoration and punishment

The relation between restoration and punishment is increasingly being debated. Among restorative justice adherents, the discussion has been furthered by Daly (2000), who put forward the opinion that restorative justice 'should embrace the concept of punishment as the main activity of the state's response to crime' (Daly 2000: 34), and by McCold (2000), who rejected the possible inclusion of coercive sanctions within the restorative frame, because that would shift restorative justice back to being punitive.

In this volume, different positions are advanced. Antony Duff in Chapter 5 considers a punitive response to crime to be indispensable, but he tries to combine this with the communicative potential of restorative responses (see also Duff 2001). For him, 'restorative justice processes are not alternatives to punitive "pain delivery": they are themselves ways of trying to induce the appropriate kind of pain' (Ch. 5: 97). John Braithwaite in Chapter 8 makes a clear distinction between both, but he reserves the label 'restorative' for deliberative processes, while accepting that restorative responses can fall short in certain cases, so that punitive justice (with possibly some restorative additions) must take over (see also Braithwaite 2002a). According to Jim Dignan in Chapter 9 coercive sanctions should also be oriented as much as possible toward reparation, but he calls them restorative punishments (see also Dignan 2002). My position, in this Chapter 10, is very close to Jim Dignan's, but rejects the term 'punishment' (see also Walgrave 2002). At first sight, this may seem a quibbling over words, but it is not, as I will try to make clear in the following subsections.

Intentional pain infliction versus awareness of painfulness

Much depends, of course, on how 'punishment' is defined. Authors like McCold (2000), Daly (2000) and Johnstone (2002) consider every painful obligation after a wrong committed to be a punishment, as does Jim Dignan (Ch. 9) in this volume. In that case, obligations in view of reparation can certainly be called punishments. There is, however, a crucial difference between obligations which are inevitably painful, like paying taxes, and obligations which are imposed with the purpose of causing pain, like paying a fine. As we shall see, the difference is crucial for socio-ethical reasons, and for communicational reasons. Therefore, rather than speaking of 'intentionally painful punishments' and 'inevitably painful punishments', I prefer, like others, to reserve the word 'punishment' for the intentionally painful obligations.

'Punishing someone consists of visiting a deprivation (hard treatment) on him, because he supposedly has committed a wrong, ...'[4] (von Hirsch 1993 :9). Three elements are distinguished: hard treatment, the intention of inflicting it, and the link with the wrong committed before. If one of these elements is lacking, there is no punishment. Intentionally inflicting pain which is not linked to a wrongful act is not punishment. Painful obligations which are not imposed with the intention of causing suffering are not punishments. 'Pain in punishment is inflicted for the sake of pain...' (Fatic 1995: 197).

The crux lies in the intention. Equating every painful obligation with punishment after a wrong done is based on a mistaken 'psychological location' of the painfulness. The key lies in the head of the punisher, not in that of the punished. It is the punisher who considers an action to be wrong and who wants the wrongdoer to suffer for it. Even if a juvenile sees the punishment first of all as a prestigious event for his reputation in his peer group, it will remain a punishment. Conversely, if he feels the obligation of reparation as being hard, and calls it 'a punishment', it actually is no punishment if the intention of the judge was not to make the juvenile suffer, but rather to request from him a reasonable contribution to reparation.

However, the relation between obliged restoration and pain is more complicated. Not taking the hardship of a restorative obligation into account could lead to draconian results. Obliging a deprived juvenile who stole and crashed a Jaguar to pay the full value of the car would condemn him to a lifetime of paying by instalment, and poverty. This would be unacceptable. Even if there is no intention to inflict pain, there must be an awareness of the painful effects, which should be taken into account. The boy will have to make an effort at reparation, which will probably transcend the material repayment. The material part will be reduced to a small amount, in view of the boy's financial, mental and social capacities, and his future. The remaining material damage to the victim should be paid by insurance or by a victims' fund.

In deciding upon the restorative obligation, its possible painfulness is thus an element. But knowing that something will hurt, and taking the suffering into account, is not the same as intentionally inflicting hurt. Pain in restorative justice is only a reason to eventually reduce the obligation, never to augment it. In retribution, on the contrary, the painfulness is the principal yardstick, and its amount may be increased or decreased in order to achieve proportionality in punishment. In restoration, a relation may be sought between the nature and seriousness of the harm and the restorative effort,[5] but painfulness can lead to its decrease only, never to its increase.

As we shall see, the importance of this difference lies in its ethical consequences. I shall argue that imposing an obligation to repair is ethically superior to intentionally inflicting pain, even if that is linked to a wrong committed. 'Repair is a very different value to punishment as hard treatment; repair does not have to hurt, though of course it often does' (Braithwaite Ch. 8: 166).

Punishment and communication as means, restoration as the goal

Punishment is a means which can be used to enforce any legal system. It is an act of power to express disapproval, possibly to enforce compliance, but it is neutral about the value system it enforces. Restoration, on the contrary, is not a means, but an outcome. The broad scope of restoration that we have in mind expresses its orientation to the quality of social life, as a normative beacon.

Traditional criminal justice conceives of punishment as the *a priori* means of the intervention, aiming to achieve a variety of possible goals. In contrast, restorative justice advances restoration in the broader sense as the objective, and chooses among a diversity of social and legal means and methods to pursue this objective. Punishment is not the most appropriate way to achieve restoration. On the contrary, the *a priori* option for punishment generally is a serious obstruction to possible restoration.[6] The priority for the procedure for determining the proportionate punishment is an often decisive intervention that pays attention to the harm and suffering done to victims; the penalty itself seriously hampers the offender's efforts toward reparation and compensation.

Especially counterproductive is the communicative poorness of the *a priori* option for punishment. Probably the most important function of criminal justice is to be a beacon of social disapproval, to show clear limits which are observable to all. After a crime has been committed, disapproval must be expressed in such a way that it is understood and accepted by all concerned. The *a priori* option for punishment in criminal justice, however, interferes with effective and constructive communication. Disapproval expressed by the criminal sentence may communicate a clear message to the public at large, but it fails to communicate adequately to the other key actors in the crime, namely the victim and the offender. Good communication needs adequate settings. This is not the case in court, where confrontation prevails over communication, in front of the judge who will at the end decide upon the kind and degree of hard treatment. The offender does not listen to the moralizing message, but tries to get away with as lenient a punishment as possible. He does not hear the invitation, but merely experiences the threat. It is the *a priori* option for inflicting hard treatment which is the major obstruction for good communication.

Hard treatment is not the only way to express blame. In daily life, in families and in schools, disapproval is routinely expressed without punishment. Morally authoritative persons without any power to punish are more effective in influencing moral thinking and behaviour than punishment. After a crime has occurred, the processes of restoration are more appropriate for communicating moral disapproval and provoking repentance, than are traditional punitive procedures and sanctions. Victim–offender mediation or family group conferences, for example, convey their intense disapproval of the crime through those who care for the offender and for whom the offender cares. As is also argued in Chapter 3 by Gordon Bazemore and Sandra O'Brien, most offenders are open to communication if they themselves experience respect and elementary understanding. They can feel empathy for the suffering of their victims (Harris 2001). Restorative settings position the harm and suffering centrally, presenting victimization as the focal concern in the norm, and this provides huge communicative potential.

Punishment, communication, repentance and restoration

In Chapter 5, Antony Duff takes an intriguing position (see also Duff 2001). In line with retributivism, punishment is considered to be indispensable, because the offender has not only caused harm, but also committed a wrong : '…punishment is the proper response to criminal wrongdoing, and … what justifies punishment is that it is deserved for that wrongdoing ' (Ch. 5: 82), or '…the guilty should be punished as they deserve and because that is what they deserve … punishment should bring them to suffer what they deserve to suffer' (Ch. 5: 96). But the imposed suffering is also a form of communication, intended to influence the offender: '…the idea of a kind of censure that aims to bring offenders to face up to and recognize the wrongs they have done; …of burdensome reparation that expresses such an apologetic and repentant recognition; …of a reconciliation, mediated by such recognition and reparation, between victim and offender' (Duff 2001: 99). Traditional punishments are rejected, but the hard treatment is linked to the offender's 'recognition of his wrongdoing, since that should be a repentant recognition, and repentance is necessarily painful' (Ch. 5: 96). It remains a retributive process, because it is aimed at being painful: 'She deserves to suffer the censure of others and her own remorse… She deserves to suffer the burden of making moral reparation' (Ch. 5: 96). The sequence 'censure – recognition of wrongfulness – repentance – reparation' is close to what is supposed to happen in ideal restorative justice processes. In writing 'we must try to censure in a way that displays our recognition of, and concern for, the offender as a fellow citizen' (Ch. 5: 93). Antony Duff even seems to suggest a kind of reintegrative shaming (Braithwaite 1989). But this does not fit into the restorative justice philosophy.

First, Duff refers to wrongfulness, as opposed to harmfulness, to consider hard treatment necessary after a crime. It is, however, not clear how wrongfulness can be understood separately from harmfulness. One can imagine moral wrongfulness which is not evidently harmful (in religious systems, for example), but we are discussing here a framework for coercive interventions in a democratic state. Purely ethical wrongfulness cannot justify authorities' intrusion upon our liberties, unless it serves to prevent harm to fellow citizens and/or public life. Even a retributivist like von Hirsch grounds the degree of seriousness of a crime on the harm to the standard of living (von Hirsch and Jareborg 1991). Granted, behaviour may be harmful by accident, or be intentional, and the wrongfulness lies in the intention of causing harm (Ch. 5: footnote 4). But still, the degree of wrongfulness will depend on the degree of harm intended, and it creates first of all an obligation upon the offender, not necessarily the need for imposing on him a degree of suffering. But that brings me to the second observation.

Second, the sequence just mentioned is certainly important , but it may be more difficult to achieve by the a priorism that it must be burdensome for the offender. As already argued above, confirmation of the norm and disapproval of the norm transgression can be carried out in other ways than through willingly imposing hard treatment. On the contrary, instead of promoting repentance, it may provoke defiance (Sherman 1993). Referring to Antony Duff's typology (2001: 115ff.), the 'already repentant offender' does not need punishment to comply with apologies and willingness to make up, the 'defiant offender' might become more defiant under the threat of punishment, and the number of 'morally persuaded offenders' persuaded by punishment will probably be reduced, because the punishment will turn 'persuadable offenders' into defiant ones.

Finally, while Antony Duff presents a truly renovating and constructive approach to the way in which crime has to be responded to, it remains a retributive approach which cannot be reconciled with the restorative one. His approach focuses on what should be done to the offender, whereas restorative justice primarily focuses on how harm can be restored. The main concern is not how the harm and suffering experienced may be repaired as much as possible, but how the wrong can be undone. This wrong, and the way to respond to it, are given, not socially debatable categories. 'The reactions of others [including the victim], and of the wrongdoer, are ... subject to normative appraisal: we must ask not just what they in fact feel, but what they should feel' (Ch. 5: 86). It clearly remains a top-down approach, not the bottom-up perspective which is fundamental to restorative justice, and wherein there is large space for mercy (see John Braithwaite in Chapter 8).

Distinguishing restorative justice ethics from punitive a priorism

We have so far argued that punishment is a means, based on the intentional inflicting of pain, while restoration is an objective for which the intentional inflicting of pain is an obstacle. A second crucial difference between both is their ethical foundation. Punishment is imposed after the transgression of any rule, even if that rule should itself be immoral. The intervention in the direction of restoration, by contrast, not only expresses disapproval, but is also indicative of the moral system underlying the disapproval. The priority given to restoration focuses on social life rather than on an abstract moral or legal system of any kind.

Ethical problems with punishment

Punishment '...involves actions that are generally considered to be morally wrong or evil were they not described and justified as punishments' (de Keijser 2000: 7). Punishment of offences by criminal justice is evidence of this, while leaving unanswered why the general ethical rule not to inflict pain on others does not apply to it.

Penal theory provides a rich and complex variety of justifications (von Hirsch 1998), which I have briefly discussed elsewhere (Walgrave 2001a). In my view, the *a priori* position that crime must be punished is both ethically questionable and instrumentally inefficient. Social rejection can be expressed in ways that do not involve punishment. Since the deliberate inflicting of pain is in principle unethical, the alternative ways to express blame should be fully exploited. The blind acceptance of punishment as a means of condemning behaviour is therefore in itself morally questionable. This position might need revision if the punitive approach should appear to be the only or the most effective way of significantly reducing the amount of victimization. But it is not. The available research leads rather to the contrary belief (Lab 1993, Sherman 1993).

The *a priori* position that crime must be punished is a typical top-down approach, based on an imposed rule of law, and does not genuinely consider the social context of possible solutions. For society at large, penal criminal justice intervention offers a strong confirmation of legal order, but public safety is badly served. Pure punishment carries the seeds of more social discord and lack of wellbeing, and thus of more crime and criminalization (Braithwaite 1999b). Victims are principally used as witnesses, but then left alone to deal with their losses and grievances (Dignan and Cavadino 1998). The priority given to the penal procedure and the penal sanction generally hinders the chances for victims to be compensated and/or restored. For the offender, the sanction involves a senseless inflicting of suffering. It does not contribute to public safety, nor to the victim's interests. It is a needless intrusion in the offender's freedom, causing an additional threat to his social future.

Let us now turn to possible ethical foundations for restorative justice.

Postmodernism and victimalization

In line with postmodern philosophy, George Pavlich rejects in Chapter 1 a general ethical foundation of restorative justice. For him, the opportunity for restorative justice lies in refusing 'a blackmail that commands us to come up with well-founded universal principles or else be condemned as unethical, immoral or just plain irrational' (Ch. 1: 2). General ethical principles are expressions of totalitarian thinking, a form of imperialism over thinking and behaviour, which we should reject. Instead, we must accept 'uncertain ethics', based on 'hospitality' oriented toward 'being with others'. We must leave the decisions on what is to be repaired, and how, to the participants' own options and visions. 'A restorative ethics could be understood as the critical work performed when subjects gather to name injustice or harm, and address promises of just patterns of being with others that are yet to come' (Ch. 1: 5).

Pavlich's option rightly rejects the pure top-down imposition of abstract ethical maxims and legal rules, to leave space for the ethical options of the participants in the restorative process. But if 'hospitality ... never exists as such – it is always to come, of the future' (Ch. 1: 9), then the question arises of what happens in the meantime. The 'critical work when subjects gather' just mentioned is possible only if the participants share some minimal common understandings, values and interest. Grounding restorative ethics on hospitality does not provide any guarantee. And that, according to George Pavlich, is the ultimate ethical issue: options based on hospitality must be taken without assurance of an ontological foundation. It is a 'key reponsibility' (Ch. 1: 16). That makes Pavlich's contribution not so stripped of rules as is suggested. Subjects must accept their responsibility with respect to achieving hospitality for others. In my view, this is a general ethical rule, oriented towards respectful and cohesive community life, moved by subjects taking their responsibility for it.

In Chapter 2 , Hans Boutellier also observes the loss of general ethical systems (see also Boutellier 2000). Unlike Pavlich, however, Boutellier considers this to be a social factor, which explains the search for a new normative minimum: 'While our consensus on the good life is privatized, our common moral understanding focuses on "evil". It is the bad behaviour which triggers the need for moral consensus' (Ch. 2: 22). Boutellier refers to Rorty's 'are you suffering?' (Rorty 1989). Instead of universalism, Rorty defends a liberal pluralistic culture, based on freedom and solidarity. Solidarity is not general, but very local and concrete: the common rejection of cruelty and suffering. Morals are 'victimalized'. ... 'victimalization defined as the process by which – on an individual level – suffering is defined as victimization, and as the process – on a cultural level – by which morality is defined as agreement on victimization' (Ch. 2: 23). It is this cultural–ethical focus on rejecting victimization which, according to Hans Boutellier, explains the growth of restorative justice in recent decades.

Boutellier may be right that the emergence of the victim as an icon in recent years has contributed to the breakthrough of practices like mediation, restitution, compensation and the like, but limiting restorative justice to such techniques is too reductionist a view. 'Victimalization' also is too narrow an ethical basis for restorative justice. First, because morals based on fear of being victimized, instead of being based on positive values to be promoted, are reduced and even negative. Secondly, because the victimization in view here is limited to individuals and does not include any reference to social life as such. It is based on the traditional liberal conception of liberty, shared by both Boutellier and Rorty, which sees collectivity as a threat for individual freedom, whereas restorative justice basically views life in community and developing individual freedom as mutually dependent.

From community to communitarianism

We believe that the search for ethical foundations of restorative justice must begin with the observation that community occupies a focal position in restorative rhetorics (Bazemore and Schiff 2001a). The priority given to restoring the harm caused by crime inevitably draws attention to the social unrest suffered by community. The living community is more directly victimized by the occurrence of an offence than is the state. Moreover, restorative interventions require a minimum of community: victim and offender must feel a minimal common interest in constructively settling together the aftermath of the crime.

However, it is difficult to get to grips with the notion of community and to fit it into a coherent normative theory on restorative justice. While recognizing great value in active citizen participation, Adam Crawford, in Chapter 6, is very critical of what he considers a kind of nostalgia which '...overidealizes as unproblematic the nature of communities' moral order' (Ch. 6: 109), saying that 'Communities are not the heavens of reciprocity and mutuality, nor are they the utopias of egalitarianism, that some might wish' (Ch. 6: 110). Daniel Van Ness, in Chapter 7, is less critical, though not blind to possible misuses. He values the involvement of non-governmental actors in the response to crime, which he calls community, and tries to find a balanced complementarity with governmental tasks.

All in all, three types of problems appear. First, even if it is not a territorial space (McCold and Wachtel 1998b: 3; Marshall 1994: 248), 'community' suggests an area, distinguishes an inside community from an outside non-community. But it is impossible to delineate it mentally, socially or territorially. It expands as far as the vague and drifting limits conceived by individual subjects (Crawford and Clear 2001). Community is a psychological entity, rather than a set of characteristics of given collectivities.

Secondly, building on communities for developing restorative responses to crime presupposes that communities really exist, which is far from evident (Braithwaite 1993; Crawford 1996; Crawford and Clear 2001). It is difficult to mobilize 'community' in the resolution of a street robbery in which victim and offender live many kilometres from one another and belong to totally different social networks. Most crimes occur in non community-like social settings, and the solution is to be found in the absence of such setting.

Thirdly, the notion of community is vulnerable to possible misuses (Pavlich 2001). Communities are not good *per se*. The supposed *niche* of community may appear to be a hotbed of suffocating social control within the community, and of exclusivism versus the outside world. In the name of community, people are subjected to unreasonable control and local stigmatization. Local communities often support repressive police forces and judges, and vote for exclusivist politicians. To the outside world, communities may develop exclusionary tendencies. These are often considered as a threat, provoking possibly violent conflicts between communities based on territory, ethnicity or religion. Community contains 'the seeds of parochialism which can lead ... to atrocious totalitarian exclusions' (Pavlich 2001: 58).

Scepticism about the notion of community does not necessarily mean rejecting the ideals promoted by most communitarians: social unity, a form of harmonious living together, based on shared values and beliefs and mutual commitment. But do we need community for promoting such ideals? We should instead promote socio-ethical attitudes and functions which are not limited to a given area defined by community (Pavlich 2001). Most communitarians in fact promote social ethics and values, not areas. That is what I understand when Daniel Van Ness describes 'communities as a challenge to assume neglected responsibilities. The sense is that people have found it easier to let the police and other government agencies handle problems rather than to become personally involved' (Ch. 7: 141). 'Community' appears as a container for ethics and social values. The ethics and values must be unpacked from their container. While being hesitant about the appropriateness of community to characterize part of social reality, I believe that communitarianism may be a useful label for a socio-ethical movement.

Towards communitarian socio-ethics for restorative justice

Restorative justice is more than a technical view on the doing of justice. It is an ideal of justice in a utopian ideal of society. In the communitarian utopia the distinction between society and community is meaningless, because collectivity is governed with a view to individual and collective emancipation, in which autonomy and solidarity are not seen as opposed, but as mutually reinforcing principles. Collective life draws its strength not from threat, coercion and fear, but from motivation, based on trust, participation and support.

A collectivity aiming at this utopia promotes as 'virtues' socio-ethical attitudes which serve it. I see three such virtues or behavioural guidelines: respect, solidarity and taking responsibility. In respect the intrinsic value of the other is recognized. The recognition may be broad. It is ethical to respect not only humans, but also nature and objects. Respect for humans recognizes the intrinsic value of a human being, made concrete through the Universal Declaration of Human Rights, for example. Respect for 'human dignity' is a bottom line obligation for all social institutions.

Solidarity is more specific than respect. It is not evident that many people feel solidarity with objects or with nature. Solidarity presupposes more commitment than does respect, because solidarity includes a form of companionship and reciprocity of support. Companionship goes with empathy and mutual trust, which is most visible in the attitudes towards those in trouble. It may be what George Pavlich meant by 'hospitality' and 'being with others' (Ch. 1). Community rhetorics often locate solidarity within the scope of a given community, but as it is now unpacked from its 'community container', solidarity is no longer limited to a given area, but is a general ethical value. '...this spirit of solidarity may be regarded as a forever-elusive promise of unpremeditated collective togetherness.' (Pavlich 2001: 67).

Responsibility links the person to his acts and its consequences. It confronts the self with its own actions. Passive responsibility means being confronted with one's actions by others; active responsibility is an aware-ness of the link between the self and the actions, and the need to behave accordingly (Bovens 1998, in Braithwaite and Roche 2001). This active form of responsibility is highlighted in John Braithwaite's Chapter 8, but it also appears in other chapters. It is essential that members of a community, or citizens, take responsibility themselves, i.e., respond actively and autonomously to the obligations created by social life, which in com-munitarian ethics must be oriented towards solidarity.

Other ethical guidelines might be superflous if members of the collectivity behaved according to these three ethical guidelines. 'Where there is sufficient community peace, there will be relatively little need for order. Where there is little peace, more order will be needed' (Van Ness, Ch. 7: 142). In my view, justice is currently advanced as a separate ethical rule only because respect, solidarity and responsibility are not sufficiently achieved.

At first glance, advancing respect, solidarity and responsibility as basics in a communitarian ethic may seem to be mere rhetoric. Don't we all value these virtues? Do we really? Let us explore their presence in retributive justice. Is respect an ethical guideline in retributivism? Respect for the victim is absent, because he is not included in the deliberations of the retributivists. Retributivism is focused on the offender. Considering the offender as a conscious moral agent, and treating him in a just (desert) way, recognizes him as a human being, and as a citizen with guaranteed rights. But the respect is not complete. The offender is not respected as a whole person with personal interests and interpretations, including a possible willingness to make up for misbehaviour. In the end, the offender has to submit to a proportionate punishment. Once the crime has been committed, respect for the person is withdrawn. The offender is judged as a moral agent to be considered guilty, but not to contribute to the finding of a constructive response to the problems caused by his crime.[7]

I do not see solidarity, companionship including willingness to extend mutual support, in retributivism. The response does not support the victim, but merely punishes the offender, which often hampers possible reparation. In restorative justice, solidarity with the victim is evident, but solidarity with the offender is also present. The offender is not excluded, but encouraged to make up for the conduct, in order to preserve his position as an integrated member of the collectivity.

Responsibility is central to retributivism. The offender is held responsible by having to respond autonomously to the obligation created by the misconduct, but again, the responsibility is incomplete. Responsibility only means accepting the negative consequences, but not searching for a constructive solution to the problems created. It is only a passive, retrospective form of responsibility. The victim is not considered responsible for anything, except maybe to report the crime and serve as a witness during the trial. Retributivism burdens the criminal justice system with the crucial responsibility to censure criminal behaviour, and to impose proportionate punishments. Restorative justice largely relies on active responsibility (Braithwaite, Ch. 8). The offender's active responsibility includes the obligation to contribute to the reparation of the harm. The victim is encouraged, but not obliged, to assume the general citizens' responsibility for trying to find peace-promoting solutions. Restorative justice also stands for responsible collectivities, bound by obligations to search for socially constructive responses within the rules of law.

This exercise of course needs more deepening and extension. It may, however, make clear that restorative justice promotes social ethical attitudes or virtues like respect, solidarity and taking responsibility to a greater degree than retributive justice, and that it is therefore more likely to contribute constructively to social life and relations. The priority for the quality of social life, as expressed in the communitarian utopia, grounds the bottom-up approach in restorative justice, which appears through the preference for informal regulations, away from imposed procedures and outcomes. The point of departure for restorative justice, as in communitarianism, is that solutions must primarily be sought through the human and social resources in social life itself. This is opposed to the top-down approach in traditional criminal justice, where decisions are imposed according to strict rules, leaving little room, if any, for the views and interests of those directly concerned.

Dominion as the bridging concept between communitarian ethics to the rule of law

The communitarian utopia is far from being realized. While justice was a derivative value only in the communitarian utopia, it must currently be advanced as a value in itself in non-ideal societies. In our existing communities and societies, where respect and solidarity are often over-ruled by self-interest and abuse of power, there is need for a framework of justice, to check processes and decisions according to a set of rights and duties (see also Crawford in Chapter 6). It is here that the difficult relation between restorative justice and the law is at its most problematic. We must find a combination, in one system, of a large margin for informal processes in line with the communitarian ethics, with rules of law and the legal mechanisms of formal control. These rules and mechanisms should them-selves maximally express the socio-ethical guidelines described above.

I start my reflection in agreement with John Braithwaite (Ch. 8), seeing dominion, or 'freedom as non-domination'[8] as the ultimate criterion by which restorative processes and values may be evaluated. Based on Braithwaite and Pettit's republican theory of criminal justice (Braithwaite and Pettit 1990), dominion is defined as 'the set of assured rights and freedoms'. Dominion is the mental and social territory of which we freely dispose, as it is guaranteed by the state and in social life. The assurance of rights and freedoms is crucial.[9] 'I know that I have rights, I know that the others know it, and I trust that they will respect it'. I am assured only if I trust my fellow citizens and the state, that they will take my rights and freedoms seriously, based on respect and solidarity. It is only then that I will fully enjoy my mental and social domain. Assurance provides the crucial distinction between the social concept of 'freedom as non-domination' and the liberal concept of 'freedom as non-interference'. In the liberal conception, the other is a possible interferer in my freedom, and therefore basically a rival in my struggle for freedom. In the republican view, the other is an ally in trying to extend and mutually assure dominion as a collective good.

This concept is crucial here, as (1) the fundamental aim of restorative justice appears to be restoring assurance in dominion, and (2) the limits of restorative justice interventions are posed by the rights and freedoms in dominion.

Restoring assurance in dominion

A good state, according to Braithwaite and Pettit, must promote dominion for its citizens. Dominion is thus not delineated, but is a value to be promoted. Dominion can be seen as a formalization of the communitarian ideal into a political theory. The communitarian utopia can be achieved only in so far as the state's dominion is developed. Conversely, the assurance of rights and freedoms is achieved only to the degree to which citizens take their responsibilities seriously in relation to respect and solidarity.

The state seeks to extend and deepen dominion by promoting equality through more democracy, education, equitable socio-economic policy, welfare policy and the like. Criminal justice is the 'defensive' institution. Crime is seen as an intrusion upon dominion, and criminal justice must act to repair it (Walgrave 2000b).[10] That is my view of the 'public wrong' which is central to Antony Duff's thesis (Ch. 5). This intrusion hurts most of all the assurance contained in dominion. A burglary, for example, is both a private and a public affair. Strictly speaking, the restitution or compensation of the concrete victim's losses could be private, to be arranged by civil law. But there is also a public side. The public matter is the loss of assurance: the burglary not only hurts the victim's trust that his privacy and possessions will be respected by his fellow citizens; the specific victim also stands as an example of what all citizens risk undergoing. If the authorities did nothing against the particular burglary, it would undermine citizens' trust in the right to privacy and possession.[11]

Public intervention after a crime is therefore not primarily needed to rectify the balance of benefits and burdens, nor to re-confirm the law. It is needed first of all to enhance assurance, by communicating the message that authorities do take dominion seriously. The intervention must reassure the victim and the public of their rights and freedoms, and to transform these rights and freedoms into being an assured, fully-fledged dominion. This happens by clearly censuring the intrusion and by involving, if possible, the offender in actions designed to restore dominion. The voluntary cooperation of the offender is more effective in restoring assurance, but only if it is backed by public institutions; necessarily, assurance not only comes from the individual offender's repentance and apologies, but also from the authorities' determination to take the assured set of rights and freedoms seriously.

So, I conclude that there cannot be complete restoration without at least a supportive participation by the state. Or in Braithwaite and Parker's words: the state's rule of law must 'percolate down' into restorative processes (Braithwaite and Parker 1999).

Limiting intervention by the rights and freedoms in dominion

Dominion is not only a value to be defended and promoted. The 'hard core' of dominion consists of actual rights and freedoms, which provide grounds for defining limits to (restorative) justice interventions. The intervention itself must assure dominion by the respect it shows itself for rights and freedoms. Braithwaite and Pettit (1990) list four constraints: parsimony, checking of authorities' use of power, reprobation of crime and reintegration of victims and offenders.

The scope of this chapter does not allow for extensive comments (see Walgrave 2000b). I must confine myself to a brief comment on the first constraint, parsimony. The second and the third constraints, checking of power and reprobation, can partly be seen as variations on traditional deontologic principles of criminal justice like 'right of defence' and 'censure', whereas the fourth constraint, reintegration, seems to be a restorative variation of typical consequentionalist goals.

The parsimony constraint is crucial to the combining of informal processes with formal controls. In republican theory, criminal justice must strive for achievable goals (repairing the intruded dominion), and is bound by the constraint of parsimony in using its coercive power. Parsimony is more restricting than satiability. We can eat until full satiation, but we can parsimoniously do with less in order to survive.

Satiability includes an obligation to set an upper limit, as required by the proportionality principle. Parsimony, however, excludes the setting of a lower limit. On the contrary, the parsimony constraint requires an active search for non-coercive ways to restore dominion. The more voluntary restorative processes result in satisfying and balanced outcomes, the less appeal is needed to coercive judicial interventions and thus, the more the parsimony principle is achieved. A fully-fledged restorative justice system should fulfil its parsimony obligation by promoting space for voluntary processes, wherein victim, offender and collectivity can seek together an agreed settlement of the aftermath of a crime that restores dominion to the greatest extent possible.

So, I do agree with John Braithwaite (Ch. 8) that proportionality in the retributive sense is an obstacle to restorative justice, and that this constraint must be replaced by setting only upper limits to possible intervention. I would, however, add that we must set proportionate upper limits. The upper limit for murder, for example, should be higher than for vandalism. If not, the upper limit for vandalism would probably be set much too high.

Whilst we have just said that the rule of law must percolate down into restorative processes, restorative justice must also percolate up into the rule of law (Braithwaite and Parker 1999). John Braithwaite speaks of 'responsive regulation' (Ch. 8, but more in Braithwaite 2002a). The regulator (the state) should be responsive to the individuals and collectivities he regulates. Legal regulation must pay full attention to, and respect what happens in, non-formalized settings. '…law enforcers should be responsive to how effectively citizens or corporations are regulating themselves before deciding whether to escalate intervention' (Braithwaite 2002: 29). As Braithwaite explains in Chapter 8, intervention after a crime should be planned according to a 'regulatory pyramid', of which persuasion, or restorative processing, is at the base, and incapacitation of 'incompetent or irrational actors' is at the top. '…what we want is a legal system where citizens learn that responsiveness is the way our legal institutions work. Once they see the legal system as a responsive regulatory system, they know there will be a chance to argue about unjust laws… The forces of law are listening, fair and therefore legitimate, but also are seen as somewhat invincible' (Braithwaite 2002: 34).

Towards a model for a restorative justice system

From ethics, we now make the step towards the concrete social institutions which are needed for ensuring the priority for restoration in the response to crime.

Particularities in legalizing restorative justice

A justice system which is primarily oriented towards doing justice through restoration has some features in common and some crucial differences from the traditional criminal justice system. Both the criminal justice and the restorative justice system express clear limits to social tolerance, hold the offender responsible for his behaviour, and use, if necessary, coercion according to legal standards.

The limits to social tolerance are clear, because the reason for the intervention refers directly to the offender's behaviour. The interventions are retrospective, which is crucial for the maintenance of legal safeguards. In penal justice, the seriousness of the crime committed is the yardstick by which decisions upon the proportionate punishment are made. In restorative justice, the seriousness of the harm caused is the criterion to set proportionate upper limits (Walgrave and Geudens 1997).

Holding the offender responsible is essential in both punitive and restorative approaches to crime. Both also can include personal and social circumstances in the sentencing. The amount of punishment or obligation to compensate will depend on personal capacities to understand[12] and material resources, degree of premeditation, and social and situational peculiarities. Such elements would evidently be considered more adequately and thoroughly in a deliberative setting, as in voluntary processes, but they are also crucial in judicial sentencing.

Both retrospectivity and (degree of) responsibility address the two crucial questions in traditional sentencing: have the facts been established and has the (degree of) guilt been established (Ashworth 1986)?

Sentencing with a view to restoration, however, adds a third question: how can the sanction contribute maximally to restoration? This question is not asked in retributive justice, because of the *a priori* option for punishment, and because it is not prospective. Restorative justice, by contrast, aims at restoring the harm, and is therefore also prospective. Again, voluntary deliberative processes are more capable of assessing harm and of considering possible restoration, but the restoration question should also be central in judicial proceedings. Restorative justice is thus retrospective and prospective at the same time.[13]

This leads to a few principles in which judicial procedures which aim to achieve restoration would deviate from traditional criminal procedures.

- Because coercive intervention must be used parsimoniously, restorative justice procedures should at all stages allow easy exits towards voluntary informal crime regulation. Diversion is obligatory wherever possible. The decision to prosecute in court must be justified with positive arguments, and not simply because 'the law has been broken'. This is so because dominion must be intruded minimally, and because the restorative calibre of voluntary agreements is higher.

- Restorative justice procedures must allow large opportunities for input by victims and others affected by the crime. This input is crucial in defining the kind and amount of harm and in finding the best possible restorative outcome. However, because of legal rights, these actors may not be given any decisive power.

- Criminal investigation should not only be focused on establishing the facts and an offender's guilt, but also on defining the harm, suffering and social unrest caused by the offence. It should also explore possible ways for negotiation, and thus for 'diversion', and for possible restorative sanctions if diversion was not possible.

- As mentioned earlier, the sanction would not link the seriousness of crime to a proportionate punishment; but the seriousness and kind of harm to a maximum of reasonable restorative effort.

Emerging contours of a model

In this volume, outlines of a possible restorative justice system have been presented by Daniel Van Ness (Chapter 7), John Braithwaite (Chapter 8) and especially by Jim Dignan (Chapter 9). I have myself described elsewhere how the Belgian juvenile justice system could be reformed into being primarily oriented toward restoration (Walgrave *et al.* 1997; Walgrave 2001b). The four models are very comparable, which suggests some unanimity on the contours of what might be a comprehensive restorative justice system. They all are located between a 'unitary model in which the restorative system is the only available', and a 'dual-track model in which both systems stand side by side' (Van Ness Ch. 7: 145). As becomes clear through the pyramids presented by John Braithwaite and Jim Dignan (Chapters 8 and 9), the models depart from according priority for voluntary deliberative processes, which, they assume, will resolve the majority of cases. They then provide several variations of coercive interventions by courts, while still keeping opportunities for (partial) reparation. Finally, security concerns may make incapacition of the offender inevitable. The levels in the pyramid roughly present different degrees in restorativeness, which are described more in detail in Van Ness's Chapter 7. Daniel Van Ness also points out that a comprehensive restorative justice model must include victim service and support, available regardless of whether the offender is apprehended and/or collaborative or not.

One striking difference in these approaches is the position they take on how to conceive judicial coercion. John Braithwaite clearly abandons restorative justice in favour of punitive and deterrent reactions when restorative justice (seen as exclusively deliberative processes) fails, while accepting that restorative values should be given as much space as possible within the punishing environment, and promoting de-escalation down the pyramid whenever possible (Ch. 8: footnote 2). Jim Dignan sticks to the primacy of the restorative process through advancing court-imposed restoration orders and restorative punishments for recalcitrant and for persistent offenders. I am rather sympathetic to Jim Dignan's option. First, because I share his concerns over John Braithwaite's position, that it would lead to a two-track model, and because it leaves unanswered severe problems with punitive responses, at least for the non-virtuous offenders. Secondly, because it seems to be inconsistent in principle to give up the socio-ethical plus value of the restorative approach when resistance is met. In my view, it applies also to non-cooperative offenders, in that the reason for rejecting their behaviour is that they harm victims, and assurance in dominion, and that the social response to it must as much as possible express that reason by aiming at maximum possible reparation of harm. It is the harm reason only which can justify the possible use of coercion, not 'deterrence'.

Contrary to Jim Dignan, however, I would not speak of restorative punishments, but of restorative sanctions. My main reasons have been explained earlier in this chapter. Let me just add here that Dignan himself must specify that the restorative punishments he has in mind are not 'conceptualized in an unambiguously punitive manner', but 'in a straight-forwardly reparative manner as a more constructive and meaningful undertaking' (Ch. 9: 184). That is exactly where I find the difference between punishment and restorative sanctions.

The outline discussed here is only a beginning. But it is time to demonstrate what a system which would do justice through its priority for restoring the harm that has been caused by a crime would look like. Such explication is timely for political and methodological reasons. First, as Van Ness writes, the increasing credibility of restorative options creates great expectations, among policy makers also. Restorative justice advocates must therefore be prepared to present a coherent view with respect to which the social, institutional and judicial environment is the most ap-propriate for implementing restorative responses within the framework of a constitutional democratic state. Secondly, exploring thoroughly the consequences of the restorative justice option is also an excellent method for exploring the potentials and possible limits of restorative justice, and in order to raise new questions. For example, Dignan's detailed description of how he conceives a comprehensive system has not only a value on its own, but it also provokes many concrete questions which oblige us to make choices and to make options explicit.

Conclusion

Restorative justice has gradually gained great credibility in recent decades, as its socio-ethical and instrumental-plus value is becoming more and more obvious, and its potential appears to extend much further than was originally believed. How far restorative justice will penetrate the pre-dominant social response to crime depends, among other things, on how it is delimited. If it is reduced to voluntary deliberative settlements, the hard core reaction to crime will be left to the traditional justice system. We have therefore argued in favour of including coercive impositions of restorative sanctions, and have called this approach a 'maximalist' version of restorative justice (Bazemore and Walgrave 1999b). I certainly believe that the restorative approach to doing justice must be implemented maximally, and not be limited by nor subordinated to the punitive *a priori*. It must, on the contrary, have the ambition to replace in the longer term the current punitive a priorism in the reaction to crime.

The possibility of achieving this depends on a number of social, cultural and political developments, but also on how restorative justice itself evolves in its methodological, theoretical, socio-ethical, legal and institutional aspects. In this volume, we have focused especially on the legal aspects of implementing restorative justice. It is a crucial issue for the future. If restorative justice is proposed as the mainstream response to crime, then it must be made a part of the principles of a democratic constitutional state, including its safeguards of rights and freedoms. This is not evident, given the unavoidable tension between the intrinsic need in restorative justice for maximizing informality in deliberation, on the one hand, and the necessity for legalization and formalization and external control, on the other.

The legal safeguards which are contained in the traditional penal justice system cannot simply be transposed. Restorative justice claims to be based on a different view of society and to offer another paradigm for doing justice. Differences, and often contrasts, exist in the socio-ethical and ideological foundations, the objectives aimed at, the means involved, the kind of responsibility invoked, the actors implicated, etcetera. Legal theory on restorative justice must therefore be reconstructed from the ground. That does not mean that existing penal theories can simply be erased. Scepticism by retributivists, for example, must be taken seriously, but their presuppostions should not be taken for granted. Due process, right of a defence, guilt and responsibility, proportionality and other principles remain respectable, but they must be critically checked as to their meaning in a restorative justice context, and possibly be re-formulated, rejected or replaced.

In my view, for example, due process and some kind of proportionality are important constraints in safeguarding rights and justice in general. Contrary to the traditional deontologic version, however, these constraints must not be seen as top-down rules on how to do justice. They must be re-formulated and integrated into the broader dominion concept which seems to integrate both safeguards for rights and freedoms, and the participatory bottom-up approach that is part of evolving social life in a communitarian direction.

The communitarian ideal must be inserted into a model of state. If there was no state, there would be no rights, and one would depend on the goodwill of others, or on one's own power, to compete with the others and to oppress them. If there was only the state, there would be no trust, and the other would be considered as a rival, a threat to one's own territory. Such a state would deteriorate into anarchy or tyranny. That is what it is all about for those who commit themselves to finding a better way of doing justice, which would be more satisfactory for the victims, more assuring for social life and more reintegrative for the offenders, and thus, more restorative for all.

It is my hope that this volume makes a contribution to this.

Notes

1. I shall use the male form as the general form. This may not be politically correct, but it is more practical to use one form coherently.
2. This is not to say that family group conferences cannot usefully be inserted into a welfare context. It is included in several welfare systems (see several chapters in Hudson *et al.* 1996). But even as a response to crime, the original FGC in New Zealand is evidently not always practised from a restorative standpoint. Several practices still operate with predominantly reintegrative aims (Stewart 1996).
3. I agree with Jim Dignan (Ch. 9) that restorative justice interventions need moral justification and limitation, but these interventions must therefore not necessarily be included in the punishment philosophy, as Jim Dignan concludes. Punishment has not, in my view, the monopoly of moral justification and legal limitation.
4. Contrary to von Hirsch, I do not add disapprobation as another characteristic. Punishment is often administered routinely, and experienced as a 'prize' to be paid, without any moral reflection at all.
5. The proportionality issue, challenged by John Braithwaite (Ch. 8), will be discussed later.
6. The long tradition of criminological research on the effectiveness of criminal punishment leads to the overall conclusion that punishment is socially not really effective. The actuarial approach to criminal justice even suggests that criminal punishment would also not function adequately as a moral agent, and thus not as an authoritative 'censurer' (Feeley and Simon 1992).
7. This is less true in Duff's approach to punishment (2001, and Ch. 5), but the problem remains the punitive a priorism.
8. In later publications, 'dominion' has been renamed as 'freedom as non-domination'. It may make it easier to oppose it to the liberal concept typified as 'freedom as non-interference', but I see no other advantage in complicating the wording. I will therefore stick to the 'old' naming, 'dominion'.
9. See also what Putnam (1993) called 'trust' in social capital.
10. The target of criminal justice must be repairing dominion, and not promoting it, as Braithwaite and Pettit advance, because promotion of dominion is an unsatiable target.
11. See also Duff: '... it is for us, collectively, to respond to that wrong – rather than leaving it for her [the victim, LW] to deal with it as a private manner' (Ch. 5: 92).

12. The difference between using personal characteristics as elements for estimating responsibilities and using them in a rehabilitative sense is well explained in Weijers, Ch. 4.
13. As Antony Duff also underlines in his Chapter 5, with regard to restorative processes.

References

Abel, R. (1981) 'Conservative Conflict and the Reproduction of Capitalism: The Role of Informal Justice', *International Journal of the Sociology of Law*, 9: 245–67.

Abel, R. (1982) 'The Contradictions of Informal Justice', in R. Abel (ed.) *The Politics of Informal Justice, Vol. 1.* New York: Academic Press.

Achilles, M. and Zehr, H. (2001) 'Restorative Justice for Crime Victims: The Promise, the Challenge', in G. Bazemore and M. Schiff (eds) *Restorative Community Justice: Repairing Harm and Transforming Communities.* Cincinnati, OH: Anderson Publishing.

Adler, C. (2000) 'Young Women Offenders and the Challenge for Restorative Justice', in H. Strang and J. Braithwaite (eds) *Restorative Justice: Philosophy to Practice.* Darmouth: Ashgate.

Ahmed, E., Harris, N., Braithwaite, J. and Braithwaite, V. (2001) *Shame Management through Reintegration.* Cambridge: Cambridge University Press.

Andrews, D. A., Bonta, J., and Hoge, R. D. (1990) 'Classification for Effective Rehabilitation: Rediscovering Psychology', *Criminal Justice and Behavior*, 17(1): 19–52.

Ashworth, A. (1986) 'Punishment and Compensation: Victims, Offenders and the State', *Oxford Journal of Legal Studies*, 6: 86–122.

Ashworth, A. (1993) 'Some Doubts about Restorative Justice', *Criminal Law Forum*, 4: 277–99.

Ashworth, A. (2000) 'Assessing the R.J. Paradigm', paper presented to the Restorative Justice Colloquium, Cambridge, 12 September.

Ashworth, A. (2000b) 'Victim's Rights, Defendant's Rights and Criminal

Procedure', in A. Crawford and J. Goodey (eds) *Integrating a Victim Perspective within Criminal Justice*. Aldershot: Ashgate.

Ayres, I. and Braithwaite J. (1992) *Responsive Regulation: Transcending the Deregulation Debate*. New York: Oxford University Press.

Ayto, J. (1993) *Dictionary of Word Origins*. London: Bloomsbury.

Badiou, A. (2001) *Ethics: an Essay on the Understanding of Evil*. London: Verso.

Baier, A. C. (1986) 'Trust and Antitrust', *Ethics*, 96: 231–261.

Bauman, Z. (1988) *Freedom*. Minneapolis, MN: University of Minnesota Press.

Bauman, Z. (1992) *Intimations of Postmodernity*. London: Routledge.

Bauman, Z. (1993) *Postmodern Ethics*. Oxford: Blackwell.

Bauman, Z. (1994) *Alone Again: Ethics After Certainty*. London: Demos.

Bauman, Z. (1995) *Life in Fragments: Essays in Postmodern Moralities*. Oxford: Blackwell.

Bauman, Z. (1997) *Postmodernity and its Discontents*. Cambridge: Polity.

Bauman, Z. (1999) 'The world inhospitable to Levinas', *Philosophy Today*, Summer, 151–167.

Bauman, Z. (2001a) *Communities Seeking Safety in an Insecure World*. Cambridge: Polity.

Bauman, Z. (2001b) *The Individualized Society*. Cambridge: Polity.

Bauman, Z. (2002) 'Violence in the Age of Uncertainty', in A. Crawford (ed.) *Crime and Insecurity: The Governance of Safety in Europe*. Cullompton: Willan.

Bayley, D. (2001) 'Security and Justice for All', in H. Strang and J. Braithwaite (eds) *Restorative Justice and Civil Society*. Cambridge: Cambridge University Press.

Bazemore, G. (1997) 'The "Community" in Community Justice: Issues, Themes and Questions for the new Neighborhood Sanctioning Models.' *The Justice System Journal*, 19(2): 193–228.

Bazemore, G. (1998) 'Restorative Justice and Earned Redemption: Communities, Victims and Offender Reintegration', *American Behavioral Scientist*, 41(6): 768–813.

Bazemore, G. (1999) 'The Fork in the Road to Juvenile Court Reform', *The Annals of the American Academy of Political Social Science*, 564(7): 81–108.

Bazemore, G. (2000) 'Community Justice and a Vision of Collective Efficacy: The Case of Restorative Conferencing', *Criminal Justice 2000*, 3.

Bazemore, G. (2001) 'Young People, Trouble, and Crime: Restorative Justice as a Normative Theory of Informal Social Control and Social Support', *Youth and Society*, 33(2): 199–226.

Bazemore, G. and Earle, T. (2002) 'Balance in the Response to Family Violence: Challenging Restorative Principles', in J. Braithwaite and H. Strang (eds) *Restorative Justice and Family Violence*. London: Cambridge University Press, (forthcoming).

Bazemore, G. and Erbe, C. (2002), 'Reintegration and Restorative Justice: Toward a Theory and Practice of Informal Social Control and Support', (forthcoming).

Bazemore, G. and Schiff, M. (2001a) 'Understanding Restorative Community Justice: What and Why Now?', in G. Bazemore and M. Schiff (eds) *Restorative Community Justice: Repairing Harm and Transforming Communities*. Cincinnati, OH: Anderson.

Bazemore, G. and Schiff, M. (eds) (2001b) *Restorative Community Justice. Repairing Harm and Transforming Communities*. Cincinnati, OH: Anderson.

Bazemore, G. and Schiff, M. (2002). *Understanding Restorative Conferencing: A Case Study in Informal Decisionmaking in the Response to Youth Crime. Final Report*. National Institute of Justice, US Department of Justice, (forthcoming).

Bazemore, G. and Umbreit, M. (2001) 'A Comparison of Four Restorative Conferencing Models', *Juvenile Justice Bulletin*.

Bazemore, G. and Walgrave, L. (eds) (1999a) *Restorative Juvenile Justice: Repairing the Harm of Youth Crime*. Monsey, NY: Criminal Justice Press.

Bazemore, G. and Walgrave, L. (1999b) 'Restorative Juvenile Justice: in Search of Fundamentals and an Outline for Systemic Reform', in G. Bazemore and L. Walgrave (eds) *Restorative Juvenile Justice: Repairing the Harm of Youth Crime*. Monsey, NY: Criminal Justice Press.

Bazemore, S. G., Pranis, K., Umbreit, M. and United States Office of Juvenile Justice and Delinquency Prevention (1997) *Balanced and Restorative Justice for Juveniles: a Framework for Juvenile Justice in the 21st Century*. Washington, DC: Office of Juvenile Justice and Delinquency Prevention.

Bazemore, G., Nissen, L. and Dooley, M. (2000) 'Mobilizing Social Support and Building Relationships: Broadening Correctional and Rehabilitative Agendas', *Corrections Management Quarterly*, 4(4): 10–21.

Beck, U. (1992) *The Risk Society*. London: Sage.

Berrien, J. and Winship C. (2000) 'Lessons Learned from Boston's Police-Community Collaboration', *Federal Probation*, 63: 25–33.

Blagg, H. (2001) 'Aboriginal Youth and Restorative Justice', in A. Morris and G. Maxwell (eds) *Restorative Justice for Juveniles*. Oxford: Hart Publishing.

Bonta, J., Rooney J. and Wallace-Capretta, S. (1998) *Restorative Justice: An Evaluation of the Restorative Resolutions Project*. Ottawa: Solicitor General Canada.

Bottoms, A. E. (2000) Oral contribution in the course of a conference on Restorative Justice: Exploring the Aims and Determining the Limits, held in Cambridge, 6–8 October.

Boutellier, H. (2000) *Crime and Morality; The Significance of Criminal Justice in Postmodern Culture*. Dordrecht: Kluwer Academic Publishers.

Boutellier, H. (2001) 'The Convergence of Social Policy and Criminal Justice', *European Journal on Criminal Policy and Research*, 9(4): 361–80.

Boyes-Watson, C. (1999) 'In the Belly of the Beast? Exploring the Dilemmas of State-Sponsored Restorative Justice', *Contemporary Justice Review*, 2(3): 261.

Boyes-Watson, C. (2000) 'Reflections on the Purist and Maximalist Models of Restorative Justice', *Contemporary Justice Review*, 3(4): 441–50.

Braithwaite, J. (1984) *Corporate Crime in the Pharmaceutical Industry*. London and Boston: Routledge and Kegan Paul.

Braithwaite, J. (1985) *To Punish or Persuade: Enforcement of Coal Mine Safety*. Albany, NY: State University of New York Press.

Braithwaite, J. (1989) *Crime, Shame and Reintegration*. Cambridge: Cambridge University Press.

Braithwaite, J. (1991) 'The Political Agenda of Republican Criminology', paper presented at the British Criminological Society Conference, York, 27 July.

Braithwaite, J. (1992) 'Juvenile Offending: New Theory and Practice'. Address to the National Conference on Juvenile Justice, Adelaide, Institute of Criminology, September.

Braithwaite, J. (1993) 'Shame and Modernity', *British Journal of Criminology*, 33: 1–18.

Braithwaite, J. (1998) 'Restorative Justice', in M. Tonry (ed.) *Handbook of Crime and Punishment*. New York: Oxford University Press.

Braithwaite, J. (1999a). 'Restorative Justice: Assessing Optimistic and Pessimistic Accounts', in M. Tonry (ed.) *Crime and Justice: An Annual Review of Research, Vol. 25*. Chicago: University of Chicago Press.

Braithwaite, J. (1999b) 'A Future where Punishment is Marginalized: Realistic or Utopian?', *UCLA Law Review*, 46: 1727–50.

Braithwaite, J. (2000) 'Repentence Rituals and Restorative Justice', *Journal of Political Philosophy*, 8: 115–32.

Braithwaite, J. and Roche, D. (2000) 'Responsibility and Restorative Justice'. In *Restorative Community Justice*. Edited by M. Schiff and G. Bazemore. Cincinnati, OH: Anderson.

Braithwaite, J. (2001) 'Youth Development Circles', *Oxford Review of Education*, 27(2): 239–52.

Braithwaite, J. (2002a) *Restorative Justice and Responsive Regulation*. New York: Oxford University Press.

Braithwaite, J. (2002b) 'Setting Standards for Restorative Justice', *British Journal of Criminology*, 42: 563–77.

Braithwaite, J. and Mugford, S. (1994) 'Conditions of Successful Reintegration Ceremonies: Dealing with Juvenile Offenders', *British Journal of Criminology*, 34(2): 139–71.

Braithwaite, J. and Parker, C. (1999) 'Restorative Justice is Republican Justice', in G. Bazemore and L. Walgrave (eds) *Restorative Juvenile Justice: Repairing the Harm of Youth Crime*. Monsey, NY: Criminal Justice Press.

Braithwaite, J. and Pettit, P. (1990) *Not Just Deserts: A Republican Theory of Criminal Justice*. Oxford: Oxford University Press.

Braithwaite, J. and Roche, D. (2001) 'Responsibility and Restorative Justice', in G. Bazemore and M. Schiff (eds) *Restorative Community Justice. Repairing Harm and Transforming Communities*. Cincinnati, OH: Anderson.

Braithwaite, J. and Strang, H. (2001) 'Introduction: Restorative Justice and Civil Society', in H. Strang and J. Braithwaite (eds) *Restorative Justice and Civil Society*. Cambridge: Cambridge University Press.

Brehm, S. S. and Brehm J. W. (1981) *Psychological Reactance: A Theory of Freedom and Control*. New York: Academic Press.

Bush, R and Folger, J. (1994) *The Promise of Mediation: Responding to Conflict Through Empowerment*. San Fransisco, CA: Jossey-Bass.

Buss, E. (2000) 'The Role of Lawyers in Promoting Juveniles' Competence as Defendants', in T. Grisso and R. G. Schwartz (eds) *Youth on Trial. A Developmental Perspective on Juvenile Justice*. Chicago, IL/London: University of Chicago Press.

Cantor, G. M. (1976) 'An End to Crime and Punishment', *The Shingle (Philadelphia Bar Association)*, 39(4): 99–114.

Caputo, J. D. and Derrida, J. (1997) *Deconstruction in a Nutshell: a Conversation with Jacques Derrida*. New York: Fordham University Press.

Cavadino, M. and Dignan, J. (1997) 'Reparation, Retribution and Rights', *International Review of Victimology*, 4: 233–53.

Cavadino, M. and Dignan, J. (2002) *The Penal System: An Introduction*, (3rd edn). London: Sage.

Cavadino, M., Crow, I. and Dignan, J. (1999) *Criminal Justice 2000*. Winchester, UK: Waterside Press.

Cayley, D. (1998) *The Expanding Prison: The Crisis in Crime and Punishment and the Search for Alternatives*. Cleveland, OH: Pilgrim Press.

Christie, N. (1977) 'Conflicts as Property', *British Journal of Criminology*, 17(1): 1–15.

Christie, N. (1981) *Limits to Pain*. London: Martin Robertson.

Cohen, S. (1985) *Visions of Social Control*. Cambridge: Polity.

Cohen, S. (1989) 'The Critical Discourse on "Social Control": Notes on the Concept as a Hammer', *International Journal of the Sociology of Law*, 17: 347–57.

Cohen, S. (2001) *States of Denial*. Oxford: Polity.

Consedine, J. (1995) *Restorative Justice: Healing the Effects of Crime*. Lyttelton, NZ: Ploughshares Publications.

Cooley, D. and Law Commission of Canada (1999) *From Restorative Justice to Transformative Justice: Discussion Paper*. Ottawa: Law Commission of Canada.

Corrado, R. R. (2001) 'Serious and Violent Offenders and their Views on Restorative Justice Options', Paper presented at the Fifth International Conference on Restorative Justice, Leuven, 16–19 September.

Cragg, W. (1992) *The Practice of Punishment: Towards a Theory of Restorative Justice*. London/New York: Routledge.

Crawford, A. (1996) 'The Spirit of Community: Rights, Responsibilites and the Communitarian Agenda', *Journal of Law and Society*, 2: 247–62.

Crawford, A. (1997) *The Local Governance of Crime*. Oxford: Clarendon Press.

Crawford, A. (1999) 'Questioning Appeals to Community in Crime Prevention and Control', *European Journal on Criminal Policy and Research*, 7(4): 509–30.

Crawford, A. (2000a) 'Situational Crime Prevention, Urban Governance and Trust Relations', in A. von Hirsch, D. Garland and A. Wakefield (eds) *Ethical and Social Perspectives on Situational Crime Prevention*. Oxford: Hart.

Crawford, A. (2000b) 'Salient Themes Towards a Victim Perspective and the Limitations of Restorative Justice: Some Concluding Comments', in A. Crawford and J. Goodey (eds) *Integrating a Victim Perspective within Criminal Justice*. Dartmouth, MA: Ashgate.

Crawford, A. (2000c) 'Justice de Proximité – The Growth of "Houses of Justice" and Victim/Offender Mediation in France: A Very UnFrench Legal Response?', *Social and Legal Studies*, 9(1): 29–53.

Crawford, A. (2002a) (ed.) *Crime and Insecurity: The Governance of Safety in Europe*. Cullompton, UK: Willan.

Crawford, A. (2002b) 'The Prospects for Restorative Youth Justice in England and Wales', in K. McEvoy and T. Newburn (eds) *Criminology and Conflict Resolution*. London: Palgrave.

Crawford, A. and Clear, T. R. (2001) 'Community Justice: Transforming Communities Through Restorative Justice?', in G. Bazemore and M. Shiff (eds) *Restorative Community Justice: Repairing Harm and Transforming Communities.* Cincinnati, OH: Anderson.

Crawford, A. and Newburn, T. (2002) 'Recent Developments in Restorative Justice for Young People in England and Wales: Community Participation and Restoration', *British Journal of Criminology*, 42(3): 476–95.

Critchley, S. (1992) *The Ethics of Deconstruction: Derrida and Levinas.* Oxford: Blackwell Publishers.

Critchley, S. (1999) *Ethics Politics Subjectivity.* London: Verso.

Cullen, F. T. (1994) 'Social Support as an Organizing Concept for Criminology: Residential Address to the Academy of Criminal Justice Sciences', *Justice Quarterly*, 11: 527–59.

Cullen, F. T. and Gendreau, P. (2000) 'Assessing Correctional Rehabilitation: Policy, Practice, and Prospects', in J. Horney (ed.) *Changes in Decision Making and Discretion in the Criminal Justice System, Vol. 3.* Washington, DC: US Department of Justice.

Daly, K. (2000) 'Revisiting the Relationship Between Retributive and Restorative Justice', in J. Braithwaite and H. Strang (eds) *Restorative Justice: From Philosophy to Practice.* Dartmouth, MA: Ashgate.

Daly, K. (2001) 'Conferencing in Australia and New Zealand: Variations, Research Findings and Prospects', in A. Morris and G. Maxwell (eds) *Restorative Justice for Juveniles.* Oxford: Hart.

Daly, K. (2002a) 'Mind the Gap: Restorative Justice in Theory and Practice', in A. von Hirsch, J. Roberts, A. Bottoms, K. Roach and M. Schiff (eds) *Restorative Justice and Criminal Justice: Competing or Reconcilable Paradigms.* Oxford: Hart Publishing.

Daly, K. (2002b) 'Restorative Justice: The Real Story', *Punishment and Society 2002*, 4(1): 55–79.

Daly, K. and Immarigeon, R. (1998) 'The Past, Present, and Future of Restorative Justice', *Contemporary Justice Review,* 1: 21–45.

Davis, G., Boucherat, J. and Watson, D. (1988) 'Reparation in the Service of Diversion: The Subordination of a Good Idea', *Howard Journal of Criminal Justice*, 27: 127–262.

Davis, G., Boucherat, J. and Watson, D. (1989) 'Pre-court Decision-making in Juvenile Justice', *British Journal of Criminology*, 29: 219–35.

Davis, G., Messmer, H., Umbreit, M. S. and Coates, R. B. (1992) *Making Amends: Mediation and Reparation in Criminal Justice.* Routledge: London and New York.

de Keijser, J. (2000) *Punishment and Purpose. From Moral Theory to Punishment in Action.* PhD thesis, University of Leyden.

Derrida, J. (1992) 'Force of Law: The "Mystical Foundation of Authority." pp. 3–67 in *Deconstruction and the Possibility of Justice*, edited by D. Cornell, M. Rosenfeld, and D. G. Carlson. New York: Routledge.

Derrida, J. (1999) *Adieu to Emmanuel Levinas.* Stanford, CA: Stanford University Press.

Derrida, J. (2000) 'Hospitality', *Angelaki,* 5: 3–18.

Derrida, J. (2001) *On Cosmopolitanism and Forgiveness*. London: Routledge.

Derrida, J. and Dufourmantelle, A. (2000) *Of Hospitality*. Stanford, CA: Stanford University Press.

Dignan, J. (1994) 'Reintegration through reparation: a way forward for restorative justice?', in A. Duff *et al.* (eds) *Penal Theory and Practice: Tradition and Innovation in Criminal Justice*. Manchester: Manchester University Press.

Dignan, J. (1999) 'The Crime and Disorder Act and the Prospects for Restorative Justice,' *Criminal Law Review*: 48–60.

Dignan, J. (2000) *Youth Justice Pilots Evaluation: Interim Report on Reparative Work and Youth Offending Teams*. London: Home Office Research Development and Statistics Directorate.

Dignan, J. (2002) 'Towards a Systemic Model of Restorative Justice: reflections on the concept, its context and the need for clear constraints', in A. von Hirsch, J. Roberts, A. E. Bottoms, K. Roach and M. Schiff (eds) *Restorative Justice and Criminal Justice: Competing or Reconcilable Paradigms*. Oxford: Hart Publishing.

Dignan, J. and Cavadino, M. (1996) 'Towards a Framework for Conceptualising and Evaluating Models of Criminal Justice from a Victim's Perspective', *International Review of Victimology*, 4: 153–82.

Dignan, J. and Cavadino, M. (1998) 'Which Model of Criminal Justice Offers the Best Scope for Assisting Victims of Crime?', in E. Fattah and T. Peters (eds) *Support for Crime Victims in a Comparartive Perspective*. Leuven: Leuven University Press.

Dignan, J. and Lowey, K. (2000) *Restorative Justice Options for Northern Ireland*. Report commissioned for the Review of the Criminal Justice System in Northern Ireland. Research Report No. 10. Belfast: Criminal Justice Review Commission/Northern Ireland Office.

Dignan, J. and Marsh, P. (2001) 'Restorative Justice and Family Group Conferences in England: Current State and Future Prospects', in G. Maxwell and A. Morris (eds), *Restoring Justice for Juveniles: Conferences, Mediation and Circles*. Oxford: Hart Publications.

Duff, A. (1988) 'The "Victim Movement" and Legal Reform', in M. Maguire and J. Pointing (eds), *Victims of Crime: A New Deal?* Milton Keynes, UK: Open University Press.

Duff, R. A. (1986) *Trials and Punishments*. Cambridge: Cambridge University Press.

Duff, R. A. (1996) *Criminal Attempts*. Oxford: Oxford University Press.

Duff, R. A. (2001) *Punishment, Communication and Community*. Oxford: Oxford University Press.

Duff, R. A. (2002) 'Punishing the Young', in I. Weijers and A. Duff (eds) *Punishing Juveniles: Principle and Critique*. Oxford: Hart.

Duff, R. A., Marshall, S, Dobash, R. E. and Dobash, R. P. (1994) *Penal Theory and Practice: Tradition and Innovation in Criminal Justice*, Manchester: Manchester University Press.

Dullum, J. and Christie, N. (1996) *Konfliktrådene*. Oslo: Institute of Criminology.

Durkheim, E. (1893) *De la division du travail social*. Paris: PUF, 1978.

Dworkin, R. (1986) *Law's Empire*. Cambridge, MA: Harvard University Press.

Eco, U. and Martini, C. (1997) *Belief or Nonbelief? A Confrontation*. New York: Arcade Publishing.

Eggermont, M. (1994) *Stomme Streken. Jongeren over hun Beleving van Straf.* Alphen a/d Rijn: Samsom H.D. Tjeenk Willink.

European Forum for Victim–Offender Mediation and Restorative Justice (ed.) (2000) *Victim–Offender Mediation in Europe. Making Restorative Justice Work.* Leuven: Leuven University Press.

Fatic, A. (1995) *Punishment and Restorative Crime-Handling.* Aldershot, UK: Avebury.

Fattah, E. (1995) 'Restorative and Retributive Justice Models, A Comparison', in H. Kühne (ed.) *Festschrift für Koichi Miyazawa.* Nomos Verlagsgesellschaft.

Fattah, E. (1998) 'A Critical Assessment of Two Justice Paradigms: Contrasting the Restorative and Retributive Models', in E. Fattah and T. Peters (eds) *Support for Crime Victims in a Comparative Perspective: A Collection of Essays dedicated to the Memory of Prof. Frederic McClintock.* Leuven: Leuven University Press.

Feeley, M. and Simon, J. (1992) 'The New Penology: Notes on the Emerging Strategy of Corrections and its Implications', *Criminology,* 30, 451–471.

Feld, B. (1999) 'Rehabilitation, Retribution and Restorative Justice: Alternative Conceptions of Juvenile Justice', in G. Bazemore and L. Walgrave (eds) *Restorative Juvenile Justice: Repairing the Harm of Youth Crime.* Monsey: Criminal Justice Press.

Fisse, B. (1983) 'Reconstructing Corporate Criminal Law: Deterrence, Retribution, Fault, and Sanctions', *Southern California Law Review,* 56: 1141–246.

Foster, J. (1995) 'Informal Social Control and Community Crime Prevention', *British Journal of Criminology,* 35(4): 563–83.

Foucault, M. (1984) *The Foucault Reader.* New York: Pantheon Books.

Foucault, M. (1988) *The Care of the Self: The History of Sexuality, Vol. 3.* New York: Vintage Books.

Foucault, M. (1994) *Ethics: Subjectivity and Truth,* P. Rabinow (ed.). New York: The New Press.

Furedi, F. (forthcoming) *The State of Emotion.*

Gaita, R. (1991) *Good and Evil: an Absolute Conception.* London: Macmillan.

Galaway, B. and Hudson, J. (1996) *Restorative Justice: International Perspectives.* Monsey, NY: Criminal Justice Press.

Garfinkel, H. (1956) 'Conditions for Successful Degradation Ceremonies', *American Journal of Sociology,* 61: 420–424.

Garland, D. (1985) *Punishment and Welfare.* Aldershot, UK: Gower.

Garland, D. (1990) *Punishment and Modern Society; A Study in Social Theory.* Oxford: Clarendon Press.

Garland, D. (1996) 'The Limits of the Sovereign State', *British Journal of Criminology,* 36(4): 445–71.

Garland, D. (2001) *Culture of Control; Crime and Social Order in Contemporary Society.* Oxford: Oxford University Press.

Giddens, A. (1990) *The Consequences of Modernity.* Cambridge: Polity Press.

Gilling, D. (2001) 'Community safety and Social Policy', *European Journal on Criminal Policy and Research,* 9(4): 381–400.

Girling, E., Loader, I. and Sparks, R. (2000) *Crime and Social Change in Middle England.* London: Routledge.

Goris, P. (2001) *Op zoek naar de krijtlijnen van een sociaal rechtvaardige veiligheidszorg.* PhD thesis, KU Leuven.

Grisso, T. (2000) 'What We Know about Youth's Capacities as Trial Defendants', in T. Grisso and R. G. Schwartz (eds) *Youth on Trial. A Developmental Perspective on Juvenile Justice*. Chicago/London: University of Chicago Press.

Grisso, T. and Schwartz, R. G. (eds) (2000) *Youth on Trial. A Developmental Perspective on Juvenile Justice*. Chicago/London: University of Chicago Press.

Hadley, M. L. (2001) *The Spiritual Roots of Restorative Justice*. New York: State University of New York Press.

Halliday, J. (2001) *Making Punishments Work: Report of a Review of the Sentencing Framework for England and Wales*. London: Home Office Communications Directorate.

Harris, M. K. (1998) 'Reflections of a Skeptical Dreamer: Some Dilemmas in Restorative Justice Theory and Practice', *Contemporary Justice Review*, 1: 57–70.

Harris, N. (2001) 'Shaming and Shame: regulating drink-driving, in E. Ahmed, N. Harris, J. Braithwaite and V. Braithwaite, *Shame Management Through Reintegration*. Cambridge: Cambridge University Press.

Hart, H. L. A. (1968) 'Prolegomenon to the Principles of Punishment', *Punishment and Responsibility*. Oxford: Oxford University Press.

Hawkins, J. D. (1999) 'Preventing Crime and Violence through Communities that Care', *European Journal on Criminal Policy and Research*, 7(4): 443–58.

Hertzberg, L. (1988) 'On the Attitude of Trust', *Inquiry*, 31: 307–22.

Hirschi, T. and Gottfredson, M. (1991) 'Rethinking the Juvenile Justice System', in T. Booth (ed.) *Juvenile Justice in the New Europe*. Sheffield: Social Services Monographs.

Hobsbawn E. (1994) *Age Of Extremes: The Short Twentieth Century, 1914–1991*. London: Abacus.

Holdaway, S., Davidson, N., Dignan, J., Hammersley, R., Hine, J. and Marsh, P. (2001) *New strategies to address youth offending: the national evaluation of the pilot youth offending teams*, RDS Occasional Paper no. 69. London: Home Office Research, Development and Statistics Directorate. Available at www.homeoffice.gov.uk/rds/index.html

Home Office (1997) *No More Excuses*, Cm 3809. London: Home Office.

Home Office (2000) *Circular Introducing the Final Warning Scheme: Revised Guidance*. London: Home Office. Available at www.homeoffice.gov.uk/yousys/youth.htm

Home Office (2001) *Criminal Justice: The Way Ahead*, Cm 5074. London: The Stationery Office.

Hough, M. (1996) 'People Talking about Punishment', *Howard Journal*, 35(3): 191–214.

Hoyle, C. and Young, R. (2002) *Proceed with Caution: an Evaluation of Police-led Restorative Justice*. York: Joseph Rowntree Foundation.

Hudson, J., Morris, A., Maxwell, G. and Galaway, B. (1996) *Family Group Conferences. Perspectives on Policy and Practice*. Annandale/Monsey: Federation Press/Criminal Justice Press.

Huls, F. W. M., Schreuders, M. M. et al. (2001) *Criminaliteit en rechtshandhaving 2000; ontwikkelingen en samenhangen*. Den Haag, CBS/WODC.

Hulsman, L. (1986) 'Critical Criminology and the Concept of Crime', *Contemporary Crises*, 10: 63–80.

227

Immarigeon, R. (1999) 'Implementing the Balanced and Restorative Justice Model: A Critical Appraisal', *Community Corrections Report*, 6: 35–47.

Johnstone, G. (2002) *Restorative Justice. Ideas, Values, Debates*. Cullompton, UK: Willan Publishing.

Jones, T., Newburn, T. and Smith, D. (1994) *Democracy and Policing*. London: Policy Studies Institute.

Karp, D. (2001), 'The Offender/Community Encounter: Stakeholder Involvement in the Vermont Reparative Boards', in D. Karp and T. Clear (eds) *What is Community Justice? Case Studies of Restorative Justice and Community Supervision*. Thousand Oaks, CA: Pine Forge Press.

Karp, D. and Walther, K. (2001) 'Community Reparative Boards in Vermont', in G. Bazemore and M. Schiff (eds) *Restorative Community Justice*. Cincinnati, OH: Anderson Publications.

Kershaw, C., Budd, T., Kinshott, G., Mattinson, J., Mayhew, P. and Myhill, A. (2000) *The 2000 British Crime Survey*. London: Home Office.

Kurki, L. (2000) 'Restorative and Community Justice in the United States', in M. Tonry (ed.), *Crime and Justice: An Annual Review of Research, Vol. 26*. Chicago: University of Chicago Press.

Lab, S. (1993) *Crime Prevention. Approaches, Practices and Evaluations*. Cincinnati, OH: Anderson.

LaPrairie, C. (1995) 'Community Justice or Just Communities? Aboriginal Communities in Search of Justice', *Canadian Journal of Criminology*, 37: 521–45.

Levinas, E. (1998) *Ethics and Infinity: Conversations with Philippe Nemo*. Pittsburgh, PA: Dusquesne University Press.

Levrant, S., Cullen, F., Fulton, B. and Wozniak, J. (1999). 'Reconsidering Restorative Justice: The Corruption of Benevolence Revisited?', *Crime and Delinquency*, 45(1): 3–27.

Liebling, A. (2001) 'Policy and practice in the management of disruptive prisoners: incentives and earned privileges, the Spurr Report and Close Supervision Centres', in E. Clare and K. Bottomley (eds) *Evaluation of Close Supervision Centres*. Home Office Research Study No. 136. London: Home Office Research, Development and Statistics Directorate.

Lord Chancellor's Department (2001) *Judicial Statistics, 2000*. London: HMSO.

Luna, E. (2002) 'Punishment Theory and the Holistic Process', *University of Utah Law Review*.

Lundman, R. J. (2001) *Prevention and Control of Juvenile Delinquency*. Oxford: Oxford University Press.

Lyotard, J-F. (1979) *La condition postmoderne; rapport sur le savoir*. Paris: Editions de Minuit.

Lyotard, J-F. (1984) *The Postmodern Condition: A Report on Knowledge*. Minneapolis, MN: University of Minnesota Press.

Lyotard, J-F. and Thebaud, J-L. (1979) *Just Gaming*. Minneapolis, MN: University of Minnesota Press.

MacIntyre, A. (1983) *After Virtue, A study in Moral Theory*. Notre Dame, IN: University of Notre Dame Press.

MacIntyre, A. (1988) *Whose Justice? Which Rationality?* Notre Dame, IN: Notre Dame University Press.

Maloney, D. (1998) 'The Challenge of Restorative Community Justice', address at the Annual Meeting of the Juvenile Justice Coalition, Washington DC, February.

Mannozzi, G. (2000) 'From the 'Sword' to Dialogue; Towards a 'Dialectical' Basis for Penal Mediation'. Paper presented on the Fourth International Conference on Restorative Justice for Juveniles, Tübingen.

Marshall, S. E. and Duff, R. A. (1998) 'Criminalization and Sharing Wrongs', *Canadian Journal of Law and Jurisprudence*, 11: 7–22.

Marshall, T. (1988) 'Out of Court: More or Less Justice?', in T. Matthews (ed.) *Informal Justice*. London: Sage.

Marshall, T. (1994) 'Grassroots Initiative' Towards Restorative Justice: the New Paradigm?, in A. Duff et al. (eds), Penal Theory and Practice. *Tradition and Innovation in Criminal Justice*. Manchester: Manchester University Press.

Marshall, T. (1995) 'Restorative Justice on Trial in Britain', *Mediation Quarterly*, 12: 217–31.

Marshall, T. (1996) 'The Evolution of Restorative Justice in Britain', *European Journal of Criminal Policy and Research*, 4(4): 21–43.

Marshall, T. (1999) *Restorative Justice: An Overview*. London: Home Office Research, Development and Statistics Directorate.

Marshall, T. F. and Merry, S. (1990) *Crime and Accountability: Victim/Offender Mediation in Practice*. HMSO: London.

Maruna, S. (2001) *Making Good: How Ex-Convicts Reform and Rebuild Their Lives*. Washington, DC: American Psychological Association.

Masten, A. and Coatsworth, J. (1998) 'The Development of Competence in Favorable and Unfavorable Environments', *American Psychologist*, 53: 205–220.

Mathiesen, T. (1974) *The Politics of Abolition*. London: Martin Robertson.

Maxwell, G. and Morris A. (1993) *Family, Victims and Culture: Youth Justice in New Zealand*. Wellington, New Zealand: Social Policy Agency and Institute of Criminology, Victoria University.

Maxwell, G. and Morris, A. (1999) *Understanding Re-offending*. Wellington, New Zealand: Institute of Criminology, Victoria University.

McCold, P. (1996) 'Restorative Justice and the Role of Community', in B. Galaway and J. Hudson (eds) *Restorative Justice: International Perspectives*. Monsey, NY: Criminal Justice Press.

McCold, P. (1998) 'Restorative justice: variations on a theme', in L. Walgrave (ed.) *Restorative Justice for Juveniles: Potentialities, Risks, and Problems for Research*. Leuven, Belgium: Leuven University Press.

McCold, P. (2000). 'Toward a Holistic Vision of Restorative Juvenile Justice: A Reply to the Maximalist Model', *Contemporary Justice Review*, 3(4): 357–72.

McCold, P. and Wachtel, B. (1998) *Restorative Policing Experiment: The Bethlehem Pennsylvania Police Family Group Conferencing Project*. Pipersville, PA: Community Service Foundation.

McCold, P. and Watchel, B. (1998b) 'Community is Not a Place: A New Look at Community Justice Initiatives', *Contemporary Justice Review*, 1(1): 71–85.

McCord, J., Spatz Widom and Crowell, N. A. (eds) (2001) *Juvenile Crime, Juvenile Justice*. Washington, DC: National Academy Press.

McDonald, J. and Moore, D. (2001) 'Community Conferencing as a Special Case of

Conflict Transformation', in H. Strang and J. Braithwaite (eds) *Restorative Justice and Civil Society*. Cambridge, UK: Cambridge University Press.

McDonald, J., Moore, D., O'Connell, D., and Thorsborne, M. (1995) *Real Justice Training Manual: Coordinating Family Group Conferences*. Pipersville Pennsylvania: The Piper's Press.

McElrea, F. (1994) 'Justice in the community: The New Zealand Experience', in J. Burnside and N. Baker (eds) *Relational Justice: Reparing the Breach*. Winchester, UK: Waterside Press.

McEvoy, K. and Mika, H. (2002) 'Restorative Justice and the Critique of Informalism in Northern Ireland', *British Journal of Criminology*, 42(3): 534–63.

McKnight, J. (1995) *The Careless Society: Community and Its Counterfeits*. New York: Basic Books.

Melton, A. P. (1995) 'Indigenous Justice Systems and Tribal Society', *Judicature*, 79: 126.

Merry, S. E. (1981) *Urban Danger: Life in a Neighborhood of Strangers*. Philadelphia, PA: Temple University Press.

Merry, S. E. and Milner, N. (eds) (1993) *The Possibility of Popular Justice*. Michigan: University of Michigan Press.

Miers, D. (2000) 'Taking the Law into their Own Hands: Victims as Offenders', in A. Crawford and J. Goodey (eds) *Integrating a Victim Perspective within Criminal Justice*. Aldershot, UK: Ashgate.

Miers, D. (2001) *An International Review of Restorative Justice*. Crime Reduction Research Series Paper 10. London: Home Office.

Miers, D., Maguire, M., Goldie, S., Sharpe, K., Hale, C., Netten, A., Uglow, S., Doolin, K., Hallam, A., Enterkin, J. and Newburn, T. (2001) *An Exploratory Evaluation of Restorative Justice Schemes*. London: Home Office.

Mika, H. (1995) 'On Limits and Needs: A Justice Agenda', *Mediation Quarterly*, 12: 293–7.

Miller, W. I. (1993) *Humiliation*. Ithaca, NY: Cornell University Press.

Moffit, T. (1993) 'Adolescent-limited and life course presistent antisocial behavior: A developmental taxonomy', *Psychological Bulletin*, 100: 674–700.

Molm, L. and K. Cook (1995) 'Social Exchange and Exchange Networks', in K. Cook, G. Fine and J. House (eds) *Sociological Perspectives on Social Psychology*. Boston, MA: Allyn and Bacon.

Moon, M., Sundt, J., Cullen, F. and Wright, J. (2000) 'Is Child Saving Dead? Public Support for Rehabilitation,' *Crime and Delinquency*, 46: 38–60.

Moore, D. and McDonald, J. (2000) *Transforming Conflict in Workplaces and Other Communities*. Sydney: Transformative Justice Australia.

Moore, D. B. (1993) 'Evaluating Family Group Conferences: some early findings from Wagga Wagga', paper delivered to the Australian Institute of Criminology Criminal Justice Planning and Co-ordination meeting, Canberra, April.

Moore, D. B. and O'Connell, T. (1994) 'Family Group Conferencing in a Communitarian Model of Justice', in C. Alder and J. Wundersitz (eds) *Family Conferencing and Juvenile Justice*. Canberra: Australian Studies in Law, Crime and Justice, Australian Institute of Criminology.

Moore, M. S. (1997) *Placing Blame: A Theory of Criminal Law*. Oxford: Oxford University Press.

Moore, R. H. (1987) 'Effectiveness of Citizen Volunteers Functioning as Counselors for High-Risk Young Male Offenders', *Psychological Reports*, 61(3): 823–30.

Mørland, L. (2000) 'Community Facilitation in the Norwegian "Mediation Service": What's Happening?', *International Review of Victimology*, 7: 243–50.

Morris, A. (2002) 'Shame, Guilt and Remorse: Experiences from the Family Group Conferences', in I. Weijers and A. Duff (eds) *Punishing Juveniles: Principle and Critique*. Oxford: Hart.

Morris, A. and Maxwell, G. (2000) 'The Practice of Family Group Conferences in New Zealand', in A. Crawford and J. Goodey (eds) *Integrating a Victim Perspective Within Criminal Justice*. Aldershot, UK: Ashgate.

Morris, R. (2000) *Stories of Transformative Justice*. Toronto: Canadian Scholars' Press.

Murphy, J. G. (1988) 'Forgiveness and Resentment', in J. G. Murphy and J. Hampton *Forgiveness and Mercy*. Cambridge: Cambridge University Press.

Nathanson, D. (1992) *Shame and Pride: Affect, Sex and the Birth of the Self*. New York: Norton.

Nelken, D. (1994) 'The Future of Comparative Criminology', in D. Nelken (ed.) *The Futures of Criminology*. London: Sage.

Newburn, T., Crawford, A., Earle, R., Goldie, S., Hale, C., Masters, G., Netten, A., Saunders R., Sharpe, K., Uglow, S. and Campbell, A. (2001a) *The Introduction of Referral Orders into the Youth Justice System: Second Interim Report*, Occasional Paper 73. London: Home Office.

Newburn, T., Masters, G., Earle, R., Goldie, S, Crawford, A., Sharpe, K, Netton, A., Hale, C., Uglow, S. and Saunders, R. (2001b) *The Introduction of Referral Orders into the Youth Justice System*. Occasional Paper 70. London: Home Office Research, Development and Statistics Directorate. Available at www.homeoffice.gov.uk/rds/index.html

Newburn, T., Crawford, A., Earle, R., Goldie, S, Hale, C., Hallam, A., Masters, G., Netton, A., Saunders, R. Sharpe, K, and Uglow, S. (2002) *The Introduction of Referral Orders into the Youth Justice System: Final Report*, Home Office Research Study no. 242. London: Home Office Research, Development and Statistics Directorate. Available at www.homeoffice.gov.uk/rds/pdfs2/hors242.pdf

Nussbaum, M. (1995) 'Human Capabilities: Female Human Beings', in M. C. Nussbaum and J. Glover (eds) *Women, Culture, and Development*. Oxford: Clarendon Press.

O'Brien, S., Karp, D., Bazemore, G. and Leip, L. (2002*) Who Are We Serving and How Are We Doing: An Analysis of Program Referrals and Performance in Balanced and Restorative Justice*, Monograph. Ft. Lauderdale, FL: Community Justice Institute, Florida Atlantic University.

Olthof, T. (2002) 'Shame, Guilt, Antisocial Behaviour, and Juvenile Justice: A Psychological Perspective', in I. Weijers and A. Duff (eds) *Punishing Juveniles: Principle and Critique*. Oxford: Hart.

Pavlich, G. (1996a) *Justice Fragmented: Mediating Community Disputes Under Postmodern Conditions*. London: Routledge.

Pavlich, G. (1996b) 'The Power of Community Mediation: Government and Formation of Self', *Law and Society Review*, 30: 101–27.

Pavlich, G. (2000) *Critique and Radical Discourses on Crime*. Aldershot, UK: Ashgate.

Pavlich, G. (2001) 'The Force of Community', in H. Strang and J. Braithwaite (eds) *Restorative Justice and Civil Society*. Cambridge: Cambridge University Press.

Pennel, J. and Burford, G. (2000) 'Family Group Decision Making: Protecting Children and Women,' *Child Welfare*, 79(2): 131–58.

Petrunik, M. G. and Shearing, C. (1988) 'The "I," the "Me," and the "It": Moving beyond the Meadian conception of self', *Canadian Journal of Sociology*, 13(4): 435–48.

Polk, K. and Kobrin, S. (1972) *Delinquency Prevention Through Youth Development*. Washington, DC: Office of Youth Development.

Pranis, K. (1998) 'Engaging the Community in Restorative Justice', Balanced and Restorative Justice Project, OJJDP, Department of Justice, available at ssw.che.umn.edu/rjp/Resources/Documents/cpra98a.pdf

Pranis, K. (2000) 'Conferencing and the Community', in G. Burford and J. Hudson (eds) *Family Group Conferencing: New Directions in Community-Centered Child and Family Practice*. New York: Aldine de Gruyter.

Pranis, K. and Bazemore, G. (2001) *Engaging Community in the Response to Youth Crime: A Restorative Justice Approach*, Monograph. Washington, DC: Office of Juvenile Justice and Delinquency Prevention, Balanced and Restorative Justice Project, US Department of Justice.

Pranis, K., and Umbreit, M. (1992) *Public Opinion Research Challenges Perception of Wide Spread Public Demand for Harsher Punishment*. Minneapolis, MN: Minnesota Citizens Council on Crime and Justice.

Presser, L. and Van Voorhis, P. (2002). 'Values and Evaluation: Assessing Processes and Outcomes of Restorative Justice Programs', *Crime and Delinquency*, 48(1): 162–88.

Putnam, R. (1993) *Making Democracy Work: Civic Traditions in Modern Italy*. Princeton, NJ: Princeton University Press.

Putnam, R. (1995) 'Bowling Alone: America's Declining Social Capital', *Journal of Democracy*, 6: 64–78.

Putnam, R. (2000) *Bowling Alone: The Collapse and Revival of American Community*. New York, NY: Simon and Shuster.

Raine, J. W. (2001) 'Modernizing Courts or Courting Modernization?', *Criminal Justice*, 1(1): 105–28.

Rawls, J. (1971) *A Theory of Justice*. Cambridge, MA: Belknap Press of Harvard University Press.

Reissman, F. (1962) 'The "Helper Therapy" Principle', *Social Work*, 10: 27–32.

Restorative Justice Consortium (1999) *Standards for Restorative Justice*. London: National Council for Social Concern on behalf of the Restorative Justice Consortium.

Restorative Justice Consortium (2002) *Statement of Restorative Justice Principles*. London: Restorative Justice Consortium.

Retzinger, S. M. and Scheff, T. J. (1996). 'Strategy for Community Conferences: Emotions and Social Bonds', in B. Galaway and J. Hudson (eds) *Restorative Justice: International Perspectives*. Monsey, NY: Criminal Justice Press.

Roberts, J. and Roach, K. (2002) 'Restorative Justice in Canada: From Sentencing Circles to Sentencing Principles', in A. von Hirsch, J. Roberts, A. E. Bottoms,

K. Roach and M. Schiff (eds) *Restorative Justice and Criminal Justice: Competing or Reconcilable Paradigms*. Oxford: Hart Publishing.

Rorty, R. (1989) *Contingency, Irony and Solidarity*. Cambridge: Cambridge University Press.

Rose, D. and Clear, T. (1998) 'Incarceration, Social Capital and Crime: Implications for Social Disorganization Theory', *Criminology*, 36(3): 471–79.

Rosenbaum, D. P. (1988) 'Community Crime Prevention: A Review and Synthesis of the Literature', *Justice Quarterly*, 5(3): 323–93.

Ross, R. (1996) *Returning to the Teachings: Exploring Aboriginal Justice*. London: Penguin Books.

Ross, R. (2000) 'Searching for the Roots of Conferencing', in G. Burford and J. Hudson (eds) *Family Group Conferencing: New Directions in Community-Centered Child and Family Practice*. New York: Aldine De Gruyter.

Sampson, R. and Laub, J. (1993) *Crime in the Making: Pathways and Turning Points Through Life*. Cambridge, MA: Harvard University Press.

Sarat, A. (1988) 'The New Formalism in Disputing and Dispute Processing', *Law and Society Review*, 21: 695–715.

Schauer, F. (1991) *Playing by the Rules: A Philosophical Examination of Rule-Based Decision-Making in Law and in Life*. Oxford: Clarendon Press.

Scheid, D. E. (1980) 'Note on Defining "Punishment"', *Canadian Journal of Philosophy*, 10: 453–62.

Schiff, M. (1999) 'The Impact of Restorative Interventions on Juvenile Offenders', in G. Bazemore and L. Walgrave (eds) *Restorative Juvenile Justice: Repairing the Harm of Youth Crimes*. Monsey, NY: Criminal Justice Press.

Schiff, M., Bazemore, G. and Erbe, C. (2002) 'Tracking Restorative Justice Decisionmaking in the Response to Youth Crime: The Prevalence of Youth Conferencing in the United States' (forthcoming).

Schneider, E. (1991) 'The Violence of Privacy', *Connecticut Law Review*, 23: 973–98.

Schwartz, I. M. (1992) 'Public Attitudes Toward Juvenile Crime and Juvenile Justice: Implications for Public Policy', in I. M. Schwartz (ed.) *Juvenile Justice Policy*. Lexington, MA: Lexington Books.

Scott, E., Reppucci, N. and Woolard, J. (1995) 'Evaluating Adolescent Decisionmaking in Legal Contexts', *Law and Human Behavior*, 19: 221–44.

Scourfield, J. and Dobash, R. P. (1999) 'Programmes for Violent Men: Recent Developments in the UK', *Howard Journal of Criminal Justice*, 38: 128–43.

Sebba, L. (2000) 'The Individualisation of the Victim', in A. Crawford and J. Goodey (eds) *Integrating a Victim Perspective within Criminal Justice*. Aldershot, UK: Ashgate.

Sennett, R. (1996) *The Uses of Disorder*. London: Faber and Faber.

Sherman, L. W. (1993) 'Defiance, Deterrence and Irrelevance: A Theory of the Criminal Sanction', *Journal of Research in Crime and Delinquency*, 30: 445–73.

Sherman, L. W. (1998) 'American Policing', in M. Tonry (ed.) *The Handbook of Crime and Punishment*. New York: Oxford University Press.

Sherman, L. (2000) 'Repeat Offending in the Canberra RISE Project: An Overview', Paper presented at the Annual Meeting of the American Society of Criminology, San Francisco, CA.

Sherman, L., Strang, H. and Woods, D. (2000) 'Captains of Restorative Justice: Experience, Legitimacy and Recidivism', paper presented to the International Conference on Restorative Justice, Tubingen 1–4 October.

Shklar, J. (1984) *Ordinary Vices*. Cambridge: Belknap Press.

Skeat, W. W. (1993) *The Concise Dictionary of English Etymology*. Hertfordshire: Wadsworth.

Smart, B. (1992) *Modern Conditions, Postmodern Controversies*. London: Routledge.

Smart, B. (1993) *Postmodernity*. London: Routledge.

Smeyers, P. (1996) 'Over 'vertrouwen' en 'zorg' als morele en als pedagogische basisconcepten', *Pedagogisch Tijdschrift*, 21: 48–68.

Steinberg, L. and Cauffman, E. (1996) 'Maturity of Judgment in Adolescence: Psychosocial Factors in Adolescent Decision-making', *Law and Human Behavior*, 20: 249–72.

Steinberg, L. and Schwartz, R. G. (2000) 'Developmental psychology goes to court', in T. Grisso and R. G. Schwartz (eds) *Youth on Trial: A Developmental Perspective on Juvenile Justice*. Chicago/London: University of Chicago Press.

Stewart, T. (1996) 'Family Group Conferences with Young Offender in New Zealand', in J. Hudson, A. Morris, G. Maxwell and B. Galaway (eds) *Family Group Conferences. Perspectives on Policy and Practice*. Annandale/Monsey: Federation Press/Criminal Justice Press.

Strang, H. and Braithwaite, J. (eds) (2001) *Restorative Justice and Civil Society*. Cambridge: Cambridge University Press.

Strang, H., Barnes, G., Braithwaite, J. and Sherman, L. (1999) *Experiments in Restorative Policing*. Canberra: ANU.

Stuart, B. (1996) 'Circle Sentencing – Turning Swords into Ploughshares', in B. Galaway and J. Hudson (eds) *Restorative Justice: International Perspectives*. Monsey, NY: Criminal Justice Press.

Stuart, B. (2001) 'Guiding Principles for Designing Peacemaking Circles', in G. Bazemore and M. Schiff (eds) *Restorative Community Justice*. Cincinnati, OH: Anderson Publishing.

Sullivan, D. and Tifft, L. (2001) *Restorative Justice: Healing the Foundations of our Everyday Lives*. Monsey, NY: Willow Tree Press.

Sullivan, D., Tifft, L. and Cordella, P. (1998) 'The Phenomenon of Restorative Justice', *Contemporary Justice Review*, 1: 1–14.

Sullivan, M. (1989) *Getting Paid: Youth Crime and Work in the Inner City*. Ithaca, NY: Cornell University Press.

Sunstein C. R. (1996) *Legal Reasoning and Political Conflict*. New York: Oxford University Press.

Taylor, G. (2002) 'Guilt, Shame and Shaming', in I. Weijers and A. Duff (eds) *Punishing Juveniles: Principle and Critique*. Oxford: Hart.

Thompson, E. P. (1975) *Whigs and Hunters*. Harmondsworth: Penguin.

Toews, B. and Zehr, H. (2001) 'Restorative Justice and Substance Abuse: The Path Ahead', *Youth and Society*, 33(2): 314–28.

Tomasic, R. and Feeley, M. (eds) (1982) *Neighbourhood Justice: An Assessment of an Emerging Idea*. New York: Longman.

Tonry, M. (1999) 'The Fragmentaition of Sentencing and Corrections in America', a paper from the Executive Sessions on Sentencing and Corrections. Washington DC: National Institute of Justice.

Tudor, S. (2001) 'Accepting One's Punishment as Meaningful Suffering', *Law and Philosophy*, 20: 581–604.

Tulkens, F. (1993) 'Les transformations du droit pénal aux Etats-Unis. Pour un autre modèle de justice', in UCL Law Faculty (ed.) *Nouveaux itinéraires en droit*. Bruxelles: Bruylandt.

Umbreit, M. (1998) 'Restorative Justice through Victim Offender Mediation: A Multi-Site Assessment', *Western Criminology Review*, 1(1): 1–29.

Umbreit, M. (1999) 'Avoiding the Marginalization and McDonaldization of Victim Offender Mediation: A Case Study in Moving Toward the Mainstream', in G. Bazemore and L. Walgrave (ed.) *Restoring Juvenile Justice: Repairing the Harm of Youth Crime*. Monsey, NY: Criminal Justice Press.

Umbreit, M. (2001) *The Handbook of Victim Offender Mediation*. San Francisco, CA: Jossey-Bass.

Umbreit, M., Coates, R. B. and Kalanj, B. (1994) *Victim Meets Offender: the Impact of Restorative Justice and Mediation*. Monsey, NY: Criminal Justice Press.

Umbreit, M. and Roberts, A. (1996) *Mediation of Criminal Conflict in England: An Assessment of Services in Coventry and Leeds*. St. Paul, MN: Centre for Restorative Justice and Mediation, University of Minnesota.

Van Creveld, M. (1999). *The Rise and Decline of the State*. Cambridge: Cambridge University Press.

Van Ness, D. (1993) 'New Wine and Old Wineskins: Four Challenges of Restorative Justice', *Criminal Law Forum*, 4: 251–76.

Van Ness, D. (2000) 'The Shape of Things to Come: A Framework for Thinking about A Restorative Justice System', paper presented at the Fourth International Conference on Restorative Justice for Juveniles, October 1–4, Tübingen, Germany.

Van Ness, D and Strong, K.H. (1997) *Restoring Justice*. Cincinatti, OH: Anderson.

Van Ness, D. and Strong, K.H. (2002) *Restoring Justice* (2nd edn). Cincinnati, OH: Anderson.

Van Ness, D., Morris, A. and Maxwell, G. (2001) 'Introducing Restorative Justice', in A. Morris and G. Maxwell (eds) *Restorative Justice for Juveniles. Conferencing, Mediation and Circles*. Oxford: Hart.

Verstraete, A., Verhoeven, H. and Vandeurzen, I. (2000) 'Introducing Restorative Justice in Belgian Prisons', paper presented at The 10th International Symposium on Victimology, August, Montreal.

von Hirsch, A. (1993) *Censure and Sanctions*. Oxford: Clarendon Press.

von Hirsch, A. (1998) 'Penal Theories', in M. Tonry (ed.) *The Handbook of Crime and Punishment*. New York/Oxford: Oxford University Press.

von Hirsch, A. and Jareborg, N. (1991) 'Gauging Criminal Harm: a Living-standard Analysis', *Oxford Journal of Legal Studies*, 11: 1–38.

von Hirsch, A., Roberts, J., Bottoms, A. E., Roach, K. and Schiff, M. (eds) (2002) *Restorative Justice and Criminal Justice: Competing or Reconcilable Paradigms*. Oxford: Hart.

Wacquant, L. (2001) 'The Penalisation of Poverty and the Rise of Neo-Liberalism', *European Journal on Criminal Policy and Research*, 9(4): 401–412.

Walgrave, L. (1994) 'Beyond Rehabilitation: in Search of a Constructive Alternative in the Judicial Response to Juvenile Crime', *European Journal on Criminal Policy and Research*, 2: 57–75.

Walgrave, L. (1998) *Restorative Justice for Juveniles: Potentialities, Risks, and Problems for Research*. Leuven, Belgium: Leuven University Press.

Walgrave, L. (1999) 'Community Service as a Cornerstone within a Systematic Restorative Response to (Juvenile) Crime', in G. Bazemore and L. Walgrave (eds) *Restorative Juvenile Justice: Repairing the Harm by Youth Crime*. Monsey, NY: Criminal Justice Press.

Walgrave, L. (2000a) 'How Pure Can a Maximalist Approach to Restorative Justice Remain? Or Can a Purist Model of Restorative Justice Become Maximalist?', *Contemporary Justice Review* 3(4): 415–32.

Walgrave, L. (2000b) 'Restorative Justice and the Republican Theory of Criminal Justice. An Exercise in Normative Theorizing on Restorative Justice', in H. Strang and J. Braithwaite (eds) *Restorative Justice: from Philosophy to Practice*. Dartmouth: Ashgate.

Walgrave, L. (2001a) 'Restoration and Punishment. On Favourable Similarities and Fortunate Differences', in G. Maxwell and A. Morris (eds) *Restoring Justice for Juveniles*. Oxford: Hart.

Walgrave, L. (2001b) *Met het oog op herstel*. Leuven: Leuven University Press.

Walgrave, L. (2002a) 'Imposing Restoration Instead of Inflicting Pain: Reflections on the Judicial Reaction to Crime', in A. von Hirsch, J. Roberts, A. E. Bottoms, K. Roach and M. Schiff (eds) *Restorative Justice and Criminal Justice: Competing or Reconcilable Paradigms*. Oxford: Hart Publishing.

Walgrave, L. (2002b) 'Not Punishing Children but Committing them to Restore', in I. Weijers and R. A. Duff (eds) *Punishing Juveniles: Principle and Critique*. Oxford: Hart Publishing.

Walgrave, L. and Bazemore, G. (1999) 'Restorative Justice: In Search of Fundamentals. In G. Bazemore and L. Walgrave. *Restorative Juvenile Justice: Repairing the Harm of Youth Crime*. Monsey, NY: Criminal Justice Press.

Walgrave, L. and Geudens, H. (1997) 'The Restorative Proportionality of Community Service for Juveniles', *European Journal of Crime, Criminal Law and Criminal Justice*, 4(4): 361–80.

Walgrave L., Geudens, H. and Schelkens, W. (1997) *Naar een herstelrechtelijk jeugdsanctierecht*. In opdracht van de Minister van Justitie. Leuven: Onderzoeksgroep Jeugdcriminologie.

Walgrave, S. and Rihoux, B. (1997) *De Witte Mars, een jaar later*. Leuven: Van Halewijck.

Walklate, S. and Evans, K. (1999) *Zero Tolerance or Community Tolerance? Managing Crime in High Crime Areas*. Avebury: Ashgate.

Walzer, M. (1983) *Spheres of Justice: a Defense of Pluralism*. New York: Basic Books.

Watchel, T. and McCold, P. (2001) 'Restorative Justice in Everyday Life', in H. Strang and J. Braithwaite (eds) *Restorative Justice and Civil Society*. Cambridge: Cambridge University Press.

Watson, D, Boucherat, J. and Davis, G. (1989) 'Reparation for Retributivists', in W. Wright and B. Galaway (eds.) *Mediation and Criminal Justice: Victims, Offenders and Community*. London: Sage.

Weijers, I. (1999) 'The Double Paradox of Juvenile Justice', *European Journal on Criminal Policy and Research*, 7: 329–51.

Weijers, I. (2000) *Schuld en Schaamte. Een Pedagogisch Perspectief op het Jeugdstrafrecht*. Houten: Bohn Stafleu Van Loghum.

Weijers, I. (2002) 'The Moral Dialogue: A Pedagogical Perspective on Juvenile Justice', in I. Weijers and A. Duff (eds) *Punishing Juveniles: Principle and Critique*. Oxford: Hart.

Weijers, I. and Duff, A. (2002) *Punishing Juveniles: Principle and Critique*. Oxford: Hart.

Weiss, C. (1997) 'How Can Theory-Based Evaluation Make Greater Headway?', *Evaluation Review*, 21(4): 501–24.

Weitekamp, E. (1999) 'The History of Restorative Justice', in G. Bazemore and L. Walgrave (eds) *Restorative Juvenile Justice*. Monsey, NY: Criminal Justice Press.

Weitekamp, E. (2001) 'Victim Movement and Restoative Justice', keynote paper presented at the Fifth International Conference on Restorative Justice in Leuven, 16–19 September.

Wiebe, R. and Johnson, Y. (1998) *Stolen Life: The Journey of a Cree Woman*. Toronto: Alfred A. Knopf.

Woolard, J. L., Reppucci, N. D. and Redding, R. E. (1996) 'Theoretical and Methodological Issues in Studying Children's Capacities in Legal Contexts', *Law and Human Behavior*, 20: 219–28.

Wright, M. (1991) *Justice for Victims and Offenders*. Milton Keynes, UK: Open University Press.

Wright, M. (1996) *Justice for Victims and Offenders: A Restorative Response to Crime* (2nd edn). Winchester, UK: Waterside Press.

Wundersitz, J. (1994) 'Family Conferencing and Juvenile Justice Reform in South Australia', in C. Alder and J. Wundersitz (eds) *Family Conferencing and Juvenile Justice: The Way Forward or Misplaced Optimism?* Canberra: Australian Institute of Criminology.

Wynne, J. (1996) 'Leeds Mediation and Reparation Service: Ten Years' Experience with Victim–Offender Mediation', in B. Galaway and J. Hudson (eds) *Restorative Justice: International Perspectives*. Monsey, NY: Criminal Justice Press and Amsterdam Kugler Publications.

Young, I. M. (1990) *Justice and the Politics of Difference*. Princeton: Princeton University Press.

Young, I. M. (2000) *Inclusion and Democracy*. Oxford: Oxford University Press.

Young, M. (1995) *Restorative Community Justice: A Call to Action*. Washington, DC: National Organization for Victim Assistance.

Young, W. and Morris, A. (1998) 'Reforming Criminal Justice: Reflecting on the Present and Imagining the Future', inaugural lecture presented at the International Youth Conference, New Zealand, October 1998.

Zauberman, R. (2000) 'Victims as Consumers of the Criminal Justice System?', in A. Crawford and J. Goodey (eds) *Integrating a Victim Perspective within Criminal Justice*. Aldershot, UK: Ashgate.

Zehr, H. (1985) *Retributive Justice, Restorative Justice*. Elhart, IN: Mennonite Central Committee, US Office of Criminal Justice.

Zehr, H. (1990) *Changing Lenses: a New Focus for Crime and Justice*. Scottdale, PA: Herald Press.

Zehr, H. (1995) 'Justice Paradigm Shift? Values and Visions in the Reform Process', *Mediation Quarterly*, 12: 207–16.

Zehr, H. (2000) 'Journey to Belonging', paper presented at the Fourth International Conference on Restorative Justice for Juveniles, Tübingen, Germany.

Zehr, H. (2002) paper presented at the Fourth International Conference on Restorative Justice, Tübingen, October 2001. Forthcoming in E. Weitekamp and H.J. Kerner, *Restorative Justice: Theoretical Foundations*. Cullompton: Willan.

Zehr, H. and Mika, H. (1997) *Fundamental Concepts of Restorative Justice*. Akron, OH: Mennonite Central Committee.

Zimring, F.E. (2000) 'Penal Proportionality for the Young Offender: Notes on Immaturity, Capacity, and Diminished Responsibility', in T. Grisso and R. G. Schwartz (eds) *Youth on Trial: A Developmental Perspective on Juvenile Justice*. Chicago/ London: University of Chicago Press.

Index

reducing through RJ, 32
restorative practices, 35
reciprocity, amends, 49
recognition, of wrongdoing, 88, 93–4
redemption rituals, 157
redemption scripts, 157
referral orders, 116–17
regulatory pyramid, 212
rehabilitational model, RJ, 31–65
 mutual transformation, 57–62
 repairing harm, 44–53
 restorative practices
  empirical data, 35–9
  normative theory, 42–4
  relational model, 39–42
 stakeholder involvement, 53–7
reintegration
 making amends, 48–50
 relationship-building, 52–3
 social support, 56–7
 theory of common ground, 60–2
 of young offenders, 80
reintegrative shaming, 54–7
relational approach, to reasoning, 187
relational rehabilitation, 33, 39–42
relationship-building
 intermediate outcomes, 50–1
 long-term impact, 52–3
 rehabilitational model of RJ, 34
 social support and the task of the
  conference, 51–2
relationships
 damage to, by wrongdoing, 85–8
 restoration, 93
 see also community-government
  relationship; family relationships;
  pro-social relationships; social
  relationships
reliance
 distinguished from trust, 78
 equal justice, 160
reoffenders, condemnation scripts, 156
repairing harm
 damaged relationships, 87–90
 principle of, 42–3
 restorative conferencing, 44–53

restorative ethics, 5–6
 as RJ principle, 32
reparation, 85, 90, 95
reparation orders, 183–4
repentance, 88, 202
replacement discourse, RJ, 186
representation, public participation,
 121–2, 125
resource, community as a, 120–1
respect, 207, 208
respectful disapproval, 54–7
 intermediate outcomes, 54
 long-term outcomes, 56–7
 task of the conference, 55–6
responses, to wrongdoing, 86–7
responsibility
 jurisprudence of, 155–8
 taking, 207, 208
 see also civic responsibility
responsive regulation, 158, 212
restoration
 as goal of the legal system, 199–202
 judicial procedures, 213–14
 and punishment
  choosing between, 83
  distinctions between, 197–9
 wrongdoing, 84–91
restorative conferencing
 community-government
  cooperation, 143
 intervention theory, 44
 mutual transformation, 57–62
 repairing harm, 44–53
 short-term encounters, 36, 37
 stakeholder involvement, 53–7
 theories in use, 38
 see also family group conferencing
restorative interventions
 community strength, 115
 evaluation of, 73
 theory of rehabilitation, 35–42
restorative jurisprudence, 150–66
 contextual justice, 158–62
 principles of RJ, 162–5
 proportionality, 152–5
 responsibility, 155–8